Technotopia

Media Philosophy

Series editors: Eleni Ikoniadou, Lecturer in Media and Cultural Studies at the London Graduate School and the School of Performance and Screen Studies, Kingston University.
Scott Wilson, Professor of Cultural Theory at the London Graduate School and the School of Performance and Screen Studies, Kingston University.

The Media Philosophy series seeks to transform thinking about media by inciting a turn towards accounting for their autonomy and 'eventness', for machine agency and for the new modalities of thought and experience that they enable. The series showcases the 'transcontinental' work of established and emerging thinkers whose work engages with questions about the reshuffling of subjectivity, of temporality, of perceptions and of relations vis-à-vis computation, automation and digitalisation as the current twenty-first-century conditions of life and thought. The books in this series understand media as a vehicle for transformation, as affective, unpredictable and non-linear, and move past its consistent misconception as pure matter-of-fact actuality.

For Media Philosophy, it is not simply a question of bringing philosophy to bear on an area usu-ally considered an object of sociological or historical concern, but of looking at how developments in media and technology pose profound questions for philosophy and conceptions of knowledge, being, intelligence, information, the body, aesthetics, war and death. At the same time, media and philosophy are not viewed as reducible to each other's internal concerns and constraints and thus it is never merely a matter of formulating a philosophy *of* the media; rather the series creates a space for the reciprocal contagion of ideas between the disciplines and the generation of new muta-tions from their transversals. With their affects cutting across creative processes, ethico-aesthetic experimentations and biotechnological assemblages, the unfolding media events of our age pro-vide different points of intervention for thought, necessarily embedded as ever in the medium of its technical support, to continually reinvent itself and the world.

'The new automatism is worthless in itself if it is not put to the service of a powerful, obscure, condensed will to art, aspiring to deploy itself through involuntary movements which none the less do not restrict it.'

Eleni Ikoniadou and Scott Wilson

Titles in the series:

Technotopia

A Media Genealogy of Net Cultures

Clemens Apprich

Translated by Aileen Derieg

ROWMAN & LITTLEFIELD
INTERNATIONAL

London • New York

Published by Rowman & Littlefield International Ltd
Unit A, Whitacre Mews, 26-34 Stannary Street, London SE11 4AB
www.rowmaninternational.com

Rowman & Littlefield International Ltd. is an affiliate of Rowman & Littlefield
4501 Forbes Boulevard, Suite 200, Lanham, Maryland 20706, USA
With additional offices in Boulder, New York, Toronto (Canada), and Plymouth (UK)
www.rowman.com

British Library Cataloguing in Publication Data
A catalogue record for this book is available from the British Library

ISBN: HB 978-1-7866-0313-5
ISBN: PB 978-1-7866-0314-2

Library of Congress Cataloging-in-Publication Data

Names: Apprich, Clemens, author.
Title: Technotopia : a media genealogy of Net cultures / Clemens Apprich.
Description: Lanham : Rowman & Littlefield International, 2017. | Series: Media
   philosophy | Includes bibliographical references and index.
Identifiers: LCCN 2017030697 (print) | LCCN 2017036039 (ebook) | ISBN
   9781786603159 (Electronic) | ISBN 9781786603135 (cloth : alk. paper) | ISBN
   9781786603142 (pbk. : alk. paper)
Subjects: LCSH: Internet—Social aspects. | Cyberspace—Philosophy. | Digital media.
Classification: LCC HM851 (ebook) | LCC HM851 .A735 2017 (print) | DDC
   302.23/1—dc23
LC record available at https://lccn.loc.gov/2017030697

Printed in the United States of America

The author is grateful to the following institutions for their support in the writing of this book.

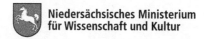

In Memory of Armin Medosch

Contents

Acknowledgements

Like net cultures, this publication is a hybrid. It is a translated, yet revised and substantially extended version of my German book *Vernetzt—Zur Entstehung der Netzwerkgesellschaft* from 2015. The first and the last chapters of this edition are new, everything in between is a thoroughly modified version of what appeared in the original edition, in order to speak to a more international audience. I want to thank my publisher in Germany, transcript, for permitting me to rework the book, as well as my English publisher, Rowman & Littlefield International, for their substantial support throughout the whole process, in particular Isobel Cowper-Coles, Eleni Ikoniadou, Scott T. Wilson and the Project Manager, Jayanthi Chander. I would also like to thank the anonymous reviewers of the book proposal for their insightful comments, as well as my colleagues and friends Claus Pias, Timon Beyes, Wendy Hui Kyong Chun, Ned Rossiter, Orit Halpern, Felix Stalder, Gerald Raunig, Jussi Parikka, Ulf Wuggenig, Götz Bachmann, Armin Beverungen, Marcell Mars, Tomislav Medak, Nishant Shah, Oliver Lerone Schultz, Josephine Berry, Anthony Iles, Felipe Fonseca, Paulo Lara, Nelly Y. Pinkrah and Inga Luchs for their comments and input. Special thanks to the Centre for Digital Cultures at Leuphana University of Lüneburg, not only for the financial and institutional support of this book project, but also for the ongoing opportunity to work with so many outstanding people. The creative and unique atmosphere of the centre has greatly influenced this work.

This book has also been influenced by a number of other sites and people. First of all, there is the Institute for New Culture Technologies/

Public Netbase in Vienna, which, during my studies in philosophy and politics, was the first place for me to go, seeking for answers regarding a society increasingly determined by new media technologies. Then there is the Ludwig Boltzmann Institute for Media Art Research in Linz, as well as the Institute for Human Sciences in Vienna, both of which were of great help to me. And most recently, there are the Post-Media Lab and Making Change, two projects to which I owe a lot. Last but not least, many of the ideas in this book are due to a multitude of encounters, conversations and discussions with people who actually shaped the history of net cultures. Although most of these are only presented in an abbreviated form here, this book would not have been possible without the thought-provoking impulses from Konrad Becker, Martin Wassermair, Wolfgang Sützl, Katja Diefenbach, Mike Bonanno, Pit Schultz, Diana McCarty, Andreas Broeckmann, Robert Sakrowski, Marleen Stikker, Joachim Blank, Karl Heinz Jeron, Brian Holmes, Rasa Smite, Eric Kluitenberg, David Garcia and Geert Lovink and, in particular, Armin Medosch, a true net pioneer and pirate, who was among the first I discussed my ideas on critical net cultures with and who offered me the opportunity to present them at an early stage. This book is dedicated to him.

Foreword

Geert Lovink

'To be honest, it's too early, too late.' 2014 Taipei Biennale – 'It's like what my friend Donald used to say: "Stick a fork in their ass and turn them over, they're done."' (Lou Reed) Death to Digital – 'In my youth, the twenty-first century was always a dream. Now it's becoming a nightmare.' Charles Esche – Antoni Muntadas: 'Warning: Perception Requires Involvement.' 'The first rule of #ProjectMayhem is you do not talk about Project Mayhem.' – 'Post-boring is the most boring,' Aiwen Yin.

In this age of the *permanent now*, it is hard to write up comprehensive histories of the present. We are told to memorise the past, remember its victims and never to forget the dark chapters of the *short twentieth century* (1914–1989). But, what about recent history? Who is going to bother and write it all down? Where are the archives of the *roaring 90s*? The watershed is 1973 and everything that happened after the heroic sixties faded away into defeat and neoliberalism entered the stage. Those who grew up in the post-hippie era know what it means to create *minor culture* in the shadow of the post-1968 theories, coping with mass media that never understood a thing, having to deal with teachers and authorities who lost the plot long time ago. In this age of accelerationism, it makes no sense to sit down and reflect on vanished websites, VHS tapes, festival posters and flyers. At best we quickly document the present and move on. Who was ever rewarded for their refined historical awareness of the past 40 years? In that sense, we are in the Age of Indifference, also known as the Nietzschean Century. There may be (dis)advantages of history for life, but who cares? It is not our own history but technology that is the driving force. Let us build monuments for tomorrow and join the glorification of action for its own sake.

Once caught in the real-time regime, living in the constant fear of missing out, all we can do is speculate about the future value of concepts. In this case we deal with the ups and downs of the network paradigm. In 2016, networks were finally pushed aside by the competing platform term, reflected in two rather different publications: Benjamin Bratton's grand design theory *The Stack* and Nick Srnicek's critical essay *Platform Capitalism*. Both use the network term frequently but no longer give it much significance. In the age of Uber, AirBnB, Google, Amazon and Facebook, networks have been downgraded to a secondary organisation level, a (local) ecology, only significant for user experience. It no longer matters whether the network has a meaning. Networks can be big or small, distributed or scale-free; as long as its data and potential surplus value can be subtracted, everything runs smoothly.

What can we hold up against this nihilist reality? The proposal would be to de-historicise and redesign the media-network-platform triangle into layersor stacks, if you like. Platforms are not our inevitable destiny. Let's sabotage Kevin Kelly's *inevitable*. In the same way as media are not merely about communication, networks are more than social media. Hence, what we learn from Apprich's *Technotopia* is to upgrade the 1990s' infrastructure approach. The commons will not be offered to us on a plate. We need a detox from the *free* services and build up cooperative alternatives to the data-centre logic of Silicon Valley. I am aware that these thoughts are *out of season*, as net critique and tactical media once were in the mid-1990s. With nowhere to hide, what could be today's equivalent of critical net cultures? You can't dwell in an ontology. If once there was a constant fear for appropriation, these days there is simply no more time and space where subversion can unfold. What is needed is a new form of shadow. Once the *meme* has been designed, there are enough real-time amplification channels available to spread the message.

The historical question we need to ask here is: Why networking became such a big topic in the outgoing decade of the twentieth century – and what this could teach us, decades later. In order to answer this question, I am going to use S. Alexander Reed's *Assimilate* (2011), which presents itself as 'a critical history of industrial music'. This classic study of the time right before the rise of critical net cultures has a multitude of personal ties with industrial music and the related performance scene such as Survival Research Laboratories. I want to mention Konrad Becker (Public Netbase, Vienna), Franz Feigl (Netband/desk.nl, Amsterdam), Menno Grootveld (Rabotnik TV/N5M, Amsterdam) and Marleen Stikker (Zomerfestijn/Digitale Stad, Amsterdam) here. The links are embodied in the numerous squats, where performances took place, but also Staalplaat Records (Amsterdam/Berlin) and the free radio stations that played industrial music. Reed's account can be used as a mirror, an inspiration to tell the story of the *short summer* of the Internet counter-culture, an avant-garde that was all too aware of its own inability to make larger claims, let alone be utopian.

Reed traces back industrial media to Italian futurism, Artaud's Theatre of Cruelty and William Burroughs' cut-up techniques. The disturbing rhythms coming out of the rust belts and deserted inner cities not only expressed the existential anger of a lost post-punk generation, it also produced early digital culture. This self-destructive Reagan/ Thatcher era also transfigures into the first generation of personal computers that were used to produce zines and sound samples. The industrial casus tell of isolated, self-producing small units. These 'UFOs', as Patrick Codenys of Front 242 calls them, are autonomous nodes with a strong desire to communicate. According to Reed, the isolation in this pre-Internet period was 'merely a geographic one: a vital connection exists between early industrial music and the global network established through the Fluxus art movement, its outgrowth of mail art, and the cassette and small press cultures that arose in the late 1970s'.[1]

Surrounded by the doom and gloom of the neo-liberal order with its permanent austerity, factory closures, takeover of global finance, environmental disasters (from acid rain to Chernobyl) and mass unemployment, it is both tempting and subversive to embrace *the new* that the baby boom generation and the powers-to-be had no clue about. Reed refers to musician La Monte Young's preference of the new over the good. 'The new is a non-directional, nonteleological one, thus differing from the traditionalist and reactionary preconceptions of "progress," which were synonymous with "good".'[2] Good was the realm of priests, academics, critics and curators, and their judgement had been predictable for ages. Chaos and mess was not their preferred ur-soup. According to the discourse police, the DIY aesthetics of the *ingenious dilettantes* was neither *professional* nor *pop* and was thus ignored.

Much like the industrial music scene, early net cultures were ambivalent about their own democratic imperative. Networking was first and foremost networks-for-us. The claim to provide 'access for all' (the infamous name of the Dutch hackers ISP that would be sold in 1998 to the former national telecom firm KPN) only come later and was an explicit counter-historical anomaly, in an age when public utilities were being split up and privatised and autonomy became synonymous with an inward-looking world view.

Reed sums up this position accurately under the term *techno-ambivalence*: 'In his 1992 collaboration with the band Ministry, Burroughs orders us to "Cut word lines. Cut music lines. Smash the control images. Smash the control machines." This cutting and smashing is by no means a rejection outright of the viral agents of mind control – words, technology, belief – but instead it's a reversal of these agent's powers upon themselves. As both the fragmented recordings to be cut up and as the recording device, machines are necessary to smash the machine, just as the vaccination is achieved through viral exposure.'[3] The ambivalence between technophobe elements (computer as the 1984 control machine) and technophile (liberating production) promises remains unsolved. Take SPK's 'Metal Dance' song, in which, according to Reed, the band 'attempts to have its revolution and dance to it too'. As Reed explains, there is submission in all its techno-newness. Physically exhausted and damaged, the female SKP singer, Sinan Leong, is enslaved to the Marxist opiate potential: 'Can't help moving to the rhythm Feel so breathless Can't shake out that breathless voice Crashing Steel Strange new sounds intoxicate me Cutting hard.'[4]

Networks, in the cultural context of the 1990s, were inhabited neither by individuals (users with a *profile*) nor by institutions. At best, they could be described as connectors between clouds of initiatives. The vanished worlds that Clemens Apprich brings vividly back to life were light years removed from the official reality of the non-government organisations; neither do they have much resemblance either with hipster startups. If any philosophy would come close to describe them, it would be the dream scape of Gilles Deleuze and Félix Guattari (ecstasy), combined with the leather jacket power politics of Michel Foucault (speed). Without exception, the *new media* collectives were products of previous social movements (squatting, feminism, ecology and anti-racism) and cannot be understood outside of that context. Following Adilkno's definition of 'the movement as the memory of the event',[5] there is a task here to reconstruct the origins of the early critical computer network initiatives. What was their event and what is the event today? It's too easy to say it ought to be located in the offline. As Apprich reminds us, key might be the social element, not the question whether the magic moment happened in real life or mediated through machines.

After Facebook, the question is no longer about scale. No matter how much we all desire to have our fair share of exposure, networks can only scale down from here. Global connectivity has reached its moment of entropy years ago (but when exactly?), and the *tactics* have now shifted to *meme design* inside a protected environment. This is where the 'organized networks' proposal of me and Ned Rossiter comes into play.[6] It is an *out-of-season* concept because its time has either not yet come, already passed or never materialises. In retrospective, we could claim that certain cultural networks of the late 1980s and early 1990s had *org net* characteristics: the actors developed strong ties, despite the fact that they did not know each other and had to work across large distances. As today's social media platforms systematically neglect (read: ban) network tools, local and regional organisation still has revolutionary potentials, beyond the existing organisational forms such as the political party and event-based occupations and other forms of protest. For some, their decisive moment will be an image burnout. For others it will be war and permanent stagnation (or permanent vacation, as it was once called). What some fear as 'balkanisation' of the net, many will celebrate as a true cultural, organisational and eventually economic empowerment.

Ultimately, network theory did not go anywhere. Its normative approach in favour of the distributed network model rendered an entire field-in-the-making irrelevant once rhizomes were replaced by scale-free platforms for the billions. What is left are network visualisations no one seems to be able to read (not even machines as maps are eye candy, generated for humans). From an organisational perspective, the network did not deliver either. It might be promising that one day vagueness and non-commitment might transform into firm, long-term engagement. But who is honestly going to wait for all these hyper-informed social media users that have no clue anymore about the basics of self-organisation?

Let's end with Jodi Dean's critique of the network form and her plea to return to the (Communist) Party as an Hegelian synthesis of dispersed short-term commitment. In *Crowd and Party* (2016), she asks: How do mass protests become an organised activist collective? 'How can acts remain intelligible as acts of a collective subject? How do people prevent their acts from being absorbed back into communicative capitalism?'[7] Social media architectures actively prevent autonomous organisation (not to mention the obvious surveillance and social control aspects). The *leaderless* Occupy-approach was only able to orchestrate one-off protests and failed to set up sustainable grassroots initiatives. Following in the footsteps of Elias Canetti, she states that 'the crowd wants to endure', and pushes this desire in a particular direction by stating that 'the party provides an apparatus for this endurance'.[8] According to Dean, what is missing in our current understanding of the party is the 'affective infrastructure of the party, its reconfiguration of the crowd unconsciousness into a political form'. According to Dean, 'The communist party operates as a transferential object for the collective action of the many.' It is all about reconfigurations and reverberations, or overtone. 'The party is tasked with transmitting the event's overtone.' It is a still-born academic exercise to presume that Lenin is going to be a role model for the social media masses. The challenge is: progressive meme design will have to start from scratch and promote an open and participatory culture that beats the alt-right imaginary.

What also needs to be addressed is the proposed transformative act of becoming a member as a way to ferment, to capture the collective event. Is it true that we all long to sign up and feel nostalgic about membership? There might be regression everywhere today, yet there are no signs for a *return* to membership organisations. The social media ideology does not address us as members, we are users with a profile. How can we alter and differentiate this dominant form of digital subjectivity? As Jodi Dean observes, the party form is no longer recognised as an affective infrastructure that can address problems. The twenty-first-century political party is precisely not a form of concentration and endurance. The question should not be party or no party. What is on the table is the strategic question: What will the institutional form of this era look like (presumed we want to reverse the current social entropy). The problem of Jodi Dean's approach is not one of analysis or urgency but one of ordinary overdetermination. Instead, the question 'what's to be done' should be an open one. Agreed, we need synchronous political socialisation, one that can overcome the feeling of being stuck in the lonely social media crowd. Let's see this as a start. It is social networking (as it is still called) that should be transformed. We need contradictory platforms that break through the unconscious numbness of the smooth interfaces. Let's build a toolkit and hack the attention economy.

It should be easy to smash the online self and its boring cult of narcissism. These are the post-network challenges.

NOTES

1. S. Alexander Reed, *Assimilate. A Critical History of Industrial Music* (Oxford/New York: Oxford University Press, 2013), 110.

2. Reed, Assimilate, 51.

3. Reed, *Assimilate*, 40. It is tempting to make a reference here to Bernard Stiegler's key concept, the 'pharmakon' (originally coming from Jacques Derrida), in which technology (and Internet in particular) is seen as both poisonous and a remedy.

4. Reed, *Assimilate*, 137.

5. Adilkno, *Cracking the Movement* (Brooklyn: Autonomedia, 1994), 16.

6. See Geert Lovink and Ned Rossiter, 'The Politics of Organized Networks: The Art of Collective Coordination and the Seriality of Demands', in *New Media, Old Media: A History and Theory Reader*, 2nd edition, ed. Wendy Hui Kyong Chun et al. (New York/London: Routledge, 2016), 335–345.

7. Jodi Dean, *Crowds and Party* (London/New York: Verso Books, 2016), 218.

8. Dean, *Crowds and* Party, 217.

Chapter 1

Introducing Technotopia

'The utopian dimension of new technology lies not before us,
but rather behind us, in the dreams and ideals of the past.'[1]

Today we live in an 'epoch of space' and, as Foucault explains in a
lecture, delivered at the Parisian Cercle d'études architecturale in 1967,
this epoch is an 'epoch of simultaneity: we are in the epoch of juxtaposition, the epoch of the near and far, of the side-by-side, of the dispersed.
We are at a moment when our experience of the world is less that of a
long life developing through time than that of a network that connects
points and intersects with its own skein.'[2] Intensified through the dissemination of digital technologies and, consequently, an overlay of a
global data space upon local physical places, the network has become
the determining morphology of this epoch. By privileging space over
time, a new complexity emerged, which can be read as the most recent
push for modernisation. In this situation, the metaphor of the network
is employed to tackle what Fredric Jameson identified as postmodern
confusion; a state of affairs, caused by a fundamental transformation of
our social interaction, political agency and economic organisation.[3] Not
only is the idea of the network considered to bring some clarity into the
postmodern world, but it also resonates with the socio-economic shift
of our time. As Wendy Chun recently suggested, 'Networks have been
central to the emergence, management and imaginary of neoliberalism, in particular to its narrative of individuals collectively dissolving society.'[4] The dissolution of the social involves the imagination

1

of neo-liberal networks, which, from now on, are supposed to adapt individuals to the new conditions of global capital. Hence, the rise of a network society can be seen as the expression of late capitalism.[5]

The book at hand follows this analysis by considering socio-technical networks as a part of our cultural imagination. In so doing, it is not so much interested in (re)discovering the *origins* of these networks in the military-industrial complex of Silicon Valley, but rather considers critical net cultures of the 1990s, associated with media-cultural initiatives such as the Critical Art Ensemble, nettime, *Telepolis*, Public Netbase, and Ljudmila, as precursors for new forms of media and social practices, which have become part of our everyday culture. In opposition to the then prominent concept of cyberspace as a virtual space, the artistic, cultural and hacktivist practices of critical net cultures sought to implement digital technologies within existing physical spaces. In retrospect, the proliferation of so-called *social media* has precisely proven this approach to be right: it is not the parallel universe of a virtual reality but rather the net as a web of socio-technical relations which has gained significance today. Yet, paradoxically, while the discourse around the Internet has exploded, the critical knowledge of these early experiments seems to have been forgotten. It is therefore important to recollect this forgotten future of the 1990s and to make it productive for the current debates about the impact of digital networks on our everyday lives.[6]

In our digital culture, the idea of a homogeneous information space is not sufficient anymore to describe the increasingly complex network sphere. As our machines are constantly connected to a global data space, it becomes more and more difficult to separate our online life from our offline life. This is the reality of a networked world, augmented with electronics, software and sensors. However, the Internet is not only a technological, but a cultural and social phenomenon as well. While the technological infrastructure is needed to establish a network on a global basis, the Internet would be no more than a loosely connected network of computers without the cultural horizon of a common meaning. Using early net cultures as a starting point allows me to take account of both the material and imaginary aspects as interdependent and to trace some of the hidden presumptions when it comes to digital networks. In particular, the antagonistic idea that the Internet is either a space of emancipation or manipulation, of freedom or control, is deeply rooted in our cultural imagination, namely the assumption that (positive or negative) social change can be derived from technology. In order to avoid such a technicistic reduction, I suggest that technology should be understood in terms of neither a utopian nor dystopian world view, but rather of what Foucault in the above-mentioned lecture called a 'heterotopia'. Heterotopias are 'counter-sites, a kind of effectively enacted utopia in which the real sites, all the other real sites that can be found within culture, are simultaneously represented, contested, and inverted'.[7] I will argue in the following pages that digital space itself constitutes such a counter site, a technotopia which represents and infiltrates reality.

EXPERIMENTAL PLAYGROUNDS

In the 1990s, numerous publications discussed a possible crisis of the city, entailing a critical assessment of the city in the age of global networking.[8] Urban space, in most of the authors' view, was no longer defined as locally tangible place, but rather by a global 'space of flows'.[9] This implied an overcoding of the city with information networks and, consequently, the superimposition of a multitude of data streams over the material architecture of the city. However, the built environment did not disappear, but the transformation of material infrastructures – from transportation and communication systems all the way to energy supplies – became irreversibly dependent on digital information networks.[10] In this sense, shift towards spatially distributed processes radically transformed the way urban space was imagined. The so-called 'mirror worlds'[11] enabled an informational representation of cities, in order to have better control over their increasingly complex reality. With electronic networks, digital maps, or the use of online systems in city administration, the digital replication of urban processes became a second reality.[12] Hence, at the turn of the millennium, the city metaphor established a new symbolic order and constituted – at least for a short period of time – the core idiom in electronic space. Not only had the city become a data space because of the mass distribution of network technologies, but the data space, generated by these technologies, was represented as a city.

By making use of the city metaphor as an organisational regime, the attempt was made to manage and control the data flood caused by digital networks. Here, the wish of gathering and structuring information within the city walls referred to the old idea of an ideal space of knowledge. The urban vision of the 1990s, exemplarily represented by digital cities (along with Amsterdam and Berlin, also Vienna and others), introduced a unique perspective, which proves to be helpful to unravel some of the ongoing controversy about the dangers, but also possibilities of data networks. By retracing this *technotopia* back to the early stage of network building, the main objective of the present book is to define net-cultural projects of the 1990s as experimental playgrounds for new forms of knowledge that are fundamental to the emergence of today's network dispositif. They not only provided metaphors needed to translate and implement technological developments, but also anticipated the modes of perception that were soon to become part of our everyday life. In this sense, the *topos* of digital cities is both a commonplace to describe our networked space and the actual site where it remains possible to experience and thus discuss the utopian and aesthetic moments of that space.

While in the early days of the Internet the city came into the net in order to structure the newly formed data space, today the net comes into the city, in order to provide the necessary data to govern it. A current example for this may be found in much-debated smart cities.[13] Rio de Janeiro, for instance, in preparation for the FIFA World Championship 2014 and the Olympics 2016, witnessed the launch of a city-wide sensor network, implemented to coordinate and control urban life from a futuristic command centre.[14] Along with communication, energy and transportation administration, the goal was to *pacify* so-called problem districts using ubiquitous computer technologies. This sort of optimisation follows the cyber-utopian dream of automatised surveillance and control systems. And in addition to state regulation, it is private enterprises that decide how technological networks are implemented and used. In relation to current media practice, this leads to a rather paradoxical situation: on the one hand, digital technologies have become more accessible and easy-to-use than ever before; on the other hand, access to the data generated by these technologies is largely controlled by a few companies. This specific form of a *digital panoptism* insidiously affects the user by employing new techniques of data mining and marketing research, while its centre remains closely guarded, and therefore, unreachable to the user. The danger of these closed systems of state agencies and Internet companies is that they do not allow alternative models to even come up, so that an open digital ecosystem is already nipped in the bud.[15]

Hence, it is essential to look back to the early days of network building – when the terms of 'possible futures' were still under negotiation – if we want to understand one of the most recent transformations in our digital culture. With my book, I revisit this critical time when the Internet was not yet an everyday reality, but when its potential was already understood and fiercely debated. The historical context of early net cultures provides us with a basis to critically engage with the current discussions about the weal and woe of the Internet, and, finally, allows us to shed light on the question of how the discourse about technology yields an epistemological model for the economic, political and social disposition of our time. This book, precisely because it is critical towards any deterministic understanding of technology, is interested in the materiality of media, in order to point to the following questions: What are the social, political and economic effects visible not only in the ephemeral practices of digital media, but also in its underlying structures? How do technological infrastructures shape culture, economics and politics in specific locales? Why did the heterogeneous and meandering net cultures of the 1990s turn into the concrete form of a network society and a new mode of governing based on digital networks?

Approaching these questions requires a genealogical investigation, which enables us to understand historical processes not as a linear sequence of events, but as a permanent confrontation of forces. In this sense, the *invention* of a worldwide computer network was not a singular act, as the still dominant narrative of the military origin of the Internet suggests. Rather the emergence of the Internet is better explained by a constant *innovation* and the combination of heterogeneous and opposing forces, from technical developments (e.g. TCP/IP versus OSI-standard), to institutional frameworks (e.g. ARPANET, NSFnet, minitel) to social and individual interests (e.g. Usenet, Hackerculture and the first Bulletin Board Systems).[16] Genealogy, formulated here in line with Michel Foucault's considerations, is not solely a matter of making an implicit knowledge visible, but rather of uncovering the processes of emergence and negotiation, the search for the dispersed *descents* that constitute the own present.[17] This book thus seeks out concrete scenes and local situations, actual topoi, which were situated in the net cultures of the 1990s and enabled the emergence of today's network society.

MEDIA GENEALOGY

The present work considers the history of networking from a media-genealogical perspective. By drawing a line from the early days of network building to today's networked reality, it becomes clear that the digital space is itself the subject of divergent and conflicting lines of descent as well as hidden relations that point towards the present in critical ways.[18] Before the Internet itself became a mass medium, there was already an independent network discourse, which would ultimately contribute to the breakthrough of digital media.[19] Catchwords like community, democracy and participation marked the discourse and provided an initial orientation in the early phase of the Internet. They organised knowledge and reduced complexity, always with the promise of making it possible to control and steer the new networked space. It was this discourse that had led to the creation of a multitude of media practices, which were not only shaped by network technologies but actually produced them, and with them our understanding of social media, user-generated content and participative platforms. If it is true that our entrance into the digital age was made some time ago and that network media have thus become an essential element of our everyday lives, then the Internet itself is not only culturally formational but also culturally formed, and it is precisely this relationship of pre- and remediation that has to be considered while examining our technological present.[20]

This kind of multilinear and non-totalising understanding of technology, which is less interested in a specific all-explaining origin than in a multitude of discursive manifestations, is something that media genealogy shares with already established media archaeology.[21] Both of them undermine traditional historicising processes for which the history of technology and media functions as a sort of teleological intellectual history. And both are equally opposed to purely present-orientated research approaches, especially since these often suffer from a striking tendency to forget history when discussing *new media*. However, while media archaeological investigation examines certain technical media apparatuses (e.g. paper, camera, film projector, radio set, computer) in their respective discourse-historic settings, media genealogy contains a research programme that focuses not so much on how such a media historical discourse *is* established, but rather how it *became* established or *becomes* established. It focuses, in other words, on the transformation from one media discursive formation to another.[22] Limiting our focus to the technical structure of media processes, to their a priori and transcendental status, can lead to the exclusion of this dynamic process and freeze the object of its study.[23] Instead of describing technical media as something 'prior, decisive, determinative'[24] through discourse analysis, media genealogy takes an interest in the set of ideas, practices and networks that together form a strategic power field for the emergence of technologies and media. In media-genealogical investigations, the media apparatuses or the definition of these apparatuses remain continually in a state of flux.[25]

Whereas previous investigations of the network society often conceived the Internet as a more or less stable media technology that is responsible for social transformation, this book takes an inversive approach: it assumes that the seemingly transient media practices have engendered networking technologies as we know them today. Consequently, the historical example of net cultures provides us with an alternative line of thought: firstly, it allows us to examine the unseen, forgotten or yet-unrealised potentials of network practices and related forms of knowledge; secondly, it makes it possible to conceptualise a media historical approach that takes into account the ever-elusive status of network technologies and, as a consequence, calls into question the alleged necessity and inevitability of the predominant network model. Such an approach, because it insists on the possibility of change, implies a consciously chosen standpoint, especially since the selection of the respective genealogical lines for describing a global socio-technical structure can always only remain fragmented and local.[26] Hence, the here proposed line is only one of many possible entry points to analyse the current state of networked cultures; a 'situated knowledge',[27] which is located in the alternative discourse of critical net cultures. Starting from these, I am ultimately interested in a rearticulation of net critique that builds on the experiences of earlier net cultures, in order to formulate a critical theory of the Internet.[28]

STRUCTURE OF THE BOOK

Starting with an analysis of Jean-François Lyotard's famous exhibition Les Immatériaux (1985), the second chapter traces postmodern ideas that emerged in the transition from an industrial to an informational society. According to Lyotard, the informatisation of society has led to a general aestheticisation of the social realm, an idea that is echoed by Jean Baudrillard's theory of simulation. His critique, which abandoned any hope of an emancipatory use of media technologies, had – I argue – a profound influence on so-called German Media Theory (e.g.

Friedrich Kittler, Norbert Bolz, Peter Weibel) and its interest in the a priori of technical media; not so much in terms of the often stated, but too simplistic accusation of techno-determinism, but rather in the context of a counter movement to the Anglo-Saxon cultural studies which were influenced by Marxist scholars (e.g. Stuart Hall, John Clarke, Tony Jefferson). While cultural studies, back in the 1980s, pointed to a social differentiation in subgroups, and, as a result, to an increase of media self-determination and representation by these groups, German Media Theory argued for a technical homogenisation of society which, ultimately and in accordance with Baudrillard, leads to the dissolution of social agency. Such a media-materialist turn was the point of critique of early net cultures and its newly established net critique, which I discuss in chapter 3. In contrast to an academic media theory, net critique was no longer only about the reflection on media conditions but rather about the co-creation of these conditions. This second disengagement opened up a new perspective for emancipatory politics: tactical media constituted an ensemble of activist, artistic and cultural practices which raised hopes of a new form of political participation. However, in its effort to re-establish an emancipatory perspective, net critique tended to cleave to the idea of a per se distributed, and therefore democratic, Internet – a *subversive affirmation* of netism which I will analyse at the end of this chapter.

The fourth chapter of the book puts the theoretical debates of early net cultures into a global context by discussing Manuel Castells remarks on a new space of flows which, from the beginning of the 1990s, has begun to dominate the traditional space of places. According to this, new demands of global capital for flexible management and just-in-time production met with technical advances in the information and communication sector, leading to a new material foundation on which the dominant economic, social and political processes were reorganised. This transformation involved a rather complex process that had nothing to do with the techno-libertarian idea of a self-emerging and self-organising systems – as can be seen by the enormous financial efforts European and American governments put into the implementation of data highways. In order to keep up with the politico-economic changes and to counter a possible loss of control, the network became a privileged concept of governance. As I will show in chapter 5, the discussion of a computer-based disurbanisation marked a general crisis of governance. Paradoxically, all hopes were pinned on those technologies that were held accountable for this crisis: On the one hand, the discourse about an alleged crisis of the city led to early attempts to structure the newly built data space with the help of the city metaphor (e.g. MIT's City of News); on the other hand, network technologies were implemented into existing urban spaces (e.g. digital cities of Amsterdam, Berlin and Vienna). At the end of this chapter, I will point out how the discourse on urban participation was then linked to a new form of governance that is based on communities, in particular within the neo-liberal narrative of a dissolving society. The *virtual community* as a mode of self-governance is characterised less by a social collectivity than by a computer-mediated connectivity.

What dominates debates about the Internet is the mystifying figure of the distributed network, thus obstructing the analysis of concrete power relations within the network dispositif. A distributed network, as it was formulated by Paul Baran in 1964, is characterised by an equal distribution of equivalent nodes. It was this idea that fuelled the belief in the democratic power of network technologies in the 1990s, most prominently expressed by the proclamation of a 'new Athenian Age' (Al Gore) as a direct result of the implementation of network technologies. Here, the techno-libertarian imagination of distributed networks goes hand in hand with the neo-liberal notion of the Internet as a self-organising and self-organised system. In chapter 6, I confront such a biotechnical notion of the Internet with recent findings in network theory, in particular scale-free networks and their intrinsic power law. This approach enables me to introduce a third dimension into the two-dimensional ontology of distributed and flat networks. The dimension of power, therefore, helps to better understand today's networked soci-ality and to uncover alternative modes of subjectification in an increasingly networked environment. As I argue in chapter 7 with reference to Gilbert Simondon, it is digital networks, understood as ensembles of human, social and technological individuals, which contain the potential to foster new forms of socio-technical collectives; they enable alternative forms of individuation that go beyond the impasse of social media and its networked self. Rather than being a fixed point within the network, situated as a node of commercial media platforms, the individual, in this perspective, becomes a transversal network itself. Such a transindividual individual does not imply the naïve belief in a distributed and per se democratic network; on the contrary, articulating the transindividual potential through network practices is understood as a political act, as a struggle for collective commons and shared resources.

The eighth and last chapter of my book outlines a critique of the political economy of the net: commercial media platforms (e.g. Facebook, Google, eBay) are not only the object of such a critique, but also a digital ecosystem based on crowd-sourced value production (e.g. Amazon's Mechanical Turk, Crowdflower, Netflix), as well as rapidly growing Smart Cities with their privatised infrastructures (e.g. New Songdo City, Masdar City, PlanIT Valley). A post-media strategy, as I am formulating it with reference to some late writings by Félix Guattari, shifts the focus to those endeavours that do not simply make use of media technologies to optimise existing socio-economical models, but consider them instead as potential forces to transform these models. Here, the development of critical infrastructures, as can be seen in some of today's most prolific art and media projects, such as free radio networks, autonomous media labs and collaborative websites, is deemed important if we want to counter the increasing privatisation and commercialisation of the Internet. They provide us with an alternative to today's predominant network model and help us to develop a new imaginary of digital cultures, its underlying practices and infrastructures. With this book, I hope to encourage students, activists, artists, practitioners and scholars to engage with such an alternative line of thinking, derived from the historical example of net cultures. While the impact of Silicon Valley on our techno-cultural imagination has already been researched sufficiently, a critical revision of early artistic, cultural and hacktivist experiments within the networked sphere is still missing. Critical net cultures can be seen as 'displaced mediators'[29] in the computer-based media upheaval of the late twentieth century: On the one hand, they were crucial in implementing network technologies and fostering a cultural understanding of these technologies; on the other hand, by opening the doors of electronic space to a wider public, they were soon overrun and displaced by commercial service providers. However, the pioneer projects of the 1990s have not disappeared, but have become part of our everyday reality, thus still containing the knowledge necessary to deepen and further extend their socio-political potential in our media practices. So, instead of simply criticising today's commercial Internet platforms, thereby repeating the same ontological presuppositions of the dominant network model, we should build upon the experience of early net cultures as a vehicle for an alternative imagination, like a boat carrying meaning through time; because the boat, according to Foucault at the end of his 1967 lecture, 'is the heterotopia *par excellence.* In civilisations without boats, dreams dry up, spying takes the place of adventure, and the police take the place of pirates.'[30]

NOTES

1. Alexander Roesler, 'Bequeme Einmischung. Internet und Öffentlichkeit', in *Mythos Internet*, ed. Stefan Münker et al. (Frankfurt a. M.: Suhrkamp, 1997), 171. Quote translated by author.

2. Michel Foucault, 'Of Other Spaces', *Diacritics* 16:1 (1986): 22.

3. See Fredric Jameson, *Postmodernism, or, The Cultural Logic of Late Capitalism* (Durham: Duke University Press, 1991).

4. Wendy Hui Kyong Chun, 'Networks NOW: Belated too Early', in *Postdigital Aesthetics*, ed. David M. Berry et al. (London: Palgrave Macmillan, 2015), 289.

5. See Manuel Castells, *The Rise of the Network Society. The Information Age: Economy, Society and Culture*, Vol. I (Oxford: Blackwell Publishing, 1996).

6. See Clemens Apprich and Felix Stalder, eds., *Vergessene Zukunft. Radikale Netzkulturen in Europa* (Bielefeld: transcript, 2012).

7. Foucault, 'Of Other Spaces', 24. Foucault's examples of heterotopias are gardens, cemeteries, psychiatric clinics, brothels, prisons, the villages of Club Mediterranée, etc.

8. Among others: Mike Davis, *City of Quartz. Excavating the Future in Los Angeles* (London: Verso, 1990). Saskia Sassen, *The Global City* (Princeton: Princeton University Press, 1991). Gotthard Fuchs, Bernhard Moltmann and Walter Prigge, eds., *Mythos Metropole* (Frankfurt a. M.: Suhrkamp, 1995). William J. Mitchell, *City of Bits. Space, Place, and the Infobahn* (Cambridge: MIT Press, 1996). Christine M. Boyer, *CyberCities. Visual Perception in the Age of Electronic Communication* (New York: Princeton Architectural Press, 1996). Stefan Iglhaut, Armin Medosch and Florian Rötzer, eds., *Stadt am Netz. Ansichten von Telepolis* (Mannheim: Bollmann, 1996). Christa Maar and Florian Rötzer, eds., *Virtual Cities. Die Neuerfindung der Stadt im Zeitalter der globalen Vernetzung* (Basel: Birkhäuser, 1997). Martin Pawley, *Terminal Architecture* (London: Reaktion Books, 1998).

9. See Manuel Castells, *The Informational City. Information Technology, Economic Restructuring and the Urban-Regional Process* (Oxford: Blackwell Publishing, 1991), 126–171.

10. For German cultural theorist Hartmut Böhme, it is, therefore, obvious that in addition to hardware (i.e. the material infrastructure of information and telecommunication systems, as well as transportation lines), the significance of software (i.e. databases and control programs) has increased tremendously (see Hartmut Böhme, 'Das Neue Jerusalem. Von der Vernetzung zur Virtualisierung

der Städte', in *Flimmernde Zeiten. Vom Tempo der Medien*, ed. Manuel Schneider et al. [Stuttgart/Leipzig: Hirzel, 1999], 309–323).

11. See David Gelernter, *Mirror Worlds* (Oxford: Oxford University Press, 1993).

12. Hartmut Böhme even sees a 'third level of being' in the digital sphere, which arises alongside the first (nature) and the second (civilisation) (Böhme, 'Das Neue Jerusalem', 315).

13. For more on this debate, see Orit Halpern et al., 'Test-Bed Urbanism', *Public Culture* 25:2 (2013): 273–306. Adam Greenfield, *Against the Smart City* (New York: Do projects, 2013). Jennifer Gabrys. 'Programming Environments: Environmentality and Citizen Sensing in the Smart City', *Environment and Planning D: Society and Space* 32:1 (2014): 30–48. Anthony M. Townsend, *Smart Cities: Big Data, Civic Hackers, and the Quest for New Utopia* (New York: W. W. Norton & Company, 2014). Duncan McLaren and Julian Agyeman, *Sharing Cities: A Case for Truly Smart and Sustainable Cities* (Cambridge: MIT Press, 2017).

14. A historical predecessor of this command and control vision can be seen in the Chilean project Cybersyn during the presidency of Salvador Allende (see Claus Pias, 'Der Auftrag. Kybernetik und Revolution in Chile', in *Politik der Medien*, ed. Daniel Gethmann et al. [Zürich/Berlin: diaphanes, 2004], 131–153).

15. See Jonathan Zittrain, *The Future of the Internet – And How to Stop It* (New Haven/London: Yale University Press, 2008).

16. According to Lewis Mumford, this could be said to be an *invention of the invention*: many technologies that are born in a certain historical moment have been already known for some time, but only the social innovation helps the technical invention to break through (see Lewis Mumford, *Technics and Civilization* [Chicago/London: University of Chicago Press, 1962]).

17. See Michel Foucault, 'Nietzsche, Genealogy, History', in *The Foucault Reader*, ed. Paul Rabinow (New York: Pantheon Books, 1984), 76–100. Genealogy, as formulated by Foucault in reference to Nietzsche, contains a research programme which goes beyond the analysis of historical discourse formations by addressing the power mechanisms that contribute to the genesis of orders of knowledge and subjects of knowledge. It seeks to 'awaken beneath the form of institutions and legislations the forgotten past of real struggles, of masked victories or defeats, the blood that has dried on the codes of law' (Michel Foucault, 'War in the Filigree of Peace: Course Summary', trans. Ian Mcleod, in *Oxford Literary Review* 4, no. 2 [1976]: 17–18).

18. For a more detailed description of media genealogy as a research method, see Clemens Apprich and Götz Bachmann, 'Media Genealogy: Back to the Present of Digital Cultures', in *Digitization: Theories and Concepts for Empirical Cultural Research*, ed. Gertraud Koch (London: Routledge, 2017), in print.

19. See *Ars Electronica Festival* in 1989 for a representative example. Gerhard Johann Lischka and Peter Weibel, eds., 'Im Netz der Systeme', *Kunstforum* 103 (1989).

20. See Richard Grusin, 'Radical Mediation', *Critical Inquiry* 42:1 (2015): 124–148.

21. See Erkki Huhtamo and Jussi Parikka, eds., *Media Archaeology. Approaches, Applications and Implications* (Berkley/Los Angeles/London: University of California Press, 2011). And Jussi Parikka, *What Is Media Archaeology?* (Cambridge/Malden: Polity Press, 2012).

22. Both media archaeology and media genealogy rely on Michel Foucault's methodological concepts: on the one hand, his investigations into the archaeology of knowledge, and on the other hand, his history of power in the genealogical sense. The two methods of questioning are not mutually exclusive, but rather should be seen as complementary dimensions of his overarching research plan: 'The archaeological dimension of the analysis made it possible to examine the forms [of problematisation] themselves; its genealogical dimension enabled me to analyse their formation out of the practices and of the modifications undergone by the latter' (Michel Foucault, *The Use of Pleasure. The History of Sexuality, Vol. 2*, trans. Robert Hurley [New York: Vintage, 1985], 11–12).

23. Because media archaeology is not a discipline with its own independent terminology, it is, of course, not possible to paint all the approaches that have until now been designated as *media archaeological* with a broad brush. For example, Siegfried Zielinski's 'anarchaeology' and 'variantology' represent a project of heterogeneous media practices that undermines a transcendental point of view about the media and can be considered close to media genealogy (see Eric Kluitenberg, 'On the Archaeology of Imaginary Media', in *Media Archaeology. Approaches, Applications and Implications*, ed. Erkki Huhtamo et al. [Berkley/Los Angeles/London: University of California Press, 2011], 48–69).

24. Geoffrey Winthrop-Young: 'Von gelobten und verfluchten Medienländern. Kanadischer Gesprächsvorschlag zu einem deutschen Theoriephänomen', *Zeitschrift für Kulturwissenschaften* 2 (2008): 113–127, here 122. Quote translated by author.

25. To be clear, this does not mean that media-archaeological approaches would be superseded by media genealogical ones, especially given that they are still very much needed for the deep analysis of discursive formations, together with their more or less stable media apparatuses.

26. '[The] historical sense is explicit in its perspective and acknowledges its system of injustice' (Foucault, 'Nietzsche', 90).

27. See Donna Haraway, 'Situated Knowledge: The Science Question in Feminism and the Privilege of Partial Perspective', *Feminist Studies* 14:3 (1988): 575–599.

28. In this sense, the book at hand differs from other publications on the topic, in particular in the context of actor-network theory (ANT) and science and technology studies (STS), because net critique itself is much more rooted in a Marxian tradition of critical theory. For a critique of techno-economic networks, rather than a critique of the political economy of the net, see Michel Callon, 'Techno-economic networks and irreversibility', *The Sociological Review* 38 (1990): 132–161. For a critique of Callon's *The Laws of Markets* see Jens Schröter, 'Performing the economy, digital media and crisis. A critique of Michel Callon', in *Performing the Digital*, ed. Marina Leeker et al. (Bielefeld: transcript, 2017), 247–275. And for a recent study on networks rather related to classical infrastructure studies, see Nicole Starosielski, *The Undersea Network* (Durham/London: Duke University Press, 2015).

29. See Jodi Dean, *Blog Theory. Feedback and Capture in the Circuits of Drive* (Cambridge/Malden: Polity Press, 2010), 26–29.

30. Foucault, 'Of Other Spaces', 22–27.

Chapter 2

Postmodern Complexity

Les Immatériaux opened its doors in the Centre Pompidou in Paris on 5 March 1985. At that time, the three-month event was the largest and most expensive exhibition in the eight-year history of the museum of modern art. The real attraction, however, was its curator: Jean-François Lyotard, who had become widely known beyond the academic field with his book *La condition postmoderne* (published in 1979),[1] who was able to realise his idea of a *non-exhibition* in the 3,000 square-metre exhibition space of the fifth floor.[2] By dissociating himself from the conventional forms of exhibition making, Lyotard wanted to 'arouse that sensibility ... that we believe already exists among the audience, but without a means of expression'.[3] For the exhibition, or rather non-exhibition, did not merely depict the work of a philosopher, but was instead itself already conceived as a philosophical work. Various thematic complexes – from architecture, nutrition, clothing, all the way to money – were treated in a total of sixty-one stations structured on the basis of five question sequences. Hence, the complex structure of the exhibition, with its overlapping corridors, sequences and zones, was intended to provide an impression of the radical change in society triggered by the increasing spread of computer technologies.

For Lyotard, the problem of non-representability of postmodernism was central in Les Immatériaux, because for him, a postmodern artist or writer is in the position as a philosopher: 'The artist and the writer are working without rules in order to formulate the rules of what will have been done. ... Postmodern would have to be understood according

to the paradox of the future (post) anterior (modo).'[4] While modern
aesthetics remains nostalgic, lamenting the failure of representation,
postmodernism must set out in search of the representation of the non-
representable. It is not a question of the non-representability of the
absent, but rather of making it possible to experience what is not yet
present. So, the transformation from industrial society to information
society was not only the object of investigation, but was itself supposed
to become tangible and visible. Alongside conventional exhibition
objects such as paintings, sculptures and videos, the show featured an
impressive arsenal of the most recent technologies – from the latest
screens to high-tech headphones to computer terminals, which were
still unique at that time – to engage as broad an audience as possible.
Ironically, the fact that these very technologies were especially prone
to errors may have unintentionally reinforced the impression of a postmodern 'complexity of things'.[5]

Although Lyotard later distanced himself from the exhibition,[6] he
saw it as an effective instrument for making it possible to experience the
restless curiosity that arises 'in the outbreak of postmodernism'.[7] Les
Immatériaux was able to give the visitors a foretaste of what is to come
by simulating and reflecting the increasing informatisation of physical
space. In particular, the city, with all of its streets, squares and paths,
its traffic and communication networks, served as model for the exhibition's scenography, in which visitors found themselves in a constant
exchange with high-tech objects, data streams and sound elements. For
Lyotard, the overlapping of urban and data space was accompanied by
a transition from the modern *metropolis* to a postmodern *megalopolis*, within which the distinction between an inside and an outside has
become obsolete.[8] In the postmodern city, which is no longer marked
by clear-cut boundaries, but rather by a mesh of relations, the network
becomes the determining figure of representation. Hence, reflecting on
the conditions of urban space also implies a reflection on the conditions
of knowledge; not least because the city has always represented the site
of thinking.[9]

DEATH OF THE SOCIAL

The term *postmodernity* was taken over from American sociology, which had used it to describe knowledge-based transformation

processes that had taken place in art, literature and science since the end of the nineteenth century. Lyotard saw in this not only a literary problem, exemplified in the nouveau roman of the post-war era, but rather an indication of the legitimation deficit of meta-narratives. For him, the postmodern is expressed as a scepticism with regard to these meta-discourses, which were previously able to legitimise philosophical, scientific, as well as political forms of knowledge: 'The narrative function is losing its functors, its great hero, its great dangers, its great voyages, its great goal.'[10] The question of legitimising knowledge through grand narratives ultimately leads Lyotard to a further question, namely that of the legitimisation of social institutions themselves. Since modernism, the political, social and cultural means of organisation have been stabilised with the help of a rationality discourse. With the discontinuation of this structuring discourse, modern modes of organisation and their institutions increasingly come under pressure, especially as the new information and communication technologies impel a restructuring of sociability. The informatisation of society consequently leads to a general aestheticisation, which, according to Lyotard, is 'the answer the megalopolis gives to the anxiety born for lack of an object'.[11]

It seems fitting to describe the art institution Centre Pompidou, in which Lyotard's exhibition Les Immatériaux took place, from such a postmodern perspective, as Jean Baudrillard did in his polemic essay 'The Beaubourg Effect'.[12] In this article, Baudrillard called the Paris museum, colloquially referred to as *Beaubourg*, a 'carcass of signs and flux, of networks and circuits', the function of which is the 'translation of an unnameable structure: that of social relations'.[13] In an endless process of recycling cultural products through the plastic pipes of the Centre Pompidou, an attempt is made to simulate and thus dissolve society. In this, Baudrillard – similarly to Lyotard – sees an 'unconditional aestheticisation'[14] that ultimately leads to the implosion of the social institutions and their power. Although this 'implosion fantasy'[15] may be exaggerated, it refers to a central point of postmodern society, namely that the 'culture of liberating violence' still invoked in May 1968 has been replaced by an implosive violence, specifically through 'hypertrophied controls that invade all the interstitial paths of facilitation'.[16] The capitalist regime thus not only expands at a global scale, but also at a social level by capturing almost all aspects of life. In late capitalism, the factory as a symbol of the industrial exploitation of human labour disseminates into culture, creativity and education.[17]

From this perspective, Lyotard's idea on the postmodern transformation of knowledge could also be understood as a critique of capitalism: the subject of the analysis is not informatisation alone, but also the concomitant commodification of knowledge. This applies to new communication forms that have been turned into the basis for an immaterial mode of production: the production of communication by means of communication describes an increasingly flexibilised mode of working that – unlike its modern predecessor – can do without 'an end product'.[18] Today's cultural and media industries have summed up such a mode of working based on communicative and cognitive abilities; in other words, a mode of working that finds fulfilment in the activity itself and therefore no longer produces any products separate from communication. In late capitalism, 'The services rendered by living labor ... resemble linguistic-virtuosic services more and more.'[19] The postmodern thus implies a capitalist mode of organisation and production that aims at the entire human individual, along with its personality, its leisure time, its linguistic capacity, its intellect and its affects. This makes the old categories of labour obsolete, which was based on a merely producing activity: it is no longer the standardised regulations and procedures that are the focal point of production, but rather what is informal about communication, in which the distinction between labour and leisure, between private and public coincides. This 'implosion of the socio-economic sphere'[20] represents one of the decisive moments of the transition to postmodernism, because the postmodern play of signs replaces production as the organising principle of modern societies.

Although Baudrillard started his scholarly life by expanding the Marxist critique of political economy with a semiological theory,[21] he soon began to attack the theoretical foundations of Marxism. Because of his disappointment with the events of May 1968, Baudrillard's thinking moved from a neo-Marxist social theory in the direction of a post-Marxist theory of signs.[22] In his view, clinging to the law of value, the law in Marxist theory, through which use objects become exchange objects, unmasks Marxism as the actual mirror image of capitalism. 'Even though a certain idea of revolution has, since Marx, attempted to find a way past the law of value, it long since became a revolution in accordance with the Law,'[23] asserts Baudrillard in his standard work *Symbolic Exchange and Death*, published in 1976. Specifically, in the revolutionary phase model of historical materialism, Baudrillard sees no genuine alternative to capital's belief in progress, since the Marxist primacy of production adheres to capitalist productivism.[24] It is this 'unbridled romanticism of productivity'[25] that Baudrillard criticises. He sees the productivist discourse as leitmotif both of the capitalist system and of its revolutionary contestation – an agreement that seems suspicious to him. Although Marx recognised the general connection between production, distribution, exchange and consumption, his analysis focused on production as the determining principle.[26] Since Marx took production as the starting point for his critique of political economy, in order to disclose the neo-classical naturalisation of exchange value, he introduced – according to Baudrillard – an essentialist principle again, namely that of the use value produced by production. Hence, a critique of exchange value on behalf of use value no longer has any critical value, since both use value and exchange value are simply two sides of the same coin: 'The discourse of production and the discourse of representation are the mirror by which the system of political economy comes to be reflected in the imaginary and reproduced there as the determinant instance.'[27] In postmodernism, there is no longer any determining principle, neither a metaphysical one (God) nor indeed a productivist one (labour/capital).

The proclaimed end of historical materialism also means an end of class struggle and thus of the historical subject: 'With Baudrillard, political theory begins with a refusal of the privileged position of the historical subject, and with an immediate negation of the question of historical emancipation itself.'[28] This movement of taking a distance to both the theoretical and the political programme of Marxism substantially influenced the postmodern debates at that time. The modern belief in progress, which is a constitutive moment in Marxism, is not solely a matter of a teleological description of the economy, but also of an all-encompassing principle, which includes science, art, culture and social welfare. Baudrillard's critique aims at this logic of constant cumulation, when he criticises the productivist fetish of Marxist theory. The economic recession phases of the 1970s, which were set off by the two oil crises, led to the realisation that modernism, in fact, knows not only perpetual progress, but has instead also been haunted by a series of regressions. Yet, for Baudrillard, postmodernity marks a specific point in history during which we are passing from a phase of explosion into a phase of implosion.[29] While Western modernity was characterised by an expansion of cultural and technological forms, of cities, states and empires, postmodern society is the site where all historical, political and social relations simply implode. With the exhaustion of the socio-economic field, the cultural perception of a promising future ultimately tipped into melancholy.

SIMULATED MASSES

In his essay 'Postmodernism, or the Cultural Logic of Late Capitalism,' the American literary critic Fredric Jameson located postmodern theories in the cultural field of late capitalism. In his view, aesthetic production has become an increasingly integral component of general commodity production, which is why theories of the postmodern have 'the obvious ideological mission of demonstrating ... that the new social formation in question no longer obeys the laws of classical capitalism, namely the primacy of industrial production and the omnipresence of class strug-gle'.[30] As a consequence, every position on postmodernism is ultimately a political statement vis-à-vis today's multinational capitalism. In this context, Jameson speaks of an aesthetic populism, expressed in a new architecture, which holds all the important characteristics of postmod-ernism. For him, the company headquarters of multinational corpora-tions with their architectonic depthlessness and superficiality embody the superstructural logic of a whole new economic world system. So, instead of insisting on an autonomous sphere of culture, he argues that the new global space of multinational capitalism must be recognised as the 'moment of truth' in our postmodern time.[31] Because of the increas-ing commodification of the cultural field, in the course of which adver-tising, communication, design, entertainment and marketing themselves become a source of profit, the classic Marxist distinction between an economic base and its cultural superstructure becomes obsolete.[32]

This is also what Baudrillard had in mind, when he attempted to radicalise the Marxist analysis of the commodity form with his critique of the sign form. Within his simulation model, the sign becomes the previously undiscovered side of the production process: not in opposi-tion to the commodity form, but rather as its final demise.[33] For Bau-drillard, the end of the capitalist exchange system ultimately implies an end of the social. In the society of simulation, social differences lose their significance, and therefore every form of political intervention becomes impossible. Pacified by an enormous surplus of information (print, radio and television), the masses no longer produce the social, but merely simulate it: 'The masses are the increasingly dense sphere in which the whole social comes to be imploded, and to be devoured in an uninterrupted process of simulation.'[34] Electronic mass media, in particular cable and satellite TV, are responsible for this process, because they represent the site of simulation. The hyper-realisation of the real in television networks implies not only a disappearance of the social, but also a disappearance of reality. In a reality produced by media, the real is replaced by signs of the real and real processes by their mediatic simulation. Of course, Baudrillard does not doubt the reality of the world as such, although he has often been accused of this, but his focus is instead on the disappearance of the reality as we know it. In a world completely staged by media, it is increasingly difficult to tell whether an event has actually taken place or not.[35]

But where does this nihilist conclusion in postmodern theory come from? For Gianni Vattimo, postmodernism is obligated to the Nietzschean idea that modernism cannot simply be overcome, because every attempt to critically overcome it is already subject to a modern way of thinking.[36] The dissolution of truth as a foundation of (rationalist) modernism is accompanied by a notion of the world as a cultural simulation. This is the insight that moves Baudrillard to define the sign as the most abstract form of the capitalist system and recognise the entire obscenity of commodity fetishism in the world of the simulated spectacle.[37] For, with the dissemination of new information and communication technologies, signs replace the reality they previously simply represented. The simulation model now shifts into the centre of the mode of production, so that the sign becomes the central category of the commodity form. Baudrillard's analysis can therefore be understood as a radicalisation, or even suspension of Marxist critique: use and exchange value are divested of their constituent oppositionality and reintroduced as broken particles in an endlessly reoccurring cycle. For Baudrillard, Marx's analysis of capitalist society represents a first in-depth investigation of the nihilist culture diagnosed by Nietzsche: 'After Baudrillard, it is impossible not to confront the political and theoretical conclusion that *Capital* isn't the reverse, but parallel, image of *The Will to Power*.'[38] In *Capital*, according to Baudrillard, Marx came across the nihilist mode of production in postmodernism, meaning that the commodity form produces abstract power in the form of signs: along with use and exchange value, it is the sign value as a third and previously hidden pole of the commodity form.

The 'fetishism of the sign'[39] impels capital, thus forming the mirror stage of capitalist production. If Marx wanted to maintain (living) labour as an autonomous sphere, in order to launch an emancipatory social theory, with his critique of this kind of naturalistic view of labour (or the use value created by it), Baudrillard also abandons any hope of liberation by taking Nietzsche's will to power as the real force of capitalist accumulation. This postmodern break with an emancipatory critique of the political economy ultimately implies an implosion of the social in the media, according to which electronically produced images, symbols and signs develop a momentum of their own. Unlike the common belief that information creates social meaning, and, consequently, transforms mass into revolutionary energy, Baudrillard argues that the overproduction of information simply devaluates social meaning. 'Instead of informing as it claims, instead of giving form and structure, information neutralises even further the "social field"; more and more it creates an inert mass impermeable to the classical institutions of the social, and to the very contents of information.'[40] In this perspective, all the well-intended attempts to reinstitute social emancipation and political liberation, as well as to resurrect a historical subject, ultimately reproduce the system in power, whose imperative is the surplus production of meaning and the endless remediation of signs.

EMANCIPATION/MANIPULATION

Although Baudrillard – like Marx – takes a stand for a wholehearted clarification of sociology as economy, contrary to the Marxist idea of a revolution through the mobilisation of the masses, Baudrillard dismisses the social as the 'zero degree of the political'.[41] It is therefore irrelevant if the masses overcome their supposed alienation, because the mass itself is the site of this alienation. This also sheds a different light on mass media, which, from a Marxist point of view, has long been considered a manipulative force: 'It has always been thought ... that it is the media which envelop the masses. The secret of manipulation has been sought in a frantic semiology of the mass media. But it has been overlooked, in this naive logic of communication, that *the masses are a stronger medium than all the media*'.[42] Hence, for Baudrillard, it is not the media that manipulate the masses, but conversely the masses that co-opt and ultimately absorb the media.

An excessive consumption of media has yielded a hyper-simulation, and, consequently, a hyper-conformity within the masses that renders political change impossible. This disengagement from the political programme of Marxism can be taken as a pessimistic response to the long-debated question of whether electronic media can be used in an emancipatory way or not. Since the 1920s – at the very latest – a new 'man of the masses' had been invoked again and again as a result of mass-media communication.[43] Especially Brecht's radio theory saw the mass distribution of radio as an opportunity to constitute listeners not only as isolated receivers of information, but also as active transmitters. For him, radio is a medium of exchange, since it organises the masses and relates individuals to one another.[44]

Brecht's vision took a cruel turn, however, when shortly afterwards National Socialism transformed the hoped-for communication apparatus into a machine of enforced conformity to advance the fascist mass mobilisation. The experience of National Socialist propaganda soon evoked the idea of an instrumental domination of technological media among the German – largely exiled – leftists. One of the most prominent examples in this respect is a chapter from Adorno and Horkheimer's *Dialectic of Enlightenment* on mass-production of culture.[45] In it, the two founders of the Frankfurt School identify post-war mass media as part of the more broadly defined cultural industries, which foster the standardised reproduction of culture and ultimately the formation of a pseudo-individuality.[46] The broad reception of the text among the movement of 1968 had a substantial influence on the perception and understanding of media technologies by leftist theory. In Germany particularly, the discussion was for a long time influenced by the idea that media is nothing more than mass manipulation. This widespread suspicion towards an emancipatory use of media technologies was finally criticised by Hans Magnus Enzensberger.[47] In his view, a socialist media theory and practice must appropriate the media for its own ends, if it does not want to remain powerless in the face of cultural industries and technological developments. '[E]very use of the media presupposes manipulation,' writes Enzensberger in 1970. 'There is no such thing as unmanipulated writing, filming, or broadcasting. The question is therefore not whether the media are manipulated, but who manipulates them.'[48] Instead of lamenting the manipulative power of the media, the left should fight for as broad an access as possible to the media, so that everyone can become a manipulator.

The electronic media, for Enzensberger, constitute a new productive force, whose practical means, in the form of copy machines, transistor radios or video cameras, are already in the hands of the masses. However, the dominant relations of production still suppress the mobilising force of the media, thus leading to a de-politicisation of the masses: 'In its present form, equipment like television or film does not serve communication but prevents it. It allows no reciprocal action between transmitter and receiver.'[49] In this sense, the transition from a simple apparatus of distribution to a medium of communication is not a technical but a political problem. With recourse to Brecht's radio theory, Enzensberger demonstrates that any transistor radio is, by the principle of its technical construction, not only a receiver, but always also a potential transmitter. The purposely maintained separation into transmitter and receiver thus only mirrors the 'basic contradiction between the ruling class and the ruled class'.[50] The division into producers and consumers of information is not technically inscribed in electronic media, but is instead the result of the political, social and economic conditions of capitalism.

In this argumentation, the Marxist idea of historical materialism is clearly evident, according to which the continuously evolving forces of production (i.e. natural, technical, scientific, organisational and intellectual resources) are being trapped by the dominant relations of production (relations of property, labour, distribution, circulation and consumption), thus forming a specific mode of production (e.g. bourgeois society/capitalism). The material-economic structure constitutes the basis of a society, from which the entire political, juridical and ideological superstructure develops.[51] For Enzensberger's Marxist-orientated media theory, it is obvious that electronic media are a component of the economic structure, in other words, part of the material base and not simply an outgrowth of its ideological superstructure: 'With the development of the electronic media, the industry that shapes consciousness has become the pacemaker for the social and economic development of societies in the late industrial age.'[52] In order to free the emancipatory potential of the new productive forces from the capitalist relations of production, a collective mode of production is needed, which is focused on the needs and interests of the masses. Enzensberger's emancipatory programme thus refers not simply to individual bricolage, such as in the basement hobby rooms of radio amateurs, but is underlying the importance of new '[n]etwork-like communications models built on the principle of reversibility of circuits', which 'might give indications of how to overcome this situation: a mass newspaper, written and distributed by its readers, a video network of politically active groups'.[53] Key to this argument is not the mere dissemination and distribution of electronic media, but their activation through a collective usage and practice.

In his response to Enzensberger's essay, Baudrillard shares his opinion that it is not enough to simply turn every receiver into a transmitter in order to break with ruling media structures. However, for Baudrillard, the mere reversal of the communication process is also insufficient, because '[r]eversibility has nothing to do with reciprocity'.[54] According to Baudrillard, the media structure itself – regardless of the dominant relations of production – hinders any form of communication, because technical media transcends 'real exchange' to the abstract level of code. Transmitter and receiver can indeed change their position, but they thereby only reproduce the simulation model of communication, within which one can choose the code of the message and the other only has the choice to accept it or not.[55] This scheme, which is rooted in information theory, 'excludes, from its inception, the reciprocity and antagonism of interlocutors, and the ambivalence of their exchange'.[56] Of course, Enzensberger also sees the danger of a mere simulation of communication, when he points out the pseudo-participation of the reader, listener or viewer in so-called 'democratic forums', in which 'he is only asked questions so that he may have a chance to confirm his own dependence'.[57] Still, for him, these manipulatory procedures are contrary to the media structure itself and have already been displaced by the emancipatory forces of electronic media, whereas Baudrillard recognises the essence of manipulation, that is the ability to disrupt all processes of exchange, within the media: 'They speak, or something is spoken there, but in such a way as to *exclude any response anywhere.*'[58] In keeping with his critique of the political economy of the sign, Baudrillard rejects Enzensberger's socialist media theory as not radical enough, especially since it continues to adhere to a 'strategic illusion' about the media. The hope of (re)appropriating electronic media for an emancipatory use ultimately remains part of the Marxist imaginary, namely to 'strip objects of their exchange value in order to restore their use value'.[59]

According to Baudrillard, it is therefore no coincidence that the *media revolution* has not taken place yet, because the possibility of such a revolution 'presupposes an upheaval in the entire existing structure of the media'.[60] As Baudrillard shows by the example of graffiti, it is the immediate 'insurrection and eruption in the urban landscape as the site of the reproduction of the code' [61] that first allows for an alternative and subversive form of media practice, since the street is 'the frayed space of the symbolic exchange of speech – ephemeral, mortal: a speech that is not reflected on the Platonic screen of the media'.[62] Accordingly, only singular 'symbolic actions' are possible, which may irritate the ruling system, but cannot overcome it. Because of this subversive affirmation, one can detect yet another version of the manipulation thesis in Baudrillard's critique – in fact a kind of hyper-manipulation within a system of total media control. The Marxist project of political organisation, which refers to an active subject, thus becomes irrelevant. 'Chief point of Anti-Marxist postmodern theory: that under postmodern conditions, the game is over. The struggle does *not* continue.'[63] But what if the highly speculative character of this postmodern media theory produces a tautology, in the sense that the critique of the 'neo-capitalist cybernetic order'[64] is itself a simulation effect? Andreas Huyssen, in this context, notes that '[s]imulation, after all, may simply be the latest version of the ideology of the end of all ideology'.[65] There is no way out of the hyper-reality of simulation, because all objections against it are denounced as being complicit with the system.

Contrary to such a fatalistic point of view, Stuart Hall argued that communication is a rather complex process, on the basis of which the received message can very well differ from the one sent out. In fact, the meaning of a message is never determined a priori, but changes with the distinctive moments of communication, namely the production, circulation, distribution, consumption and reproduction of signs. In order to be meaningful, a message has to be de-coded according to the dominant code, thereby reproducing the hegemonic set of meanings. However, to have an effect, the meaning has to be articulated in practice, thereby producing difference. Hence, the process of encoding and decoding messages – Baudillard's mode of symbolic exchange – is not ahistorical, but deeply entangled to the socio-economic power relations of a specific time and place.[66] This finally opens the way for a non-deterministic definition of the media: while both, the deep suspicion towards the manipulative power of the media, as well as the wide-eyed hope of its emancipatory potential, cleave to the idea that social change – positive or negative – can be directly derived from technological structures, Hall's 'politics of signification' allow us to go beyond such a technicist reduction. In addition to the manipulation and emancipation paradigm, a third paradigm arises from Marxist media theory, namely that of politics, which considers media as apparatuses of hegemony.[67] Here, the question is not anymore whether media technologies are inherently emancipatory or manipulative, but they are considered to be both, terrain as well as means of politics within a hegemonic struggle over meaning. Embedded in the social, cultural and institutional power structure, media play a crucial role in our cultural imaginary, all the more, as they transport social knowledge (in terms of images, values, categories, classifications and lifestyles) and therefore contribute to the construction of dominant, but also antagonistic, forms of identity (along the lines of class, race and gender).[68] If we want to understand politics related to media – whether traditional mass media or new Internet media – we have to question any deterministic shortcut, because ultimately it is in political sphere, not in the media, where emancipation or manipulation takes place.

NOTES

1. The book was basically a study, commissioned by the Academic Council of the Government of Québec, about the conditions of knowledge in the – by then and according to the Council – most economically and technologically advanced societies (Jean-François Lyotard, *The Postmodern Condition: A Report on Knowledge*, trans. Geoff Bennington and Brian Massumi [Minneapolis: University of Minnesota Press, 1984]).

2. Of course, the realisation of the exhibition also required other people, especially the co-curator Thierry Chaput, and the scenographer Phillipe Délis.

3. Jean-François Lyotard et al., *Immaterialität und Postmoderne* (Berlin: Merve, 1985), 11. All quotes from this book translated by author.

4. Jean-François Lyotard, 'Lyotard, Answering the Question: What Is Postmodernism?' trans. Regis Durand, in *The Postmodern Condition: A Report on Knowledge* (Minneapolis: University of Minnesota Press, 1984), 81.

5. The concept of a non-exhibition exceeded the frustration tolerance of many visitors. Especially the experimental audio guide, which attempted less to explain the respective stations, but rather to charge them with additional meaning, was a subject of numerous complaints. The fact that the headphones needed for this were only available for a fee, led to a series (see Nathalie Heinich, 'Les Immatériaux Revisited: Innovation in Innovations', *Tate's Online Research Journal* 12 [2009], accessed March 15, 2017, www.tate.org.uk/research/publications/tate-papers/les-immateriaux-revisited-innovation-innovations).

6. See Antony Hudek, 'From Over- to Sub-Exposure: The Anamnesis of Les Immatériaux', in: *Tate's Online Research Journal* 12 (2009), accessed March 15, 2017, http://www.tate.org.uk/research/publications/tate-papers/12/from-over-to-sub-exposure-the-anamnesis-of-les-immateriaux.

7. Lyotard et al., *Immaterialität*, 11.

8. See Jean-François Lyotard, 'The Zone' in *Postmodern Fables*, trans. George Van Den Abbeele (Minneapolis/London: University of Minnesota Press, 1997), 17–32.

9. See Georg Simmel, 'The Metropolis and Mental Life (1903)', in *The Blackwell City Reader*, ed. Gary Bridge et al. (Oxford and Malden, MA: Wiley-Blackwell, 2002), 11–19.

10. Lyotard, *Postmodern Condition*, xi.

11. Lyotard, 'The Zone', 27.

12. See Jean Baudrillard, 'The Beaubourg-Effect: Implosion and Deterrence', trans. Rosalind Krauss et al., *October* 20 (1982), 3–13.

13. Baudrillard, 'Beaubourg-Effect', 3.

14. Ibid., 8.

15. John Rajchman, 'Les Immatériaux or How to Construct the History of Exhibitions', *Tate's Online Research Journal* 12 (2009), accessed March 15, 2017, http://www.tate.org.uk/download/file/fid/7271.

16. Baudrillard, 'Beaubourg Effect', 12.

17. See Gerald Raunig, *Factories of Knowledge, Industries of Creativity*, trans. Aileen Derieg (Los Angeles: semiotext(e), 2013). In the light of computer-based informatisation in postmodernism, Fredric Jameson already spoke of a cultural logic of late capitalism (see Fredric Jameson, *Postmodernism, or, the Cultural Logic of Late Capitalism* [Durham: Duke University Press, 1991]).

18. Paolo Virno, *Grammar of the Multitude*, trans. Isabella Bertoletti et al. (Los Angeles: semiotext(e), 2004), 58.

19. Virno, *Grammar*, 58.

20. Isabell Lorey, 'VirtuosInnen der Freiheit. Zur Implosion von politischer Virtuosität und produktiver Arbeit', *grundrisse. Zeitschrift für linke Theorie & Debatte*, 23 (2007): 4–10. English translation available online, accessed August 8, 2016, http://eipcp.net/transversal/0207/lorey/en.

21. See Jean Baudrillard, *Le Système des Objets* (Paris: Gallimard, 1968).

22. See Jean Baudrillard, *The Mirror of Production*, trans. Mark Poster (St. Louis: Telos Press, 1975). This disappointment, which Baudrillard shared with a large number of French leftist intellectuals (including Michel Foucault, Gilles Deleuze, Félix Guattari, Jacques Derrida and Gianni Vattimo), was not least of all the result of the passive stance of the Communist Party of France during the May revolts in 1968, in which Baudrillard saw an indication of a Marxist conservatism.

23. Jean Baudrillard, *Symbolic Exchange and Death*, trans. Iain Hamilton Grant (Los Angeles/London/New Delhi: Sage, 1993), 22.

24. Marx demonstrated that classical economy necessarily became entangled in contradictions when attempting to explain the origin of profit, because it did not recognise the central position of labour as the sole source of surplus value. In order to resolve the problem of value production, he himself made a distinction between the commodity form of labour and living labour power. This ultimately led to an essentialist explanation of labour, because living labour was declared as being the only source of value production in society: 'His [Marx's] labor theory of value expressed perfectly the nature of capitalist reductionism, its tendency to convert every social activity into just one more form of work ... comparable with every other kind of work' (Harry Cleaver, 'Sozialismus', in *Wie im Westen so auf Erden. Ein polemisches Handbuch zur Entwicklungspolitik*, ed. Wolfgang Sachs [Reinbeck: Rowohlt, 1993], 345–372; available in English online, accessed 8 August 2016: http://la.utexas.edu/users/hcleaver/socialismessay.html).

25. Baudrillard, *Mirror*, 17.

26. See Karl Marx, 'Ökonomische Manuskripte 1857/1858', in Karl Marx and Friedrich Engels, *Werke* 42 (Berlin: Dietz, 1983), 34.

27. Baudrillard, *Mirror*, 20.

28. Arthur Kroker, 'Baudrillard's Marx', in Arthur Kroker and David Cook, *The Postmodern Scene. Excremental Culture and Hyper-Aesthetics* (Hampshire/London: MacMillan 1988), 175.

29. See Jean Baudrillard, 'Review of Marshall McLuhan's *Understanding Media*', in *The Uncollected Baudrillard*, ed. Gary Genosko (London/Thousand Oaks/New Delhi: Sage Publications, 2001), 39.

30. Jameson, *Postmodernism*, 3.

31. Ibid., 49.

32. See Nick Dyer-Witheford, *Cyber-Marx. Cycles and Circuits of Struggle in High-Technology Capitalism* (Urbana/Chicago: University of Illinois Press, 1999), 368.

33. See Jean Baudrillard, *For a Critique of the Political Economy of the Sign*, trans. Charles Levin (St. Louis: Telos Press, 1981).

34. Jean Baudrillard, *Simulacra and Simulation*, trans. Sheila Faria Glaser (Ann Arbor: The University of Michigan Press, 1994), 68. The simulation consists of a multiple order of artificial sign worlds, which Baudrillard calls simulacra. The first order of simulacrum corresponds to the stage of imitation, as it is expressed, for instance, in the maps of the Renaissance era and their pictorial representations of a territory. The second-order simulacrum functions as a reproduction of the first order: in this context, Baudrillard mentions a fable by Jorge Luis Borges, in which the cartographers of a kingdom make such a perfect copy of a state territory that the map and the territory match; not in form of a replica, but as an identical reproduction. Today, however, even this fable is outdated, because we have now reached a phase in which the map no longer refers

to a territory, but precedes it. Such a third-order simulacrum is no longer that of a territory, because it no longer recognises any referential being or substance.

35. See Jean Baudrillard, *The Gulf War Did Not Take Place*, trans. Paul Patton (Indianapolis: Indiana University Press, 1995).

36. See Gianni Vattimo, *The End of Modernity*, trans. Jon R. Snyder (Baltimore: John Hopkins University Press, 1991), 164.

37. In his theory of the spectacle, Guy Debord already recognised that the spectacle has become the abstract equivalent of all commodities. It assumes the function of money, which one only looks at, because every use value in it has been obliterated. Guy Debord, *The Society of the Spectacle*, trans. Donald Nicholson-Smith (New York: Zone Books, 1994), 49.

38. Kroker, 'Baudrillard's Marx', 180.

39. Ibid., 184.

40. Jean Baudrillard, *In the Shadow of the Silent Majorities ... or The End of the Social*, trans. Paul Foss et al. (New York: Semiotext(e), 1983), 25.

41. Baudrillard, *Shadow*, 18.

42. Ibid., 44.

43. See Wolfgang Hagen, 'Discharged Crowds. On the Crisis of a Concept', in *Social Media – New Masses*, ed. Inge Baxmann, et al. (Zürich/Berlin: diaphanes, 2016), 127.

44. See Bertolt Brecht, 'The Radio as an Apparatus of Communication', in *Brecht on Theatre: The Developments of an Aesthetics*, ed. John Willett (New York: Hill and Wang, 1964), 51–52.

45. See Theodor W. Adorno and Max Horkheimer, 'The Culture Industry: Enlightenment as Mass Deception', in Theodor W. Adorno and Max Horkheimer, *Dialectic of Enlightenment*, ed. Gunzelin Schmid Noerr (Stanford: Stanford University Press, 2002), 94–136.

46. See Adorno and Horkheimer, 'Culture Industry', 125.

47. See Hans Magnus Enzensberger, 'Constituents of a Theory of the Media', in *The New Media* Reader, ed. Noah Wardrip-Fruin et al. (Cambridge/London: MIT Press, 2003), 261–275.

48. Enzensberger, 'Constituents', 265.

49. Ibid., 262.

50. Ibid.

51. See Karls Marx and Friedrich Engels, 'Die Deutsche Ideologie', in Karls Marx and Friedrich Engels, *Werke* 3 (Berlin: Dietz, 1990), 26–27. To be clear, Marx and Engels do not consider the relation between base and superstructure simply as a relation of causality, but rather as a dialectical interrelationship. Thus, it is not a question of a one-dimensional determination of culture by the economy, but rather of the observation that the revolutionary potential of a society is to be found in the existing conflicts between the productive forces and the

production conditions within the base – and not, for instance, in the ideology that the society holds for itself.

52. Enzensberger, 'Constituents', 261. Although Marx regards streets, railways and telegraph systems less as means of production, but rather as means of transport and communication, which also flow into the production process, but do not have the same essentialist quality (see Karl Marx, 'Ökonomische Manuskripte 1857/1858', in *Werke*, Vol. 42 Karl Marx, Friedrich Engels [Berlin: Dietz, 1983], 431).

53. Enzensberger, 'Constituents', 267. As Noah Wardrip-Fruin explains in a brief introduction to Enzensberger's essay, this passage strongly calls to mind the concept of the 'rhizome' that appeared a few years later in *A Thousand Plateaus*. With this concept, Gilles Deleuze and Félix Guattari formulate an alternative to models of knowledge that represent the world in the form of (hierarchically organised) books. The rhizome, by contrast, is based on the principles of connection and heterogeneity. Following the global justice movement of the 1990s, the rhizome then became a metaphor for network-like organisation and information structures, which made use of new media technologies: 'In this case, new media have been used both to support the alternative organization of a social movement (more a network than a hierarchy) and to provide a different model of media consumption'. (Noah Wardrip-Fruin, 'Introduction to "Constituents of a Theory of the Media"', in *The New Media Reader*, eds. Noah Wardrip-Fruin et al. [Cambridge/London: MIT Press, 2003], 260).

54. Jean Baudrillard, 'Requiem for the Media', in *The New Media* Reader, ed. Noah Wardrip-Fruin et al. (Cambridge/London: MIT Press, 2003), 286.

55. The transmitter–receiver model, which goes back to the work of Claude E. Shannon, describes the communication process as the transfer of a message from a transmitter to a receiver. For this, a channel is needed, over which the signal, carrying the information that composes the message, is sent. Semiotics considers culture as communication in this context, whereby communication is understood as sending messages based on socially accepted codes. These are the very codes that represent a system of symbols and thus establish a certain model of domination: 'The entire conceptual infrastructure of this theory is ideologically connected with dominant practice, as was and still is that of classical political economy. It *is* the equivalent of this political economy in the field of communications' (Baudrillard, 'Requiem for the Media', 254).

56. Baudrillard, 'Requiem', 285.

57. Enzensberger, 'Constituents', 266.

58. Baudrillard, 'Requiem', 281.

59. Ibid., 280.

60. Ibid., 281.

61. Baudrillard, *Symbolic Exchange*, 101.

62. Baudrillard, 'Requiem', 284. In his essay 'Immediatism' Hakim Bey also refers to the necessity of playfully trying out new forms of immediacy (see Hakim Bey, 'Immediatism', in Hakim Bey, *Immediatism. Essays by Hakim Bey* [Edinburgh/San Francisco: AK Press, 1994], 7–12). Invoking the immediate community, which is supposed to enable 'authentic experience' in the face of the abstract violence of capital, is always in danger, however, of ending in mere escapism.

63. Dyer-Witheford, *Cyber-Marx*, 170.

64. Jean Baudrillard, *Simulations* (New York: Semiotext(e), 1983), 3.

65. Andreas Huyssen, 'In the Shadow of McLuhan: Jean Baudrillard's Theory of Simulation', *Assemblage* 10 (1989), 9.

66. See Stuart Hall, 'Encoding, Decoding', in *The Cultural Studies Reader*, ed. Simon During (London/New York: Routledge, 1999), 507–517.

67. See Oliver Marchart, 'Marx und Medien – Eine Einführung', in *Media Marx*, ed. Jens Schröter et al. (Bielefeld: transcript, 2006), 53–55. The concept of hegemony goes back to Antonio Gramsci, who therewith describes the ability of dominant groups or classes to establish their interests in such a way that they are finally regarded as general interests by subaltern groups and classes as well. Hegemony refers to a politically produced consensus that constitutes the common sense of a given historical period. Gramsci, thus, eludes the determinism of the Marxist base-superstructure-model, by explaining power not only from domination of the means of production, but also locating it in the cultural consent of a society (see Antonio Gramsci, *Prison Notebooks*, ed. and trans. Joseph A. Buttigieg and Antonio Callari [New York: Columbia University Press, 2011]).

68. See Stuart Hall, 'The Rediscovery of "Ideology": Return of the Repressed in Media Studies', *Cultural Theory and Popular Culture – A Reader*, ed. John Storey (Essex: Pearson, 2006), 124–155.

Chapter 3

Net Cultures

The massive spread of personal computers in the 1980s triggered a debate about the changing technical conditions of the production of social knowledge. While cultural studies in the Anglophone world emphasised the differentiation of subjectivity through the autonomous use of media technologies, the discussion in the German-speaking world unfolded in reverse: the so-called German Media Theory[1] argued for a technical homogenisation of social systems, shifting the attention towards the media-technological a priori of culture.[2] Instead of describing media from an ideology-critical, or socio-historical point of view, this specific strand of media theory is interested in the antecedent, defining, and determining function of media. 'Within this type of media analysis, institutions play as important a role as technologies, and modes of coding and notation, archiving, and the transfer of data are as crucial as questions of the political or strategic impacts of media,' as Eva Horn wrote in a special issue of Grey Room on the subject.[3] Even though such an approach does not necessarily imply an understanding of media as an ontological concept, that is the often-repeated accusation of media-determinism, there remains a 'forbidden pleasure' when dealing with media theory of German provenance, in particular in relation to today's emerging algorithmic cultures.[4]

The reason for this may be found in the father figure of German Media Theory, Friedrich Kittler, who from early on provoked the humanities with his radical posthumanism. In reference to Foucault's famous statement and in the light of postmodernism's attempt to destabilise the omnipotent subject position of Western philosophy, he claimed that with the introduction of the computer, 'man will vanish like a face drawn in the sand on the shore of the sea'.[5] For Kittler, media technologies not only constitute a power in themselves, but also create the human subject. Hence, not media are the extension of man, as Marshall McLuhan had suggested,[6] but in fact man is the extension of media. The postmodern thesis of the 'death of the subject' is once more radicalised by German media philosophy, thereby accepting, or even welcoming, the loss of human agency. Here, Baudrillard's influence is more than evident,[7] even more so since the media-materialist turn dropped any emancipatory agenda in favour of a less maculate theory of the epistemic and technological conditions of media assemblages. As a consequence, most of German media theorists were no longer interested in a hermeneutical programme of decoding the cultural, political and social meaning of messages, but rather in making the material functions of media, namely that of storage, transmission and processing, themselves visible. The social, in this perspective, was considered to be no more than 'one of the bureaucratic shackles'[8] of our time, which ultimately hampers the attempt of bringing the media-technological basis of culture to light.

However, and similar to Baudrillard's proclaimed end of ideology and therefore any critique of ideology, German Media Theory was superseded by the events of 1989. The inability to adequately react to the upheaval revealed its biggest blind spot, namely that of the political. In the wake of the fall of the Berlin Wall, a media-technological reorientation was taking place, not least because of the newly enabled exchange between East and West Europe, as well as the revival of social movements in the 1990s. The Internet became the epitome of this transformation and led to a re-evaluation of the media question.[9] Politically active individuals and groups made use of the rapidly growing computer network in order to bring about cultural and social change. Media were thus not any longer seen as mere technologies of communication, but rather as apparatuses of the political. The sovereign use of media, made possible by the emergence of low-cost network technologies, eventually became a central component of a newly established and largely pragmatic media critique, which began to spread throughout Europe and beyond. Whereas the post-1968 concept of alternative media worked on the principle of a counterpublic,[10] thereby only mirroring the mainstream mass media, the idea of sovereign media allowed for a self-positioning within the cultural field and a revitalisation of critical theory vis-à-vis the media-technological sphere.[11]

NET CRITIQUE

The Internet discourse of the 1990s was marked by the 'Californian Ideology',[12] a techno-liberalist amalgamation of hippie culture and New Economy, which was propagated primarily by the cyberculture magazines *Mondo 2000* and *Wired*. According to Richard Barbrook and Andy Cameron, the core of this ideology contained a bizarre mixture of technological determinism and libertarian individualism, combined with an anti-statism typical of the US counterculture. Despite, or precisely because of its inconsistency, the belief in individual freedom through technological progress became the operating system of a 'virtual class'[13] that was able to establish a discursive hegemony in the Internet economy. The close interconnections between countercultural currents in San Francisco and the high-tech industries in nearby Silicon Valley engendered a cybercultural imaginary that had a strong influence on the so-called dot-com phase.[14] Hence, at the 'electronic frontier', the old American dream of the Wild Wild West merged with the new promises of the World Wide Web, reinforcing the (colonial) desire to liberate the individual from all social constraints.[15]

Counter to commercially orientated cyberculture, a critical stance soon formed that was called the 'European answer to Wired' by cultural theorist McKenzie Wark.[16] Organised around the Internet mailing list *nettime*, net critique arose in the mid-1990s as an explicitly non-academic project, in order to discuss the dangers, but also political opportunities of the Internet. Throughout Europe, a critical net culture scene emerged, manifesting itself in a multitude of newly established media centres (e.g. De Balie in Amsterdam, Public Netbase in Vienna, Backspace in London, Ljudmila in Ljubljana, E-Lab in Riga), media art festivals (e.g. Ars Electronica in Linz, Dutch Electronic Arts Festival in Rotterdam, transmediale in Berlin), magazines (e.g. *Arkzine* in Zagreb, *Mute* in London), Internet radios, techno clubs, mailing lists and other projects. The broad field of interest necessitated a transdisciplinary and transinstitutional approach, which made it possible to break with the established boundaries in the art, culture and media world. Net critique functioned as a kind of interface in this new media-cultural art movement, by providing a bold mix of postmodern theory, institutional critique, media activism, hacker and DIY cultures. Its theoretical and practical interventions reacted to an academic media theory 'dominated by speculative thinking',[17] whose preferred medium was still the printed word. In contrast, net critique did not want to take an outside perspective, but wanted to develop a theory about and within the Internet, the software and the cables.

As Dutch media theorist and net activist Geert Lovink pointed out, 'the aim of creating an international, interdisciplinary and networked critical discourse, able to reflect and intervene in the fast changing daily economics and politics of the Internet'[18] had led to a critical Internet culture, which differed fundamentally from the dominant cyberculture. Net critique advocated Internet access for all, not only for a few happy *digerati*,[19] while focusing at the same time on the socio-economic programme of the Californian Ideology, as it was also expressed in established media theory.[20] The self-imposed delimitation was said to lead to a strengthening of the commercially influenced cyberculture, especially since media theory supplied the widely unquestioned metaphors that information-capitalism needed to introduce its market-based concepts. Net critique saw this as an attempt to tame the anarchic character of the Internet and to discipline the wild-growing knowledge production associated with it. Distancing itself from the commercial orientation of the media sector, it also attacked the academic realm for being ineffective in producing the necessary critique to counter this commercialisation.[21]

In this sense, one could speak of a second disengagement: while postmodern media theory of the 1980s (e.g. Jean Baudrillard, Friedrich Kittler and Norbert Bolz) turned away from a Marxist critique of ideology, net critique of the 1990s rejected this speculative media theory in order to regain political agency. This sort of a dialectical movement opened up a new perspective to the effect that it was no longer merely about the theoretical reflection on the media-technological conditions, but rather about the active co-creation of these conditions. 'Jean Baudrillard's elaborations on simulation were useful in the 1980s when the media scape exploded', writes Lovink in his book *Dark Fiber*, but '[a]pproaching the millennium everything seemed simulated and Baudrillard's elaborations started to sound conservative and out of touch with the actual Internet reality'.[22] Beyond this postmodern conservatism, net critique emphasised the necessity of re-establishing a critique of ideology, in particular because 'the idea of a pure global communication, assisted by software algorithms and decentralized network architectures, are themselves mythological constructs, loaded with ideology'.[23] In order to call into question the narratives, myths and ideological patterns accompanying the network discourse, the aim was neither to spread a new techno-euphoria nor cultural pessimism, but rather to formulate a critical position that was able to intervene in the media processes themselves. Hence, whereas the aforementioned technicist arguments tend to explain social developments – both positive and negative – from technological processes, such a net-critical position recognises the embeddedness of social practices within technologies.[24]

At a time when the network discourse began to explode, net critique followed a largely pragmatic approach towards new media technologies, in order to keep up with the technological developments and not to leave the field entirely to the New Economy. This is relevant insofar as net culture initiatives were among the first to open the Internet to a broader public, by offering public access points, as well as technical and educational support. In Europe, but also in the United States and elsewhere, non-commercial Internet Providers (e.g. Backspace, Centre for Culture & Communication, De Digitale Stad, Internationale Stadt, Ljudmila, Silver Server, Public Netbase, The Thing, XS4ALL) did not only offer Internet access, but also a platform for the self-determined use of new media technologies. The idea was to position net critique at the centre of action and to open up spaces of creation and experimentation: '[R]ather than just doing critical reading and theorizing, practitioners go on to develop participatory events that demonstrate the critique through an experiential process.'[25] Critical net cultures emerged in this process and soon began to influence the economic, legal and political debates surrounding the Internet.[26] Because of this engagement, net cultures played a crucial role in implementing network technologies in society and fostering a cultural imaginary, which then became omnipresent with the establishment of the Internet as a mass medium.[27]

TACTICAL MEDIA

As 'minor media',[28] net cultures were able to challenge the dominant cyberculture with a critical perspective. For a short period of time, a political perspective opened up within the post-1989 situation, which was able to take up the legacy from alternative community media of previous decades, but without assuming the same kind of ideological rigour.[29] A perky dilettantism, expressed in dirty aesthetics and do-it-yourself practices, became a characteristic feature of early net cultures. Not the big strategic stakes, but the small edges and minoritarian positions were considered to make a difference.[30] Tactical media, thus, designated an ensemble of techniques and practices at the intersection of theory, art, culture, activism and media, blended into a set of 'digital micro-politics'.[31] For many, this pluralistic approach entailed a liberating moment, especially since tactical media practitioners did not want to be reduced to a certain field, whether it was art or science, activism or politics: 'There was a feeling of relief that those involved in tactical media could be any kind of cultural hybrid. ... Many felt liberated from having to present themselves to the public as a specialist in order to be experts.'[32] The possibility of digging one's own channel in the information landscape created a new media awareness, which in turn opened up new fields of agency. Not least, the exchange between East and West Europe that was made possible after the fall of the Berlin Wall led to a reanimation of media activism, with the ancillary effect that the art and cultural scene was ploughed up by it. This moment marked the birth of a new generation of media activists, for whom the tactical was an opportunity to express their resistance to the emerging neo-liberal powers without having to confront them directly.[33]

One of the birthplaces of tactical media was the Amsterdam festival Next Five Minutes (N5M), where, in the early and mid-1990s, Internet activists met with radio- and video-makers to discuss issues related to art, activism and new media technologies.[34] While the conference was initially centred entirely on the reunification of East and West Europe, it soon began to shift its focus to the media boom set off by the massive spread of digital technologies. Tactical media can therefore be seen as a result of both, the new political situation at the beginning of the 1990s and the transition from analogue to digital electronic media, because of which the technical equipment necessary for autonomous media production became increasingly cheap. As it says in the 'ABC of Tactical Media', written for N5M in 1997: 'Tactical Media are what happens when the cheap "do it yourself" media, made possible by the revolution in consumer electronics and expanded forms of distribution (from public access cable to the Internet) are exploited by groups and individuals who feel aggrieved by or excluded from the wider culture.'[35] In Europe, where a lively scene of pirate TV and radio stations existed, the introduction of the World Wide Web led to numerous initiatives seeking to open up their own media spaces. '[A]lways in search of an enemy',[36] strategic fields were to be temporarily occupied in the sense of hit-and-run tactics. This was all the more the case as the electronic data space was considered to be the new site of political struggle. Or, as the Critical Art Ensemble (CAE) formulated it: 'As far as power is concerned, the streets are dead capital!'[37] According to the CAE, power does not manifest itself anymore in the form of palaces, governmental buildings or company headquarters, but rather dissolves and circulates in global data streams. To be effective, relevant politics must therefore attack the centres of power where it matters to them the most – in the electronic circuits of digital networks.[38]

This was proven to be not just an empty threat: in the course of the 1990s a multitude of media-activist tactics, such as attacks on the informational infrastructure of governments and corporations (so-called 'denial of service' attacks), were employed to challenge the powers of neo-liberal governance. Interrupting the opponent's flows of information, however, was only a partial aspect of tactical media. The goal was rather to 'cross borders, connecting and re-wiring a variety of disciplines and always taking full advantage of the free spaces in the media that are continually appearing because of the pace of technological change and regulatory uncertainty'.[39] In this sense, Alexander Galloway distinguishes between an orthodox definition of tactical media – as it is primarily associated with the CAE and N5M – and a more general understanding of tactical media projects.[40] Especially cyberfeminism, which arose in the context of tactical media, can be seen as a new mix of artistic and activist practices. Instead of appropriating commercial or governmental media spaces on a temporary basis, cyberfeminists of the 1990s aimed to transversally connect alternative spaces, in order to adapt them for their cause. This form of feminism considered itself a response to both the largely male fantasy of media guerrilla warfare and the usually technophobic orientation of feminist movements in the 1970s and 80s. Whereas media technologies were long considered to be part of the order of male domination, cyberfeminists wanted to intervene in and open up 'technologically complex territories that have been overcoded to a mythic degree as a male domain'.[41] Along these lines, the British philosopher Sadie Plant tells a women's history of technology, which does not simply distance itself from patriarchal historiography, but rather unveils the history of technology as fundamentally female.[42]

The early 1990s saw a growing awareness of feminist politics, which resonated with the nonlinear and distributed model of tactical media. Alternative modes of media production therefore promised to break with – or at least destabilise – the old, linear narrative of patriarchy. The link between the network and women, between the digital machine and female bodies was a frequently recurring motif in cyberfeminist discourses. 'The clitoris is a direct line to the matrix',[43] as the Australian artist group VNS Matrix wrote in its 1991 cyberfeminist manifesto. It was this cheeky appropriation and inversion of hegemonic rhetoric, the intervention in the existing order, which allowed the cyberfeminists to not only occupy, but actually traverse the male domain of media and technology.[44] During the first Cyberfeminist International (CI), which took place during the 'Hybrid Workspace' at the documenta X in Kassel, the potentiality of this kind of disruptive politics was discussed, in particular the question if and how the patriarchal conditions of the Internet – its code, language and structure – could be deconstructed. What is noticeable about this meeting is the largely negative, albeit ironic, self-description of the movement, as it was expressed in the '100 Anti-Theses' of cyberfeminism.[45] Not only is cyberfeminism not a practice or a theory, but it is also not to be reduced to a specific form of organisation. The pluralist approach of these 'happy negatives'[46] was intended to inscribe a new, multifaceted text into the electronic net, in other words, to liberate the Internet from its militaristic male origins and transform it into a non-hierarchical, anti-identitarian, transversal communication platform.

Nettime

One of the central places where the discourse of early net cultures took place was the mailing list nettime, which was initiated in 1995 by Pit Schultz and Geert Lovink.[47] The central component of nettime is that the international, English-speaking mailing list Nettime-l, which had about 500 subscribers in 1997, grew to approximately 2,000 subscribers by 2001, and today has 4,699 subscribers (as of April 2017). In addition, there are lists in Dutch, Romanian and South-Slavic languages, as well as a separate list for announcements, which together make up the 'mailing lists for networked cultures, politics and tactics'.[48] The origins of nettime go back to a meeting in Spessart, near Frankfurt am Main, Germany: from 16 March to 19 March, 1995, the 'Media ZK' (ZK being the German abbreviation for central committee) convened under the title 'terminal theory of the 1990s – secret knowledge for all'.[49] The ironic allusion to a supposedly arcane knowledge in the hands a few should not conceal the fact that the organisers were quite serious in their intent of developing a common media strategy of net cultures, in order to intervene into the hegemony of 'Wired ideology'.[50] figure 3.1

But the attempt to build up an autonomous communication infrastructure failed at first, largely because of the technophobe atmosphere during the meeting, as Pit Schultz recalled in an interview with the author.[51] Shortly afterwards, some of the protagonists of Spessart met again at the Venice Biennale in the same year. The international orientation of the art festival, as well as the active *recruitment* by the founders of nettime, helped the project to gain more visibility and ultimately attracted the interest of net activists from all around Europe.[52] The transnational e-mail exchange that followed resulted in the implementation of a regular mailing list in late October 1995, whose agenda was

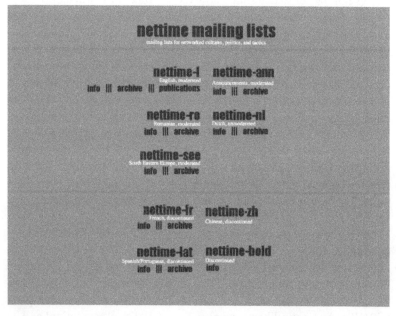

Figure 3.1   Screenshot of nettime, mailing lists for networked cultures, politics and tactics.

quite clear from the start: 'From its genesis, nettime was to embody the project of "net criticism" in order to counter the unbearable lightness of Wired magazine.'[53] It was precisely this mix of net critique and tactical media that soon made the list one of the international hubs to debate the implications of techno-libertarian cyberculture. A crucial characteristic of the discourse was the practice of 'collaborative text-filtering' (nettime): as was common in the early days of the Internet, content from the net was posted to the mailing list to be subsequently discussed. This commentary function was an appropriate means for producing a critique of and on the net.[54]

Similar to newsgroups, having been around since the introduction of the Usenet in the 1980s,[55] mailing lists are usually grouped around certain themes, which is how they establish social bonds of trust among the list members.[56] This is crucial, because unlike most centralised services of Web 2.0 mailing lists are usually operated on independent and decentralised servers.[57] As a consequence, the person who sets up the sever, also holds the key to the configuration of the mailing list, which allows him or her to determine how the list functions: whether posts to the list are immediately visible (unmoderated), for instance, or whether they first have to be approved by a moderator (moderated). In the case of nettime, the list was initially unmoderated, so that the content posted was not checked before it was sent to the list. New subscriptions were checked, however, so that not everyone had access to the list. What was remarkable about this semi-public list community was the fact that even those positions found a place, which were rejected by the majority of the members. Thus, one of the most active posters in the early days of nettime was John Perry Barlow, co-founder of the Electronic Frontier Foundation (EFF) and former lyricist of the rock band the Grateful Dead, who made no secret of his techno-libertarian opinions – not only on the list, but also in nettime meetings during various conferences and festivals.[58]

Only a few weeks after Barlow attended the second Next5Minutes conference in Amsterdam beginning of 1996, he presented the 'Declaration of the Independence of Cyberspace' at the World Economic Forum in Davos, Switzerland.[59] The manifesto, which was a response to the American 'Telecom Reform Act',[60] corresponded in large parts with *Wired*'s techno-libertarian narrative of a 'digital revolution' and its liberating effects for the individual. Barlow saw in cyberspace an *independent* space, which had to be protected from the old power structures, in particular the state. In a post-industrial, knowledge-based economy, information was supposed to be free and exchanged in a self-regulated market of ideas. This techno-libertarian vision of info-capitalism, which clearly followed the neo-liberal idea of a spontaneous social order, rejected governments as uninformed and illegitimate powers of the past. On nettime, a fierce debate sparked off about the implications of Barlow's declaration of independence. For the most part of list members, capitalism was by no means a 'natural order of things' and the electronic space therefore was not to be considered independently from the existing political, social and economic power relations. On the contrary, following the tactical media-approach, new technologies were supposed to be used to intervene in real conflicts. Instead of disengaging from the *old world*, the Internet was seen as a medium to reanimate the democratic discourse and public sphere, as well as the possibility of political participation in real space.[61]

The constant negotiation regarding the alignment and focus of nettime was at the centre of the first and, to date, the only conference organised by and for mailing list members: 'The Beauty and the East' took place from 21 May to 23 May 1997 in Ljubljana, Slovenia, and assembled 120 of the roughly 500 subscribers at that time.[62] During the meeting, it soon became clear that nettime was no longer a simple mailing list, but had grown into a kind of 'European Avant Garde'.[63] As such, however, it had difficulties to leave the narrow framework of a mailing list community and become a part of a bigger movement. While the popular discourse around the Internet exploded, expectations on and within nettime grew, not least because the applicability of tactical media gradually reached its limits. Issues concerning net art and media activism were thus passionately and controversially discussed in Ljubljana, as well as the special role of cultural institutions in places that were previously part of the Eastern Bloc (including Riga, Tirana, Novi Sad, Belgrade or Ljubljana). Consequently, the hoped-for consolidation of net critique with its own festivals, conferences and institutions did not take place, a circumstance, which might also be due to the fact that net critique itself took a very critical stance towards any institutional form of organisation. This hit a sore point in the debate of early net cultures, namely the role of state-funded institutions in the artistic and cultural sector.[64] figure 3.2

A somehow unintended restructuring of nettime took place soon after the meeting in Ljubljana: Because of a dispute that broke out over the

Figure 3.2   Peter Lamborn Wilson at nettime press conference in Vienna (1997).

net art project 'name.space',[65] the decision was made to moderate the
mailing list, so that from September 1997 onwards incoming messages
were first checked, before being passed on to the list. As Pit Schultz
explained the measure: 'The production of "information" along the
borderline of noise means to constantly refine a social context, maybe
an artificial one, what some call immanent, I mean with rules which are
self-evident, and are interdependent in a dynamic way.'[66] According
to this, an immanent discursive control in (online) communication is
achieved not only by technical, but also by social, protocols. By demar-
cating the field of possible communication – from open/unmoderated
to closed/filtered – both sets of protocological control define the rules
of the game, within which the mailing list is constituted as a *discourse
community*. The attempt to limit the amount of noise on the list thus led
to a gradual enclosure: 'In the next period of consolidation (1998–99)
nettime became a more structured (and moderated) forum where political and cultural aspects of technology and Internet development were

discussed.'[67] Whereas the list was characterised in its early years primarily by the desire to develop an alternative to the 'Californian Ideology', the collapse of the dot-com bubble and the peak of neo-liberal globalisation at the turn of the millennium led to a thematic broadening and brought political-economic issues into focus. However, these subjects were now also discussed on newly built communication platforms, such as the Indymedia network founded in the late 1990s. The aim to establish a transnational network of activists within the global sphere of multinational corporations was something that early net cultures shared with the emerging global justice movement, with the effect that 'globalization issues (Seattle) were much larger than net criticism and surpassed nettime'.[68] Consequently, net critique as an independent project was swallowed by the so-called anti-globalisation movement and its successors, even though the list itself has remained to be an important node in critical Internet culture till date.

CRITIQUE OF NET CRITIQUE

In the light of what has been said so far, critical net cultures of the 1990s can be described on the basis of – at least – three attributes: firstly, the autonomous *theory practice* that was mainly positioned outside of the established academic, artistic and cultural institutions; secondly, the exchange between East and West Europe, made possible by the fall of the *Iron Curtain* and the spread of new network technologies; thirdly, the opposition to a techno-libertarian cyberculture, as it was expressed in the *Californian Ideology*. In particular, the latter can be seen as a constituent element of critical net cultures and its hegemonic struggle over meaning, which, from the perspective of hegemony theory, necessitates the construction of an enemy.[69] However, despite the openly shown aversion to *Wired* magazine, there seemed to be a hidden and unarticulated accordance between net critique and its techno-liberal opponent, namely the shared belief in the transformative power of networks. In this sense, net critique was not questioning 'the values of Internet pioneers from the pre-dotcom age'[70] (i.e. decentrality, anonymity and free exchange of ideas), but rather their commercialisation and institutionalisation. While net critique certainly challenged the technodeterminist views of *Wired*, it was very supportive of new modes of self-organisation, which were based on bottom-up, rather than top-down decision-making processes.

Such a network-based model was often considered to be more natural and spontaneous than its traditional counterparts, in particular governmental and non-governmental institutions, thereby mirroring Barlow's techno-libertarian declaration of independence.[71]

The institutional critique within large parts of early net cultures ultimately led to a reanimation of the network model. This had already been in use in the 1970s and 1980s to describe so-called *grassroots movements*, a concept of horizontal ad-hoc networking that was taken up by tactical media theorists and practitioners, in order to link 'new media practices to grassroots impatience with old left hierarchies, overflowing anger against governments and businesses, and an urge to rethink the art of campaigning on the fly'.[72] Tactical media did not attempt to assume a hegemonic position within the field of art, culture and society, but rather preferred hit-and-run tactics to long-term strategic goals; thus always in danger of falling away from its own claims of radical media politics. However, the rhetoric did not always match the reality, as can be seen in the attempts to build up sustainable networks at a national and European level (e.g. the Virtual Platforms in Austria and the Netherlands, as well as the European Cultural Backbone). In fact, the proclaimed opposition between tactics and strategy was widely inconsistent: both, the *rebellious consumer* and the *presumptuous producer* were considered to be central to the practices of tactical media, which, eventually, did indeed aim for 'the creation of spaces, channels and platforms'.[73] Well aware of this inconsistency – maybe even making use of it – the claim was nonetheless that tactical media was a short-term concept, which 'surfs on the waves of events, enjoying the opening up of scenes and borders, on the lookout for new alliances'.[74] The assumption that tactical media could not be organised led to an emphasis on political forms limited by time and space, such as the Temporary Autonomous Zone,[75] formulated by Hakim Bey and highly popular among the youth and protest cultures of the 1990s and early 2000s. Yet, this flight into a temporal and provisional reversal of power structures can itself be read as an expression of capitalist realism, that is, the global political situation at the turn of the millennium, which lacks any coherent alternative to dominant capitalism.[76]

The fragmentation of political struggles promoted the self-understanding of tactical media as a tech-savvy avant-garde able to gain a clear edge with the help of new technologies: 'Many net activists thought that with their use of media they were quicker, cleverer, more effective, and simultaneously more invisible than their hegemonic counterparts, in other words governments and corporations.'[77] For Katja Diefenbach, the blind spot of critical net cultures thus consisted in the equation of a somehow elitist escapism with popular theories of subversion. As a 'self-declared elite',[78] tactical media practitioners created a notion of themselves as a resistive vanguard, thereby often ignoring the fact that any social situation is always multivalent and cannot be reduced to a common denominator – such as the Internet. This does not imply that net critique did fall into the trap of a techno-teleological belief in progress; on the contrary, it always insisted on the pragmatic use of media technologies, the dirty aesthetics of tactical media and the co-creation of network politics. However, the site of social change, that is the 'place of decision-making, representing and restructuring future power structures',[79] was clearly located in the network. Net critique, which from the beginning questioned a mere deduction of social life form technical structures, ultimately did not go against the primacy of the network, which promised no less than a technological upheaval of social relations. The network, or to be more precise, the idea of a distributed and thus democratic network has become the ineluctable reality, within which the Internet appears to be the main aspect of economic, social and political transformation.

Hence, net critique was grouped around the same central myth, which was set into the world by the adepts of the Californian Ideology: namely that the mere implementation of new information and communication technologies – above all the Internet with its various applications (e.g. e-mail, Usenet and World Wide Web) – would help to dissolve the old power structures and enhance democracy. Here, the actual strength of the network model comes to the fore, namely its ability to absorb the critique directed against it and to incorporate it into its own model, with the effect that 'the subversive promises given with regard to the new technologies got broken, while the net managed to assert itself as the dominant model of organisation'.[80] That is not to say that net critique failed and Californian Ideology simply spread out all over the planet, but it shows that the discursive power of critical net cultures was not sufficient enough to truly challenge the hegemonic ideas in relation to network technologies. Even more so, as the popular figures of subversion, such as the hacker or the media guerillero, which initially embodied the hope for radical change, were soon celebrated by the information economy as representatives of a new work ethic, freed from the burdens of the industrial age with its rigid structures, work contracts and political organisations.[81] This mirror stage of a techno-liberal cyberculture may also be the reason why tactical media outlets were all too easily overrun by commercial enterprises at the turn of the millennium, or, as in some cases, even turned themselves into media enterprises.[82]

NOTES

1. The label German Media Theory was applied a posteriori by North American scholars to describe this very diverse current of media theory. As an 'impossible discipline', it started as a discursive strategy out of other disciplines, in particular film, communication and literature studies, to undermine the idea of an autonomous and sovereign media subject (see Claus Pias, 'Was waren Medien-Wissenschaften? Stichworte zu einer Standortbestimmung', in *Was waren Medien?*, ed. C. Pias [Zürich/Berlin: diaphanes], 7–30).

2. See Geoffrey Winthrop-Young, 'Von gelobten und verfluchten Medienländern. Kanadischer Gesprächsvorschlag zu einem deutschen Theoriephänomen', *Zeitschrift für Kulturwissenschaften* 2 (2008): 113–127.

3. Eva Horn, 'Editor's Introduction: "There Are No Media"', *Grey Room* 29 (2008): 6–13, here 7.

4. See Matthew Fuller, 'The Forbidden Pleasures of Media Determinism', in *Media After Kittler*, ed. E. Ikoniadou et al. (London: Rowman & Littlefield, 2015), 95–110.

5. Friedrich Kittler, 'Fiktion und Simulation', in *Philosophien der neuen Technologien*, ed. Ars Electronica (Berlin: Merve, 1989), 79. Quote translated by the author. Friedrich Kittler put Foucault's discourse analysis one step lower, so to speak, by pointing out the necessity of applying discourse-analytical methods to material media (e.g. paper, records, film, typewriters and screens). Not only texts should thus be examined, but also media technologies with which these texts were written (see Friedrich Kittler, *Discourse Networks 1800/1900*, trans. Michael Metteer [Stanford: Stanford University Press, 1990]).

6. See Marshall McLuhan, *Understanding Media. The Extensions of Man* (Cambridge: MIT Press, 1994).

7. The French media theorist's influence on his German colleagues is not to be underestimated, as is evident, for example, in an anthology for a symposium held during the Ars Electronica 1989. In it, Kittler speaks of the 'triumph of simulation' (Kittler, 'Fiktion und Simulation', 65), and Peter Weibel, former head of Ars Electronica, speaks of media tools as perfect 'simulations of natural organs' (Peter Weibel, 'Territorium und Technik', in *Philosophien der neuen Technologien*, ed. Ars Electronica [Berlin: Merve, 1989], 99. Quote translated by author).

8. Kittler, 'Fiktion und Simulation', 131.

9. Here, Kittler and most of his disciples did not have an answer, because they still hold fast onto the computer as a single medium, rather than a globally operating network (see Stefan Heidenreich, 'The Situation After Media', in *Media After Kittler*, ed. E. Ikoniadou et al. [London: Rowman & Littlefield, 2015], 136–139).

10. See Oskar Negt and Alexander Kluge, *Public Sphere and Experience. Towards an Analysis of the Bourgeois and Proletarian Public Sphere*, trans. P. Labanyi et al. (Minneapolis/London: University of Minnesota Press, 1993).

11. See Geert Lovink, 'The Theory of Mixing', in *Radiotext(e)*, ed. N. Straus (New York: Autonomedia/Semiotext(e), 1993), 114–122.

12. See Richard Barbrook and Andy Cameron, 'The Californian Ideology', in *Proud to be Flesh: A Mute Magazine Anthology of Cultural Politics after the Net*, ed. Josephine Berry Slater et al. (London: Mute Publishing in Association with Autonomedia, 2009), 27–34. The term Californian Ideology was not formulated by *Wired* and its associates as self-description, but is instead a polemical term, used to distance oneself from this ideology. In principle, there are two versions of the Californian Ideology: on the one side there is the notion of the virtual community as an anti-commercial continuation of the new left (see Howard Rheingold, *The Virtual Community. Homesteading on the Electronic Frontier* [New York: Harper Perennial, 1994]), on the other there is the laissez-faire capitalism of the new right-wing with an emphasis on free market and individual freedom (here especially Newt Gingrich, George Glider or Alvin Toffler). Both versions overlap in their rejection of a 'strong state' and are conjoined by a common faith in technological determinism (see Barbrook and Cameron, 'The Californian Ideology', 29).

13. See Arthur Kroker and Michael A. Weinstein, 'Data Trash: The Theory of the Virtual Class', *ctheory* (1994), accessed March 25, 2017, http://ctheory.net/book2.asp?bookid=3.

14. See Fred Turner, *From Counterculture to Cyberculture: Stewart Brand, the Whole Earth Network, and the Rise of Digital Utopianism* (Chicago: University of Chicago Press, 2006).

15. See Oliver Marchart: 'Was ist neu an den Neuen Medien? Technopolitik zwischen Lenin und Yogi-Bär', in *Netzkritik*, ed. nettime (Berlin: ID-Archiv, 1997), 89–100.

16. See 'MedienKunstNetz', accessed March 25, 2017, http://www.medien-kunstnetz.de/works/nettime.

17. Geert Lovink, 'From Speculative Media Theory to Net Criticism' (paper presented at ICC, Tokyo, December 19, 96), *nettime*, accessed August 26, 2016, http://www.nettime.org/Lists-Archives/nettime-l-9701/msg00032.html.

18. Geert Lovink, *Dynamics of Critical Internet Culture* (Amsterdam: INC, 2009), 7.

19. The word *digerati* is a portmanteau, derived from the words *digital* and *litarati*. It describes the technical elite of the early Internet days, in particular those connected to *Wired* magazine.

20. See Sabeth Buchmann, 'Nur soviel: Das Medium ist nicht die Botschaft. Kritik der Medientheorie', in *Im Zentrum der Peripherie. Kunstvermittlung und Vermittlungskunst in den 90er Jahren*, ed. Marius Babias (Dresden/Basel: Verlag der Kunst, 1995), 79–102.

21. See Geert Lovink and Pit Schultz, 'Aufruf zur Netzkritik. Ein Zwischenbericht', in *Netzkritik*, ed. nettime (Berlin: ID-Archiv, 1997). Although it was not explicitly mentioned by representatives of net critique, this of course addresses the old opposition between theory and practice, as it was discussed by Louis Althusser (see *For Marx* [London/New York: Verso, 2005]) or Pierre Bourdieu (see *The Logic of Practice* [Stanford: Stanford University Press, 1990]). In their interpretation, theory is always already a practice, and practices conversely develop their own theories. Following Jacques Rancière, however, it could also be added that this *theory-practice problem* is itself a theoretical one, which ultimately promotes *intellectualism* (see Jacques Rancière, *Althusser's Lesson*, [London/New York: Continuum, 2011]).

22. Geert Lovink, *Dark Fiber. Tracking Critical Internet Culture* (Cambridge: MIT Press, 2002), 266.

23. Lovink, *Dynamics*, 26.

24. See Lovink, *Dynamics*, 21.

25. Critical Art Ensemble, *Digital Resistance. Explorations in Tactical Media* (New York: Autonomedia, 2001), 8.

26. In the mid-1990s, media and net-cultural initiatives joined together at the national and European level to form translocal networks (including virtual platforms in the Netherlands and Austria, and the European Cultural Backbone). These associations served, not least of all, conventional lobbying work, in order to influence economic and social policy decisions in relation to net- and media cultures. The individual initiatives and institutions soon ran into the limitations of their capacities, though, so that an actual alliance of net culture initiatives could not be established at the European level (see Andreas Broeckmann, 'Reflections on Building the European Cultural Backbone', in *Public Netbase: Non Stop Future, ed. Branka* Ćurčić et al. [Berlin: Revolver, 2008], 254–255).

27. It could be argued that the Internet is, in fact, not a mass medium, since it does not fulfil, or only partially fulfils, the central functions of mass media, such as periodicity (publication at regular intervals), publicity (accessible to everyone), universality (diversity of topics) and topicality (attracting the attention of society as a whole) (see Wolfgang Hagen, 'Discharged Crowds. On the Crisis of a Concept', in *Social Media – New Masses*, ed. Inge Baxmann et al. [Zürich/Berlin: diaphanes, 2016], 123–134). In the following lines, I will, however, speak of a mass medium, because the Internet certainly does have

a mass-media character: major, meanwhile global, *media events* (such as the mass phenomenon of new TV shows or Internet memes) cannot be imagined without the Internet (and its respective services such as streaming sites). In addition, Internet corporations (e.g. Facebook, Google, Twitter, Amazon and eBay) determine how we relate to one another and thus contribute to the production of subjectivity on a mass basis.

28. See Inke Arns und Andreas Broeckmann, 'Minor Media Normality', in *ZKP4* (1997), accessed April 1, 2017, http://www.mikro.in-berlin.de/wiki/tiki-index.php?page=Minor+Media+Normality#card_1490110306675_5129.

29. The community media of the late 1960s can be seen as a test bed for a participatory media environment, which, at that time, was based on television as the central medium. Especially in the United States, where legal regulations created the technological and financial basis for community access television (CATV), free and non-commercial programmes were the order of the day. The rapid development of video and cable technologies in the 1970s ultimately enabled the so-called *camcorder revolution* of the 1980s, which was supposed to hijack the centralised television system (see Tung-Hui Hu, 'Truckstops of the Information Superhighway: Ant Farm, SRI, and the Cloud', *Media-N: Journal of the New Media Caucus* 10:1 [2014], accessed April 1, 2017, http://median.newmediacaucus.org/art-infrastructures-hardware/truckstops-on-the-information-superhighway-ant-farm-sri-and-the-cloud).

30. For an overview of tactical media projects, see Rita Raley, *Tactical Media* (Minneapolis: University of Minnesota Press, 2009).

31. Lovink, *Dark Fiber*, 254. According to Foucault, the 'microphysics of power' is relational, a power circulating between bodies, entities and institutions that cannot be fixed in terms of a specific system of rules. Hence, also the state is ultimately a manifestation of these power practices and contingent forces. Not only coercion and violence constitute the balance of power, but equally freedom, self-determination and consensual forms of action. Similar to Gramsci, Foucault states: 'I don't claim at all that the State apparatus is unimportant, but it seems to me that ... power isn't localised in the State apparatus and that nothing in society will be changed if the mechanisms of power that function outside, below and alongside the State apparatuses, on a much more minute and everyday level, are not also changed' (Michel Foucault, *Power/Knowledge. Selected Interview and Other Writings 1972–1977* [New York: Pantheon Books, 1980], 60).

32. Critical Art Ensemble, *Digital Resistance*, 5–6.

33. The term *tactical* refers to Michel de Certeau's distinction in his book *The Practice of Everyday Life* (Michel de Certeau, *The Practice of Everyday Life* [Berkeley and Los Angeles: University of California Press, 1984]). Whereas strategic power seeks to occupy and defend a territory by all means

necessary, the powerless are left only with the option of penetrating into these strategic fields with the help of tactical means.

34. The conference series took place four times in total: The first edition, held in January 1993, was still under the influence of the events that followed the collapse of Real Socialism in Central and East Europe. In March 1996, the second N5M dealt with the onset of the early Internet boom. Just before the Kosovo conflict, in March 1999, the third N5M addressed the issues of modern media wars, as they had become apparent since the First Iraq War in 1991. The last edition of N5M, held in September 2003, examined the effects of 9/11 on social movements. Despite the far-reaching influence of N5M, the festival never had regularly scheduled meetings or an institutionalised structure (see Geert Lovink, *Zero Comments: Blogging and Critical Internet Culture* [New York/ London: Routledge, 2008], 187).

35. David Garcia and Geert Lovink, 'The ABC of Tactical Media' (posted May 16, 1997), *nettime*, accessed September 6, 2016, www.nettime.org/Lists-Archives/nettime-l-9705/msg00096.html.

36. Garcia and Lovink, 'The ABC'.

37. Critical Art Ensemble, *Electronic Civil Disobedience and Other Unpopular Ideas* (New York: Autonomedia & Critical Art Ensemble, 1996), 11.

38. This position, known as *hacktivism*, goes back to the Electronic Disturbance Theater (EDT). The EDT developed the 'FloodNet-Tool', which was able to shut down individual websites using a Java script. In so-called *virtual sit-ins*, a multitude of activists would repeatedly call up the targeted site until the server broke down. The actions were intended to be a new form of civil disobedience, as was formulated by the Critical Art Ensemble, several members of which also belonged to the EDT (see Critical Art Ensemble, *Electronic Civil Disobedience*, 17).

39. Garcia and Lovink, 'The ABC'.

40. See Alexander R. Galloway, *Protocol: How Control Exists after Decentralization* (Cambridge/London: The MIT Press, 2004), 175–176.

41. Faith Wilding and Critical Art Ensemble, 'Notes on the Political Condition of Cyberfeminism', *Art Journal* 57:2 (1997): 47–59.

42. See Sadie Plant, *Zeros + Ones: Digital Women + The New Technoculture* (New York: Doubleday, 1997). A prominent figure who permeates the entire book is the British mathematician Ada Lovelace. She was the daughter of Lord Byron and assistant to the engineer Charles Babbage, for whom she wrote the first program for his Analytical Engine (a mechanical computer which never got finished). This is why she is regarded as the 'first programmer in the world' – long before her male colleagues, for which reason the programming language Ada is dedicated to her.

43. VNS Matrix, 'Cyberfeminist Manifesto for the 21st Century', accessed September 14, 2016, http://www.obn.org/reading_room/manifestos/html/ cyberfeminist.html.

44. The range of cyberfeminism was quite broad: on the one hand a theoretical–philosophical orientation as with Sadie Plant or Rosi Braidotti, on the other a more political-activist line, as with VNS Matrix, Old Boys Network, or CashGirl. In addition, there were a number of media artists like Linda Dement or Cornelia Sollfrank, who made use of Internet technologies to bring new ideas and themes into this largely male-dominated field (see Marie Ringler, 'Im Interview mit Clemens Apprich', in *Vergessene Zukunft. Radikale Netzkulturen in Europa*, ed. Clemens Apprich et al. [Bielefeld: transcript, 2012], 271–275).

45. See Old Boys Network, '100 Anti-Theses', accessed 14 September 2016, http://www.obn.org/reading_room/manifestos/html/anti.html.

46. Garcia and Lovink, 'The ABC'.

47. The name was chosen by Pit Schultz to describe his idea of a network-specific time. 'The time of nettime is a social time, it is subjective and intensive, with condensation and extractions, segmented by social events like conferences and little meetings, and text gatherings for export into the paper world. Most people still like to read a text printed on wooden paper, more than transmitted via waves of light. nettime is not the same time like geotime, or the time clocks go. Everyone who programs or even sits often on a screen knows about the phenomena of being out of time; time on the net consists of different speeds, computers, humans, software and bandwidth; the only way to see a continuity of time on the net is to see it as an asynchronous network of synchronized time zones' (Pit Schultz, 'From the Archives: Introduction to nettime' [posted May 7, 2001], accessed April 1, 2017, https://nettime.org/Lists-Archives/nettime-l-0105/msg00036.html).

48. The lists in Chinese, French and Spanish/Portuguese are no longer active, nor is a completely unmoderated *nettime* channel (*nettime-bold*). In addition to *nettime*, there existed (and partly still exists) a variety of other mailing lists, which were crucial to early net cultures; for example *rhizome* (focus on new artistic practices), *Syndicate* (exchange between East and West Europe), *Faces* (strengthening the visibility of women in network cultures) and *7–11* (focus on net art).

49. The meeting in Spessart took place at the invitation of Andreas Kallfelz, who was head of the cultural institution Verein 707 in Frankfurt am Main. As part of the celebrations for the tenth anniversary of Verein 707, Pit Schultz and Geert Lovink organised the event. In addition to Kallfelz, Schultz and Lovink, the participants included Hans-Christian Dany, Jochen Becker, Florian Schneider, Verena Kuni, Felicia Herrschaft, Stefan Beck, Barbara Strebel, Florian Zeyfand, Ed van Megen, Gereon Schmitz, Joachim Blank, Armin Haase, Ute Süßbrich, Janos Sugar, Dietmar Dath, Barbara Kirchner, Christoph Blase, Wolfgang Neuhaus, Ludwig Seyfarth and Mona Sarkis (see Geert Lovink, *Dark Fiber*, 110).

50. Lovink and Schultz, 'Aufruf zur Netzkritik', 8.

51. See Pit Schultz, 'Im Interview mit Clemens Apprich', in *Vergessene Zukunft. Radikale Netzkulturen in Europa*, ed. Clemens Apprich et al. (Bielefeld: transcript, 2012), 76.

52. Pit Schultz organised a three-day workshop as part of the *Club Berlin* in Venice, where the issues from the first meeting in Spessart were further discussed. Participants in the discussion this time included David Garcia, Heath Bunting, Geert Lovink, Diana McCarty, Vuk Cosic, Paul Garrin, Gereon Schmitz, Nils Röller, Suzana Milevska and Katja Reinert.

53. Lovink, *Dark Fiber*, 83.

54. Because of the practice of 'collaborative text filtering' established on *nettime*, the emergence and development of net critique itself must be considered as a collective effort on the part of all list members, even though many of the texts ultimately published and quoted here bear the names of the first two list moderators, Geert Lovink and Pit Schultz.

55. Usenet is a worldwide computer network with thematically specific discussion forums (so-called newsgroups). Its beginnings go back to the end of the 1970s, and unlike the even older Bulletin Board Systems (BBS) or today's web forums, Usenet is based on a decentralised server architecture. (see Michael Hauben and Ronda Hauben, *Netizens. On the History and Impact of Usenet and the Internet* [Los Alamitos: IEEE Computer Society Press, 1997]).

56. See Rasa Smite, *Creative Networks, in the Rearview Mirror of Eastern European History* (Amsterdam: INC, 2012), 28–29.

57. The free software Majordomo, which was programmed by Brent Chapmann in 1992, initially constituted the technical basis of nettime. It allowed to automatically forward e-mails to a list of subscribers, whereas each subscriber could simply reply to each e-mail, thereby creating thematic threads. When nettime moved to its new server in October 2007, the list implemented the software GNU Mailman, which has largely replaced Majordomo as most popular mailing list software.

58. These meetings in *real life* took place regularly, especially in the early phase of nettime. Following Spessart and Venice (as mentioned above), the list community met at the second MetaForum conference in Budapest (October 1995), at the second Next5Minutes conference in Amsterdam/Rotterdam (January 1996), at the fifth Cyberconf in Madrid (June 1996), the third MetaForum conference in Budapest (October 1996) and during the Hybrid Workspace at the documenta X in Kassel (June–September 1997), among others.

59. See John Perry Barlow, 'A Declaration of the Independence of Cyberspace', (1996), accessed March 25, 2017: https://www.eff.org/cyberspace-independence.

60. The Communications Decency Act (CDA) was part of the American Telecommunications Act from 1996, whose main goal was to regulate pornographic and other offensive content on the Internet. A number of activists and civil rights movements, such as the American Civil Liberties Union (ACLU)

and the Electronic Frontier Foundation (EFF), considered it an attempt to censor the electronic space. Their protest led to a revision of the CDA, so that no Internet provider would have to fear being held responsible for the actions of its customers. The Internet community reached a similar success in 2012 as the Anti-Counterfeiting Trade Agreement (ACTA), which was intended to enforce copyright, was rejected by the European Parliament following massive protests.

61. Aside from the techno-libertarian stance, the manifesto also met with criticism because of Barlow's use of an inclusive *we*, which encompassed the whole net community as opposed to the representatives of the allegedly *old world*. For Diana McCarty, 'Barlow's *We* was not inclusive, and reeked of the techno elite's belief in their own right to power' (see Diana McCarty, 'Nettime: the legend and the myth', [1997], accessed March 25, 2017: http://www.hackerart.org/corsi/fm03/esercitazioni/demaio/artic2.html).

62. The event was carried out by the Ljubljana Digital Media Lab (in short: Ljudmila), an initiative for the promotion of media art and net culture founded in 1994. Especially in the early years, Ljudmila served as an independent Internet provider, which was able to provide affordable net access to art and cultural institutions. Like many comparable media initiatives in the former East Bloc, Ljudmila was financed by George Soros' *Open Society Institute*, a fact, which was controversially discussed at the *nettime* conference in Ljubljana (see Tilman Baumgärtel, "Beauty and the East" – Nettime-Treffen in Ljubljana. Von Onkel Soros' aufmüpfigen Kindern', (1997), accessed September 14, 2016: www.heise.de/tp/artikel/3/3086/1.html).

63. See McCarty, 'Nettime'.

64. See the discussion on nettime triggered by the Piran Manifesto (Vienna Ad-hoc Committee, 'The Piran Manifesto', [1997], accessed March 25, 2017, http://www.nettime.org/Lists-Archives/nettime-l-9705/msg00147.html).

65. The American media artist Paul Garrin founded the enterprise *name. space* in 1996, in order to accommodate the growing need for Internet addresses. Garrin wanted to break the monopoly of *Network Solutions Inc.*, a company responsible for assigning Top Level Domains (TLD), and establish a Permanent Autonomous Network with a freely accessible TLD registration system. Although many doubted the technical feasibility of the project, name. space nevertheless succeeded in sparking off an international debate (including coverage in the *NYT*, *Economist*, *Die Zeit*) about the practice of assigning Internet addresses. On *nettime*, Garrin's own communication practices (he started spamming the list with *advertising material*, among other things) were met with criticism, and a *flame war* erupted in the summer of 1997 (especially between Paul Garrin and Gordon Cook). The consequence of this was that the list was moderated from that point on (see Lovink, Dynamics, 114–117).

66. Pit Schultz, 'The Origins of the Nettime Mailing List. Pit Schultz Interviewed by Pauline van Mourik Broekman', in *Proud to be Flesh. A Mute*

Anthology of Cultural Politics after the Net, ed. Josephine Berry Slater et al. (London: Mute Publishing, 2009) 46–51.

67. Lovink, *Dark Fiber*, 71.

68. Ibid., 107. In fact, the list has grown constantly and has a unique standing as a site of critical net debate today. As such, *nettime* is also the subject of varying interpretations, especially in reference to the initial avant-gardist vision (see Ted Byfield, 'nettime – Fortsetzung folgt ...', *Vergessene Zukunft. Radikale Netzkulturen in Europa*, ed. Clemens Apprich et al. [Bielefeld: transcript, 2012], 39–45).

69. See Chantal Mouffe, *Agonistics: Thinking the World Politically* (London/New York: Verso, 2013), 7.

70. Lovink, *Dark Fiber*, 2.

71. See John Perry Barlow, 'Re: <nettime> The Piran Nettime Manifesto', (posted May 27, 1997), accessed March 25, 2017, http://www.nettime.org/Lists-Archives/nettime-l-9705/msg00157.html.

72. Brian Holmes, 'Swarmachine. Activist Media Tomorrow', *Third Text* 22:5 (2008): 525.

73. Garcia and Lovink, 'The ABC'.

74. Lovink, *Zero Comments*, 187.

75. See Hakim Bey, *T.A.Z. The Temporary Autonomous Zone, Ontological Anarchy, Poetic Terrorism* (Brooklyn: Autonomedia, 1991).

76. See Mark Fischer, *Capitalist Realism. Is there no alternative?* (Winchester: Zero Books, 2009). The radical pluralism of tactical media, which would not allow itself to be pinned down to certain positions, was also criticised from within its own ranks. The feminist artist Faith Wilding wrote, for instance, that cyberfeminism was in danger of playing into the hands of a 'net quietism' and falling back behind goals already achieved by 'old-fashioned' feminism (see Faith Wilding and subRosa, 'Where is Feminism in Cyerfeminism', [2006], accessed April 1, 2017, www.neme.org/392/cyberfeminism).

77. Katja Diefenbach, 'Im Interview mit Clemens Apprich', in *Vergessene Zukunft. Radikale Netzkulturen in Europa*, ed. Clemens Apprich et al. (Bielefeld: transcript, 2012), 179. Quotes translated by the author.

78. See Baumgärtel, 'Beauty and the East'.

79. Lovink and Schultz, 'Aufruf', 6. Quote translated by author.

80. Diefenbach, 'Interview', 182. Quote translated by author.

81. See Pekka Himanen, *The Hacker Ethic. A Radical Approach to the Philosophy of Business* (New York: Random House, 2002), 155–178.

82. This was, for instance, the case with the Amsterdam Internet Provider XS4ALL, which was founded in 1993 as an offshoot of the hacker magazine *Hack-Tic*.

Chapter 4

Space of Flows

In his three-volume work on the information age, sociologist and urban theorist Manuel Castells describes the origins of a societal structure based on informational networks.[1] According to Castells, the concurrence of three mutually independent and historically contingent events in the late twentieth century led to the rise of the network society: first, the restructuring of capitalism after the end of the East-West conflict, which brought new demands from capital for flexible management and a globalisation of finance, production and trade; then society's demand for individual freedom and open communication, which goes back to the libertarian currents of the countercultural movements since the 1960s; and finally the progress in the computer and telecommunications sector, which enabled the development of entirely new media systems.[2] These socio-technical transformation processes led to a network-based sociability, which became palpable especially in the global city centres of capitalism. At the end of the twentieth century, adaptability and flexibility was seen as the new imperative, followed by a whole generation of young, creative and mobile people. This development triggered a shake-up of previous structures of meaning: 'In such disconcerting, yet magnificent times, knowledge becomes the only source to restore meaning, and thus meaningful action.'[3] Confronted with the neo-liberal restructuring of urban life and space, accompanied by new telecommunication, transportation and security systems, it was, not least of all, the knowledge of early cyberculture that provided a first orientation in the emerging network society.[4]

Networks, or the imagination of networks, offered a way to structure the postmodern space that is characterised by a 'loss of orientation'.[5] They promised to add clarity to the new situation and to adapt the individuals to the conditions of global capital, while at the same they triggered the desire for new forms of democratic self-organisation. The social transformation, instructed by the neo-liberal idea of a dissolving society, was supposed to be achieved through technical connectivity, which made it possible to reassemble the individuals along the lines of an 'electronic agora'.[6] The network thus became central to the imaginary of neoliberalism, not least because with the Internet a nearly omnipotent tool was found that seemed to make good on the techno-liberal promises.[7] However, despite the fact that the global data network has become the fastest growing technological infrastructure of all time, spreading all around the globe, techno-liberalism and its ideological set pieces have repeatedly encountered local distortions. In Europe, critical net cultures, experimenting with alternative media practices, drew less from the entrepreneurial, but rather the artistic and cultural field. Their success helped to popularise the network idea and thus facilitated the transformation of social, economic and political aspects according to the new model. This sort of an affirmative subversion eventually resulted in an independent techno-ideology, with the effect that the notion of the network became even stronger.[8]

The network discourse was able to organise knowledge in the early phase of the Internet and yield a multitude of media practices, which have become part of our everyday media life. Today, the network is an umbrella term encompassing all possible subfields: hardware and software, infrastructure and meaning, technical invention and social innovation. In other words, it can no longer be reduced to a single origin, nor can it be described as a more or less stable medium, but rather has to be understood as a bundle of various media technologies and practices, which all take place in and on the Internet. Hence, we have to look into the many origins of the network discourse, the accompanying negotiations and decisions, the knowledge and signs, and the alternative, often hidden or little regarded sites of its emergence. In fact, we have to revisit the concrete places, where the technotopian vision of a worldwide computer network was first formulated and encountered. The history of digital networking can thus be understood as a gradual overlapping of a local 'space of places' by a global 'space of flows'.[9] Yet, as Castells showed in *The Informational City*,[10] this does not mean that information and communication technologies have simply super-seded or even dissolved our material world. What has happened instead is that the new technological paradigm, effected by means of global information, communication and transportation systems, has restruc-tured the spatial logic of local places, thereby affecting the experience of people living in these places.

DATA HIGHWAY

The ARPANET, commissioned in 1968 by the Advanced Research Projects Agency (ARPA), was initially implemented at the University of California (UCLA) and connected with a computer at the Stanford Research Institute in early 1969. Until December 1969, four nodes formed the first translocal computer network, which grew to thirty-seven computers by 1972. While one of the origins of the ARPANET can clearly be found in the military context – ARPA, respectively, DARPA (since 1972) is an agency of the US Department of Defense – the early involvement of universities had no less influence on the development and direction of the network. In fact, it was primarily for the practices within the academic community, such as the sharing of research results or the technology transfer, that the ARPANET turned into a global data network. After the military section broke off as MILNET in the mid-1980s, it was due to this environment that evermore networks – in addition to ARPANET, especially the National Science Foundation Net-work (NSFNET) – joined together and opened up to civilian use (e.g. through Usenet or Bulletin Board Systems). Without this multilayered network structure and the embedded media practices, the emergence of the Internet as a *network of networks* cannot be explained. Even more so, since the World Wide Web (WWW),[11] introduced at the beginning of the 1990s, has transformed the Internet into global mass medium.

The Internet, as we know it today, is both a technical and a social network: On the one hand, it entails a computational infrastructure, made possible by the implementation of the Transfer Control and Inter-net Protocols (TCP/IP).[12] On the other hand, it constitutes a horizon of meaning, which draws from the knowledge of early Internet cultures. This matters to the extent that certain values are transported via the computer network, which have had a crucial influence on the setup and structure of the Internet. Particularly the idea of an open process of development, as it is expressed in the 'Requests for Comments',[13] is reflected in almost all of today's Internet standards and can be seen as one of the main reasons for the success of this universal networking machine. In this sense, the Internet does not simply represent yet another part of the computer; it cannot be reduced to the technical structure of computational processes.[14] Instead, it has to be seen in the light of the praxeological and dynamic sides of those processes. Because of the complex history of this socio-technical assemblage, the Internet is not a random network, but a very specific one with the values that are characteristic of it – such as the principle of openness, diversity and neutrality.[15]

A question that occupied the developers and users of the early Internet was how the dreamed-of virtual world could be transferred to the actual world of technical possibilities. The cyberspace of that time was anything but a promising land: narrow bandwidths, beeping modems and limited Internet access defined the experience. And yet science fiction and high tech conjoined with the old dream of an unlimited 'electronic frontier'.[16] For the net pioneers of the 1990s, there was a new place to discover behind the countless cables and server rooms of the worldwide computer network, which 'called for a series of new metaphors, new rules and patterns of behaviour'.[17] Well-known catchphrases such as participation, community and citizenship were rearticulated, in order to make full potential of the new network technologies. They formed the basis for new institutional rules that did not define themselves solely through the production and distribution of material goods, but also, and to the same extent, through the sharing of common ideas, information and practices.[18]

Nevertheless, the idea of autonomous and independent communities bootstrapping the Internet is misleading, because it was the state, not least of all, which invested considerable sums in developing the necessary infrastructure. In the United States, setting up a national information superhighway was one of the central concerns of the first Clinton administration. Under the direction of Vice President Al Gore, the 'National Information Infrastructure' (NII) was initiated in 1993 to create new incentives for the private sector: 'Our goal is not to design the market of the future. It is to provide principles that shape that market. And it is to provide the rules governing this difficult transition to an open market for information.'[19] As had been the case with comparable infrastructure programmes before (e.g. the Interstate Highways in the

1950s), the push for modernisation was coupled with the promise to create new markets, so that ultimately the progress of society was seen as a consequence of its economic performance.[20] The state, after it had invested in the data networks for decades, was supposed to make way for a new economy, which was believed to replace the industrial-style, centralised, top-down bureaucratic planning by 'a more open, democratic, decentralized style'.[21] In this sense, building a data highway was considered the completion of a Third Wave,[22] that is a new cycle of technological innovation holding the potential to transform society the same way as the Agricultural and the Industrial Revolution had done before. A post-industrial, knowledge-based society promised nothing short of the emergence of a whole new civilisation, built on the techno-libertarian spirit of Silicon Valley.

That this was not solely a American vision becomes evident from the Europe and the Global Information Society report, approved by the European Council in 1994.[23] The report, written under the chairmanship of European Commissioner Martin Bangemann, saw in the new information technologies the potential needed to *'improve the quality of life of Europe's citizens, the efficiency of our social and economic organisation and to reinforce cohesion'*.[24] Not only Europe's competitive position in the global market, but also the social integration of the continent were, according to Bangemann, contingent on these new technologies. And similar to Al Gore's plans, the claim was made to free the entrepreneurial spirit from the constraints of state monopolies, and, to that end, to unleash a new information society, which 'should be entrusted to the private sector and to market forces'.[25] The report thus can be seen as a direct response to the NII initiative. Both documents corresponded with the techno-libertarian ideas of that time, according to which the digital revolution was a natural necessity, enabling unconstrained competition and therefore – despite some critical voices – must always 'go forward'.[26] Hence, only a few years after the collapse of the Eastern Bloc, it was clear to the European Council that the blessings of a new network society could be achieved only by means of global capitalism.[27]

This, of course, was contrary to the agenda of critical net cultures, whose attempt it was to develop an alternative vision of the Internet and to foster bottom-up approaches within the networked space. 'The necessity of an open European net culture was not understood. ... The task of governments and the EU was to regulate, not to stimulate.'[28] However, the popularity of net cultures contributed to the general hype around the Internet, which was eventually used to implement a European model of the data highway, so as not to lose the connection to the United States. As the artist and net activist Marko Peljhan recalls: 'When the EU discovered the new technologies for themselves, they increasingly gentrified net culture by simply taking over our ideas.'[29] Hence, the transformation towards the network society was accompanied by the seizure and subjugation of net cultures' discourse. But instead of implementing their idea of autonomous and independent media production, as it was expressed in the tactical media movement, governments in Europe and the United States committed themselves to the neo-liberal agenda, according to which the new technologies should be adapted according to the needs of global capital. While the state was no longer considered a regulating instance, but rather a henchman of the market, the Internet became the new socio-technical basis, upon which capitalism was supposed to resolve all its former problems.[30]

NETWORK SOCIETY

In an environment networked by information and communication technologies, space and time condense into a new material basis, on which the dominant social practices are reorganised through information flows. This means that sociality is integrated in a space of flows, which 'links up distant locales around shared functions and meanings on the basis of electronic circuits and fast transportation corridors'.[31] From this perspective, technology does not precede society, but is interwoven with it. Because social practices have become increasingly networked over the course of the past decades, so has the space that forms the foundation for the economic, political and symbolic structures of society. The space of flows is not placeless, but consists of concrete nodes, whose characteristics are defined by the 'functions to be fulfilled by each network'.[32] On the basis of Castells' theory, three functions of the space of flows can be distinguished: firstly, the networks provide the technological infrastructure, in other words the material support for flows of information (circulation); secondly, network nodes materialise in specific places, according to the needs of the network (relation); and third, the social actors keep the flows of the network going with their social, but also cultural and economic, practices (communication).[33]

What is essential here are not the single functions for themselves, but rather their interaction with one another. Thinking of circulation, relation and communication as a functional ensemble within the network society allows us to better understand the interaction of global and local processes. Hence, the dissemination of information and communication technologies since the 1980s, together with the transformation of the political world systems after 1989, led to a restructuring of capitalism, shifting the focus towards an open, free-market information economy. The network society as a specific expression of the information age is thus distinguished by a structural change within the modes of production: 'In a word, what is facilitated by information technologies is the interconnection of activities, providing the basis for the increasing complexity of service industries, which exchange information relentlessly and ubiquitously.'[34] Information has always been central to distinctive modes of production, but it is with new media technologies that a new mode of development has formed, 'in which information generation, processing, and transmission become the fundamental sources of productivity and power because of new technological conditions emerging in this historical period'.[35] So, while every society is based on information, informationalism, which is the technological paradigm that has subsumed the previous paradigm of industrialism, is the key characteristic of the network society.[36]

The emergence of informationalism as a new technological paradigm does not, however, imply that industrialism disappears as part of the material basis of society, but rather that it loses its central function in the discourse of technology – as can be seen in the two policy papers discussed before. The network society is thus a multidimensional social structure, in which local networks, each with their own values, logics and interests, form the nodes for a globally operating network. Non-participation in the network leads to a structural marginalisation, especially since almost all areas of everyday life – from education to political articulation to the financial sector – are by now dependent on it. The increasing dominance of the space of flows over the space of places is thus also the expression of capitalism, which has found a model to reconfigure itself in the transition from the industrial to the informational mode of development. In fact, informationalism subsumes and transforms the old centres of industrialism from within, leaving behind a very disparate and fragmented social space: 'So, the new culture of urban integration is not the culture of assimilation into the values of a single dominant culture, but the culture of communication between an irreversibly diverse local society connected/disconnected to global flows of wealth, power, and information.'[37] The form of social organisation that becomes evident here is less collective, but rather connective; in other words, it is tied to the respective information network and its socio-technical protocols.[38]

HYPERSPACE

Although we are dealing with a spatial dispersion of economic activities today, the restructuring of the world economy after the collapse of the Soviet Union did not bring in its wake a democratisation of the global market, but rather led to a new geography of centrality and marginality.[39] Not only are the (neo-)colonial categories of a *highly developed* North and a *less-developed* South still in place, but since the 1990s the invisible border between connected and disconnected places runs right through continents, countries, and even cities. As a matter of fact, the most recent wave of globalisation has indeed offered an opportunity for places from the so-called *emerging economies* (cities like Bangalore, Manila, Nairobi or São Paulo) to become central nodes within the global space of flows, whereas quite often cities that used to be important industrial centres (like Detroit, Manchester, Liverpool or Osaka) have suffered a disproportionate downfall.[40] For urban sociologist Saskia Sassen, the success or failure of cities to participate in the global economy depends on their ability to mobilise strategic resources, especially 'the consolidation of an economic core of top-level management and servicing activities … alongside the general move to a service economy and the decline of manufacturing'.[41] This implies new forms of territorial centralisation between, but also within global cities. The urban information economy is thus divided into a highly qualified labour force integrated in the global space of flows, and lesser qualified low-wage jobs disconnected from the major economic processes.[42] Hidden behind the shiny façades of the global city centres is the devalued labour sector, which is nonetheless needed for the operation and maintenance of the physical infrastructure.

The space of flows integrates only certain districts of the global city with all its hyperconcentrated facilities (e.g. the International Tech Park in Bangalore or the City of London), while the rest of the city remains in its specific locality. According to Castells, this development corresponds to the 'fundamental urban dualism of our time'[43]: on the one side a cosmopolitan elite, who participate in the global network society, on the other the place-bound masses, who are excluded from it. This situation is further exacerbated by the changing role of the nation state, which was previously responsible for balancing divergent interests of different social groups. The reregulation of nation-state sovereignty at the supra- and transnational level has shifted the power to global flows, which are composed of 'personal micro-networks that project their interests in functional macro-networks throughout the global set of interactions in the space of flows'.[44] The globalised city thus spatialises the binary logic of the network, which works according to the principle of inclusion and exclusion: Everything that is valuable to the network is incorporated and put to use; what is not useful does not exist from the perspective of the network and must therefore be ignored or excluded.[45]

As can be seen from this, the debate about the changing role of the city interfered with a debate about the pros and cons of digital networks. The discussion usually took place in two camps: that of the *net-enthusiasts*, who propagated a widespread implementation of digital technologies to free the city and its inhabitants from the industrial burden of crime-haunted and traffic-jammed megacities, and that of the *reality-fetishists*, who clinged to the idea of the traditional urban structure with its public spaces and built architecture.[46] For the latter, new media were held responsible for the alleged crisis of the city, because with them central urban functions began to migrate to the data networks. 'We experience this global urban disruption instantaneously and continuously with every telecasted news report, yet we remain incapable of immediate action, frozen in front of our computer terminals.'[47] As a consequence, the city, the cornerstone of the bourgeois society, was supposed to disintegrate 'into the cybernetic representation of the virtual world of computers'.[48] For urban historian M. Christine Boyer, this debate marks a transition from the modern to the postmodern city, which replaces the traditional Western concept of space, architecture and the machine, with data-driven and network-based forms of social as well as spatial organisation. The constant flow of information, goods and people traverses the city, thereby constantly changing its character. Beginning of the 1990s this also conjured the image of a ghettoization of inner cities and an exodus from the constraints of the city,[49] as can be seen from notorious discussions about the ongoing suburbanisation of urban space in the form of *edge cities* or *urban sprawls*.[50]

In this transitional phase, several – not only conservative – observers saw a fundamental shift in our culture of meaning: whereas modernism's focus was on the functionally zoned city, postmodernism stands for a fragmentation of the urban space. Such a shift is accompanied by a change in the way we perceive and thus shape the world. Modern architecture with its representational buildings made of concrete, steel and glass are thus replaced by a postmodern architecture, 'whose forms are so neutral, so pure, so diaphanous, that they do not pretend to say anything'.[51] The postmodern city gets overlaid by information and communication networks, which fragment and recompose it according to the needs of the dominant economic processes. Consequently, what we see is less a disappearance of material space due to information technologies, but rather a permanent overcoding, which leads to a reconfiguration of this space by data flows and ultimately to an isolation of our embodied experiences.[52] This observation coincides with Fredric Jameson's idea that 'postmodern hyper-space' is marked by a new complexity, diversification and disorientation, making it harder for us to grasp our reality: 'My principal point here [is] that this latest mutation in space … has finally succeeded in transcending the capacities of the individual human body to locate itself, to organize its immediate surroundings perceptually, and cognitively to map its position in a mappable external world.'[53] In late capitalism, our surroundings are determined by factors that are global and thus no longer comprehensible to the human mind. This has a direct influence on the ability of individuals to find their way in their respective social space. The modern city, which was ultimately characterised by its centrality, and therefore its clarity, is superseded by a global and largely decentred information and communication network, in which we 'are submerged in its henceforth filled and suffused volumes to the point where our now postmodern bodies are bereft of spatial coordinates and practically (let alone theoretically) incapable of distantiation'.[54] A position outside of postmodern space is thus impossible, which makes a critique or reflection of the whole system increasingly difficult.[55]

The challenge of grasping, investigating and criticising a global system on the basis of distributed networks urged Jameson to propose the idea of a global cartography, which allows our cognition and perception to regain their grip on the postmodern world. Quite similar to net critique, such a 'cognitive mapping' entails the disengagement from postmodernism's assertion of a dissolving society, in order to be able to reformulate a radical approach to cultural politics. Instead of explaining social developments from technical processes and thus practically neutralising them, Jameson takes the position that 'our faulty representations of some immense communicational and computer network are themselves but a distorted figuration of something even deeper, namely the whole world system of present-day multinational capitalism'.[56] By linking our ideological with our cognitive position, he tries to unlock the contemporary constraint to envision the world and thus to act upon it. In his view, the network is not the ultimately determining instance in social life, but rather a central metaphor in the cultural imagination of late capitalism, because 'it seems to offer some privileged representational shorthand for grasping a network of power and control '.[57] Hence, the rise of the network to describe our world is not a technological necessity; instead, it corresponds to a society that has started to see itself as a network.

NOTES

1. See Manuel Castells, 'The Rise of the Network Society', in *The Information Age: Economy, Society and Culture Vol. I* (Oxford/Malden: Blackwell, 1996); Manuel Castells, 'The Power of Identity', in *The Information Age: Economy, Society and Culture Vol. II* (Oxford/Malden: Blackwell, 1997); Manuel Castells, 'End of Millennium', in *The Information Age: Economy, Society and Culture, Vol. III* (Oxford/Malden: Blackwell, 1998).

2. See Manuel Castells, *The Internet Galaxy. Reflections on the Internet, Business, and Society* (Oxford: Oxford University Press, 2002), 2. The concept network society results from this overlap, although Castells stresses that it does not cover the whole meaning of informational society – which would have to be expanded with components like state and social movements (see Castells, 'The Rise of the Network Society', 21).

3. Manuel Castells, 'Cities, the Informational Society and the Global Economy', in *The Global Cities Reader*, ed. Neil Brenner, et al. (London/New York: Routledge, 2006), 136.

4. See Pierre Lévy: *Cyberculture*, trans. Robert Bononno (Minneapolis/London: University of Minnesota Press, 2001). Similar to Lyotard's study on the postmodern condition, Pierre Lévy was commissioned by the Council of Europe to write a report on the state and culture of cyberspace. In it, Lévy

characterises cyberculture as 'the universal without totality' (see Lévy, *Cyberculture*, 91–102), which makes it the legitimate successor of enlightenment for him. In contrast, net cultures define themselves through their postmodern plurality, especially since they do not want to establish a universal principle.

5. Paul Virilio, 'Speed and Information: Cyberspace Alarm!' in *Reading Digital Culture*, ed. David Trend (Malden/Oxford: Blackwell, 2001), 24.

6. Howard Rheingold, *The Virtual Community. Homesteading on the Electronic Frontier* (New York: Harper Perennial, 1994), 14.

7. See Wendy Chun, 'Networks NOW: Belated too Early', in *Postdigital Aesthetics. Art, Computation and Design*, eds. David M. Berry, Michael Dieter (London: Palgrave Macmillan, 2015), 290.

8. See Oliver Marchart, *Die Verkabelung Mitteleuropas. Medienguerilla – Netzkritik – Technopolitik* (Vienna: edition selene, 1998), 21. The question of the extent to which these kinds of *local singularities* in the network discourse took place or are still taking place in other regions, especially in the so-called Global South, cannot be answered here. The present work explicitly assumes a European perspective, which can only be applied to this part of the world and makes no claim to the interpretation of other experiences.

9. See Manuel Castells, 'The Rise of the Network Society', 453–459.

10. See Manuel Castells, *The Informational City. Information Technology, Economic Restructuring and the Urban-Regional Process* (Oxford: Blackwell, 1991).

11. The World Wide Web (WWW), an information space where documents and other resources are identified by Uniform Resource Locators (URLs) and interlinked by the Hypertext Transfer Protocol (HTTP), was first conceptualised by Tim Berners-Lee in 1989. He also created the first web browser in 1990 while working for the European Organization for Nuclear Research (CERN).

12. The Transmission Control Protocol (TCP) was developed by Robert E. Kahn and Vincent Cerf in the 1970s for the Advanced Research Projects Agency (ARPA). It determines the paths along which data is exchanged among computers. Together with the Internet Protocol (IP), which makes computers in a network addressable, it forms the foundation for today's Internet (see Barry M. Leiner, Vinton G. Cerf, David D. Clark, et al., 'A Brief History of the Internet', in *The Internet Society* [1997], accessed December 21, 2016, www.internetsociety.org/internet/what-internet/history-internet/brief-history-internet).

13. A Request for Comments (RFC) is an official document of specifications by the Internet Engineering Task Force (IETF) and the Internet Society (ISOC), the principal standards-setting bodies for the Internet. It is authored in the form of a request to comment on methods, research or innovations applicable to the working of the Internet and Internet-connected systems.

14. See Friedrich Kittler, 'Das Internet ist eine Emanation: Ein Gespräch mit Friedrich Kittler', in *Stadt am Netz. Ansichten von Telepolis*, ed. Stefan Iglhaut, et al. (Mannheim: Bolmann, 1996), 196–203.

15. See Christopher M. Kelty, 'Against Networks', *spheres*. *Journal for Digital Cultures* 1 (2014), accessed December 21, 2016, http://spheres-journal. org/against-networks. It was also the principle of openness, which ultimately helped TCP/IP, the protocol issued by the Open Systems Interconnection Reference Model (OSI), to win out over the rather centrally controlled and comparatively rigid model of the International Standardization Organization (ISO).

16. See John Perry Barlow, 'Crime and Puzzlement' (1990), accessed December 21, 2016: https://w2.eff.org/Misc/Publications/John_Perry_Barlow/ crime_and_puzzlement.1.txt.

17. Stefan Bollmann, 'Einfürhrung in den Cyberspace', in *Kursbuch Neue Medien. Trends in Wirtschaft und Politik, Wissenschaft und Kultur*, ed. Stefan Bollmann (Cologne: Bollmann, 1995), 164. Quote translated by author.

18. This position can be read from some of the position papers of that time, which often served as models for national policy programmes to promote the ICT field; for example, the six-point-plan 'Misera Media', (1995), the Amsterdam Agenda (1997) or the Yellow Paper (1998).

19. Albert Arnold Gore, 'Remarks on the National Information Infrastructure at the National Press Club', *ibiblio* (1993), accessed December 21, 2016, http://www.ibiblio.org/nii/goremarks.

20. Associated with the information superhighway was also a specific American highway culture, which entails 'the freedom of the road, a constantly moving, physical fragmented existence' (Tung-Hui Hu, 'Truckstops of the Information Superhighway: Ant Farm, SRI, and the Cloud', *Media-N: Journal of the New Media Caucus* 10:1 (2014), accessed April 1, 2017, http://median. newmediacaucus.org/art-infrastructures-hardware/truckstops-on-the-information-superhighway-ant-farm-sri-and-the-cloud). In this sense, the Internet would resemble the distributed network of the highway system – at least in the imagination of some net pioneers.

21. Alvin Toffler, Previews and Premises (Montréal: Black Rose Books, 1984), 50.

22. See Alvin Toffler, *The Third Wave* (New York: Bantam, 1984)

23. See Martin Bangemann et al., 'Bangeman Report: Europe and the Global Information Society', *CORDIS* (1994), accessed March 25, 2017, http:// cordis.europa.eu/news/rcn/2730_en.html.

24. Bangemann et al., 'Report'.

25. Ibid.

26. Ibid.

27. Also in 1,995, the 'Magna Carta for the Knowledge Age' was proposed by New Gingrich, the former head of the US Republican party. The carta, which had an essential influence on Internet policies in the States and Europe, invoked the whole rhetoric of the Third Wave world: 'The bioelectronic frontier is an appropriate metaphor for what is happening in cyberspace, calling to

mind as it does the spirit of invention and discovery that led ancient mariners to explore the world, generations of pioneers to tame the American continent and, more recently, to man's first exploration of outer space' (Esther Dyson, George Gilder, George Keyworth, Alvin Toffler, 'Cyberspace and the American Dream: A Magna Carta for the Knowledge Age', The Progress and Freedom Foundation [1,995], accessed December 22, 2,017: www.pff.org/issues-pubs/futureinsights/fi22magnacarta.html).

28. Geert Lovink, *Dark Fiber. Tracking Critical Internet Culture* (Cambridge: The MIT Press, 2002), 86.

29. Marko Peljhan, 'Im Interview mit Clemens Apprich', in *Vergessene Zukunft. Radikale Netzkulturen in Europa*, ed. Clemens Apprich et al. (Bielefeld: transcript, 2012), 83. Quote translated by author.

30. See Jens Schröter, 'The Internet and "Frictionless Capitalism"', *Triple C* 10:2 (2012): 302–312.

31. Manuel Castells, 'Epilogue: Informationalism and the Network Society' in *The Hacker Ethic and the Spirit of the Information Age*, Pekka Himanen (New York: Random House, 2001), 155–78.

32. Castells, 'The Rise of the Network Society', 444.

33. Castells' functional analysis of the network society was also the subject of manifold criticism. One critique is that Castells' concept of 'global flows' reduces economic globalisation to a partial aspect, whose actual impact on the local overall economy is hard to describe (see Frank Eckardt, *Soziologie der Stadt* [Bielefeld: transcript, 2004], 92–93).

34. Castells, *The Informational City*, 142.

35. Castells, 'The Rise of the Network Society', 20.

36. See Castells, 'The Rise of the Network Society', 14.

37. Manuel Castells, 'Space of Flows, Space of Places: Notes Towards a General Theory', in *The Cybercities Reader*, ed. Stephen Graham (London: Routledge, 2004), 92.

38. And with Lefebvre it could be said that 'every society ... produces a space, its own space' (Henri Lefebvre, The Production of Space, trans. Donald Nicholson-Smith [London: Blackwell, 1991], 31).

39. See Saskia Sassen, *The Global City: New York, London, Tokyo* (Princeton: Princeton University Press, 1991).

40. There can be no doubt, however, that the old centres of colonial power (e.g. Berlin, London, Tokyo) are still disproportionally advantaged and therefore also dominate the world economy. Especially because the network infrastructure (e.g. undersea cables) continues to be embedded along historical lines, thereby reinforcing (post-)colonial tendencies (see Nicole Starosielski, *The Undersea Network* [Durham/London: Duke University Press, 2015], 12).

41. Saskia Sassen, *Global City*, 250–251.

42. See Saskia Sassen, 'The Global City: Strategic Site/New Frontier', in *Democracy, Citizenship and the Global City*, ed. Engin F. Isin (London: Routledge, 2000), 53.

43. Manuel Castells, 'European Cities, The Informational Society, and The Global Economy', *Journal of Economic and Social Geography* 84:4 (1993), 255.

44. Castells, 'The Rise of the Network Society', 416. Here, Manuel Castells objects to Saskia Sassen's concept of the global city, which, in his opinion, is not appropriate for covering the complexity of today's urban reality. Most cities have global components, and particularly the cities that are counted among the strategic nodes of the global network are primarily distinguished by their local ties (see Felix Stalder, Manuel Castells. *The Theory of the Network Society* [Cambridge/Malden: Polity, 2006], 163).

45. See Manuel Castells, 'Informationalism, networks, and the network society: a theoretical blueprint', in *The Network Society. A Cross-Cultural Perspective*, ed. Manuel Castells et al. (Northampton: Edward Elgar Publishing, 2004), 36–45. Similar and more recent: Keller Easterling, *Extrastatecraft: The Power of Infrastructure Space* (London: Verso, 2014).

46. See Florian Rötzer, *Telepolis. Urbanität im digitalen Zeitalter* (Mannheim: Bollmann, 1995), 8.

47. M. Christine Boyer: *CyberCities. Visual Perception in the Age of Electronic Communication* (New York: Princeton Architectural Press, 1996), 10.

48. Boyer, *CyberCities*, 9.

49. See Florian Rötzer, 'Auszug aus der Stadt', in *Virtual Cities. Die Neuerfindung der Stadt im Zeitalter globaler Vernetzung*, ed. Christa Maar et al. (Basel: Birkhäuser, 1997), 11–16.

50. In William Gibson's novel *Neuromancer* (1984), cyberspace was also described as a *sprawl*, that is, an urban area without a centre, invoking the idea of an uncontrolled, and therefore dangerous, space.

51. Castells, 'The Rise of the Network Society', 450.

52. See Castells, *The Informational City*, 126.

53. Fredric Jameson, *Postmodernism, or, The Cultural Logic of Late Capitalism* (Durham: Duke University Press, 1991), 46. Fredric Jameson ties this feeling of a loss of control to a building that for him was typical of postmodernism: the Bonaventure Hotel in Los Angeles. Similar to the Centre Pompidou in Paris, described by Baudrillard (see Baudrillard, 'The Beaubourg-Effect: Implosion and Deterrence', trans. Rosalind Krauss et al., *October* 20 [1982], 3–13), this is a postmodern hyperspace: 'I am tempted to say that such space makes it impossible for us to use the language of volume or volumes any longer, since these last are impossible to seize. Hanging streamers indeed suffuse this empty space in such a way as to distract systematically and deliberately from whatever form it might be supposed to have; while a constant busyness

gives the feeling that emptiness is here absolutely packed, that it is an element within which you yourself are immersed, without any of that distance that formerly enabled the perception of perspective or volume. You are in this hyperspace up to your eyes and your body' (Jameson, *Postmodernism*, 82–83).

54. Jameson, *Postmodernism*, 48–49.

55. Edward W. Soja warns against a totalisation of 'postmodern urbanisation process'. In this sense, 'There is no purely postmodern city, no place that can be investigated and understood completely from a postmodern critical or interpretative perspective' (Edward W. Soja, 'Postmoderne Urbanisierung', in *Mythos Metropole*, ed. Gotthard Fuchs et al. [Frankfurt a.M.: Suhrkamp, 1995], 145. Quote translated by author).

56. Jameson, *Postmodernism*, 37.

57. Ibid., 38.

Chapter 5

Digital Urbanism

Since the 1990s, the network has become one of the determining concepts of our time. By linking the individually tangible space of places with the highly abstract space of flows, it bridges the imaginary gap that has resulted from the postmodern 'loss of orientation'.[1] Consequently, the city, which can be seen as an interface between the local and the global, was also envisioned in network terms: 'Founding a capital today means that at highway intersections and in train stations, in time tables and computer networks, a new "hub" arises, which centralizes the flow of energy and information.'[2] The city is presented as a node of various networks, from streets, canals and information networks to the conduits of water and electricity systems. And even though a systematic networking of the city had already started with the Industrial Revolution, computer-based networks brought a qualitative turn, which 'leaves behind the boundaries of the physical location and achieves a virtual universality, a new placelessness'.[3] This process of virtualisation was thought to affect the perception of space, as well as the urban image itself, resulting in a new imagination of the city. Kevin Lynch, in his classic *The Image of the City*,[4] presents the city as a complex, ever-shifting space where people are unable to map their position within the urban totality. To (re)appropriate a spatial sense, the individual subject must mentally map his or her surroundings in a consistent and comprehensible way. Rather than falling into the gloomy ideas of urban sprawls and depraved cities, Lynch wanted to use architectural knowledge to counter the fear of disorientation. Such a mental map was then also the model for Jameson, when he argued that the cognitive map was an appropriate means to cope with the increasingly complex structure of postmodern society.

The same technologies that were held responsible for the crisis of the city, ultimately also carried the hope of a revival of the city: 'Indeed, it is now being argued that being released from reality and all of its messy and uncontrollable chaos enables the virtual to recover reality, even while, paradoxically, it implicates a withdrawal from it'.[5] This kind of digital urbanism was apparent in a vast number of newly coined words: Cybercity,[6] City of Quartz,[7] Virtual Cities,[8] Digital Cities[9] and Telepolis[10] arose as a reaction to the looming danger of a 'digital de-urbanisation'.[11] In his book, the *City of Bits*, William J. Mitchell, describes the new land of hope stretching out behind the servers: 'Early computers had been like isolated mountain valleys ruled by programmer kings. ... But networking fundamentally changed things ... by linking the increasingly numerous individual fragments of cyberturf into one huge, expanding system.'[12] To make it easier to navigate in these new and complex data worlds, the city metaphor was employed as a symbolic order. Hence, the city walls were supposed to offer protection against the overwhelming flood of information and provide a first orientation in cyberspace. Unlike the 'digiphiles and digiphobes, with their contending visions of utopia and dystopia', the city in this context is represented as an organisational regime, which holds the promise to create a new *e-topia*.[13]

This technotopian vision of a global digital network, which goes beyond the idea of the computer as single medium, was closely linked to the idea of an electronic agora, understood as a new social space. Whereas traditional meeting places of the city depended on some sort of local centrality (e.g. the market place, the town hall and the sports stadium), cyberspace made it possible to simultaneously communicate in distance on a time-shared basis. In this vision, however, two different concepts were often mixed: on the one hand, info cities, representing closed data spaces, which were entered by single users employing pre-programmed interfaces; on the other hand, digital cities, conceptualised as urban infrastructures, which emerged through the social practices of its users and whose interfaces were therefore seen as processual.[14] In particular the latter, because of its emphasis on intersubjectivity, marked the transition from a network-mediated gathering space to a new participatory media environment, which fundamentally differed from the idea of a homogenous space, represented by the information superhighway.[15] Here, the influence of early net cultures is obvious; in accordance with them, digital cities fostered the idea of self-regulating communities, which ultimately led to a new mode of governance.

INFO CITIES

While engaging with the digital sphere, the image of the city with its organising principles proved to be useful to grasp the complex and unintelligible space environment of computer-generated space. Therefore, computer interfaces had to be developed which made the navigation through cyberspace feasible. So-called 'mirror worlds' were supposed to enable a new kind of 'whole-sightedness',[16] as computer scientist David Gelernter put it. Like a microscope, or rather telescope, these software-ensembles had the task to render data space into something observable and therefore comprehensible. Since the electronic space consists of an endless series of zeroes and ones, the question arose of how this space was to be imagined. In contrast to the global village, which still conveyed the image of a manageable unit, the city metaphor was better suited to cope with the new complexity of a networked space. It helped to establish a new symbolic order and constituted – at least for a short period of time – to core idiom of cyberspace. Hence, not only had the city become a data space with the massive dissemination of digital and network technologies, but the data space, generated by these technologies, was now represented as a city.

In the early 1990s, a postgraduate student at the Technical University of Vienna, Andreas Dieberger, coined the term 'information city'[17] to describe a spatial user interface. In order to grapple with the problem of 'getting lost in hyperspace',[18] Dieberger's city metaphor attempted to make the structure of information systems easier to understand by drawing a cognitive map of the information space. He proposed, similar to Lynch and Mitchell before, to use architectural knowledge about the structured environment of the city in order to build an interface that helps to navigate hypertext. The information city thus defines 'an ontology of spaces and connections that is useful ... to create structure in an unstructured information domain'.[19] By implementing the hierarchical concept of the city, Dieberger was able to develop a rich set of navigational tools to make the data space not only visible, but also legible to the user. For him cyberspace, like the city, was constructable and therefore controllable: 'An important advantage of ... city metaphors is that they define several levels of enclosed spaces.'[20] The elements of a city (e.g. the district, the neighbourhood, the block and the building) were seen as 'ideal sources for metaphors that describe strong encapsulations and access control'.[21] What makes this proposal interesting is that it presents a diegetic conception of data space, in other words a conception that attempts to immersively involve the user in a pre-structured environment.[22] In contrast to a passive immersion in painting, scenography or film, the information city allowed the users to interact with the virtual environment surrounding them. The interface was thus defined as a portal, with the help of which it was possible to enter this immersive urban space.[23]

Although Dieberger's information city was never realised, there were a number of projects in the 1990s that came very close to his idea. Especially the *City of News*, developed at the Massachusetts Institute of Technology (MIT), made use of the immersive approach to structure data space. Similar to Dieberger's concept, an information environment was created, within which the users could draw on their experiences in actual cities: websites were visualised as buildings which themselves

Figure 5.1   MIT Media Lab's City of News (1997).

were grouped to urban districts according to their specific content (e.g. the finance district, the shopping district and the district of science). In order to retrieve the content, a browser was developed that 'organizes information as it fetches it, in real-time, in a virtual three-dimensional space which anchors our perceptual flow of data to a cognitive map of a (virtual) place'.[24] In this sense, the *City of News* can be understood as an alternative to conventional data management systems, which require an exact search term and an understanding of the basic structure of the database. Not only was the city a dynamic space, where every new website was represented by a new building, which, in turn, grew with every click, but because of its immersive logic, the cognitive map literally invited its users to search by strolling. Herein lies the old promise of an ideal order of knowledge, which was to be achieved through a spatial principle of organisation. 'City of News certainly participates in the utopian dimension of this historical line of thought as it carries within itself a hope for an ideal space of information sharing and consumption.'[25] Associated with this was the notion of a functionally zoned city, going back to a variety of works in modernist architecture and urban planning (e.g. Le Corbusier, Ebenezer Howard, Archigram and EPCOT), where the city is characterised by an organisational regime of inclusion and exclusion.

Herein lies a significant foreclosure of the possibilities of cyberspace as a potentially open and non-hierarchical space: the idea of info cities corresponds to a virtual parallel space, which is constituted by its boundaries and frontiers. Similar to the idea of the controllable city, it is primarily concerned with the construction of a spatial order using individual memories and experiences. Hence, Dieberger's information city, as well MIT's *City of News*, was still in line with the notion of the information superhighway, which 'privileges the individual user exploring a relatively homogenous information space'.[26] In this vision, the user ranges all alone through the virtual streets of the info city, always in search for human traces, which he or she only catches sight of in the form of abstract data sets. Although virtual meeting points are sometimes included in these models, they are always only a means to an end, which is ultimately the ideal organisation of knowledge for the single user. However, in contrast to this solipsistic conception of a virtual space, the city metaphor also evoked an image that was less driven by the idea of an individual knowledge space, but rather by the one of a collective data space.

DIGITAL CITIES

Instead of simply transferring the metaphor of the city to the net, in order
to produce meaning through order, critical net cultures were more interested in implementing digital networks in physical space. Digital cities,
as they were founded in the environment of European net cultures in
the mid-1990s, consisted of both, the actual places within the respective
city, which functioned as open access points (e.g. clubs, cultural centres
and libraries), and the representation of this city in electronic space, in
the form of small pictograms (e.g. street cafes, post offices or schools),
thus simulating a proximity with the familiar surroundings. Cyberspace,
in this context, was imagined as a collective and heterogeneous space;
in contrast to the simplifying story of the information highway, which
merely extrapolated the modernist desire for an omnipotent machine
(now the PC instead of the car) to explore the last frontier, the digital
city was composed of its users and their activities, thereby anticipating
today's notion of user-generated social networks.

The idea of setting up digital cities in physical as well as electronic
space goes back to the North American freenets, which had already
been implemented in the 1980s to serve as open information and communication platforms for existing communities. 'These community
networks ... are intended to advance social goals, such as building community awareness, encouraging involvement in local decision-making,
or developing economic opportunities in disadvantaged communities,'[27]
as Douglas Schuler, a pioneer of community media, wrote about the
attempt to reinvigorate communities by installing computer networking technologies in public facilities. Although the spread of commercial Internet providers in the 1990s enabled more and more people to
access the global network from their home, the demand for free and
non-commercial access to the Internet had a strong impact on the next
generation of media activists, not least because in the early years of the
World Wide Web, the dial-up fees were expensive and often unafford-
able particularly for low-income groups.[28]

The idea of an *access for all* was then also an essential component
of the digital cities in Europe, which in many cases appeared as independent Internet providers even before their commercial competitors.
The digital cities were conceived as interactive information systems,
constituted by the practices of its inhabitants. The idea of such an open
space, the ordering of which was not instructed by an already defined

ontology, but rather related to the outside world, was based on the desire of individuals and groups to build their own online environment. Social requirements mixed with technical premises, creating a new form of processual interface. Whereas the info cities were defined by an enclosed and immersive space, to which one could access only through a pre-programmed portal, the digital city was distinguished by a constant opening. As a postmodernist sprawl, it diffused into the physical space of the city, as public terminals were set up in libraries, clubs, schools, post offices and administration buildings. This conscious inversion of an ideal knowledge space, which was still constitutive of the info cities, ultimately created the notion of a non-diegetic and socially produced space.[29] In the following paragraphs, three examples from Amsterdam, Berlin and Vienna will be presented to trace some of the assumptions associated with this space.

De Digitale Stad

De Digitale Stad (DSS) in Amsterdam, founded on 15 January 1994, was initiated by the cultural centre De Balie and the hacker collective Hacktic Network[30] for the duration of ten weeks. The reason for this was local elections, which were seen as an occasion to test new forms of civic participation by means of electronic media. Instead of simply disseminating information, local authorities saw an opportunity to actually involve citizens in the political process. As Geert Lovink underlines, this attempt to revitalise participative processes must be considered in the specific context of the Netherlands in the 1990s: 'The Digital City story tells of the difficulties in building up a broad and diverse Internet culture within a Zeitgeist of the "absent state" and the triumph of market liberalism.'[31] Independent cultural initiatives, which had partly grown out of the autonomous and squatters' movement of the 1980s, had to find new ways of surviving beyond the structures of state support. For this reason, the Amsterdam situation engendered new forms of creative industries early on, which relied on the entrepreneurial self-initiative of the citizens of Amsterdam, thus advancing the neo-liberal idea of self-managing communities. With this, however, the classical institutions ended up in a crisis of legitimation, which is why the digital city was supposed to promote a dialogue between politicians and citizens.[32]

Figure 5.2   Screenshot of De Digitale Stad Amsterdam (1994–2000).

Although the hoped-for exchange between city officials and their public failed to materialise, the DDS soon achieved such a popularity as a communication platform among citizens that the experiment was extended. Starting off with small financial support from the City of Amsterdam and the Ministry of Economy, the project developed into Europe's largest freenet with over 50,000 users by mid-1997, offering free e-mail addresses and free server space for each of them.[33] Along with the information portals for public institutions and offers from local retailers and businesses, DDS became Amsterdam's central entry point to the global world of computer networks. With the introduction of the World Wide Web, the text-based system was replaced by a graphical interface, which was intended to serve as a first orientation, and gave the whole project an identity of its own. The city metaphor allowed for a digital representation of the social structure of Amsterdam, and, at the same time, enabled its citizens to access information available on the net. This was less a matter of simulating the city, but rather a metaphorical transcription of the dynamics and diversity of urban processes. The emphasis of the digital city as a public sphere, where information is shared and discussed, can also be understood as an implicit continuation of previous democratisation efforts, as is evident, for instance, in the commentary from Joost Flint, the first coordinator of the DDS: 'The city is traditionally the place for free speech, communication, and assembly, and therefore it seems most appropriate for putting the technical possibilities of the Internet into a generally comprehensible form, and also for probing the social and political aspects of the medium at the same time.'[34]

In addition to this socio-political function, the city metaphor also conveyed some nostalgic features. 'It wants to resurrect the lost splendour of the city, not by covering up existing constructions with postmodern facades or by increasing protection, but by consistently expanding its artificial character,' as Geert Lovink noted at the Ars Electronica Symposium in 1995.[35] This sort of a *digital constructivism* was also evident in the interface, which was characterised by its innovative design. The DDS was neither a pure doubling of Amsterdam nor the mere representation of its data space. In fact, the city metaphor was used to embrace the full complexity of the project: 'This metaphor permits working on a strict, clear plan, where functionality and user-friendliness dominate, as well as on a maze of alleys and small streets, where dark, illegal and adventurous things happen.'[36] In contrast to the info city, which was distinguished by its transparency and omnipresence, it was most of all the peripheral zones of the digital city – and less its centre – which held the promise of being able to represent the net in its whole complexity. After the transfer of the digital city to the graphical World Wide Web, the interface consisted of a honeycomb-like pattern, which made it possible to expand the structure without developing a centre. Each honeycomb symbolised a district with a thematic focal point assigned, whereas four opposite corners marked links to neighbouring districts and the four other corners were designated to the neighbourhoods between the districts, which served as 'settlements' of the users.[37]

This kind of playful symbolisation was also due to the rise of the creative economy in Amsterdam: graphic and web designers were encouraged to implement their ideas on the platform, which in turn became more popular among its users. The project was thus able to grow beyond the initial computer and hacker scene, providing a playground for all sorts of culturally and politically active people. As Marleen Stikker, co-founder and first 'mayor' of DDS, explained in an interview: 'All those ideas you had heard so often from the US about the new information society, tele-democracy, electronic citizenship, suddenly became a reality on DDS.'[38] For her, the metaphor of the city seemed especially suitable to do justice to the notion of a public sphere, even though structural inequalities remained, as was shown in a first survey of DDS: the average inhabitant of the digital city was about thirty years old, usually male, well educated, and close to the liberal democratic party.[39]

Partly because of this limitation, partly because of the entry of commercial Internet providers, the digital city came under increasing

Figure 5.3   General map of De Digitale Stad Amsterdam (1994–2000).

pressure. So, when the already small public subsidies dried up, the DDS had to change from a non-profit organisation to a 'mixed business model'.[40] However, '[t]he growing number of users, with growing individual requirements, and little patience for "idealistically" induced technical deficiencies, as well as the need to deliver a better performance to the paying (institutional) customers made this predicament even more acute'.[41] In March 2000, at a time when the population reached a peak of 160,000 users, the digital city was turned into a commercial company, whose new customers had little to do with the original community and its concerns. Despite this abrupt change, it should be noted that the DDS was from the start an expression of the creative industry and entrepreneurial spirit emerging at that time. Hence, the 'flight into capital' ultimately seemed to be a logical consequence of its founding context.[42]

With the growing media sector – and the jobs created with it – many of the active users soon lost interest in the voluntary work. Instead of a new public sphere, a media scene emerged, which preferred to devote itself to commercial aims. The Amsterdam model can therefore be regarded as an example of the overall development of the 1990s, in which critical net cultures were taken over by commercial media companies and subjected to the laws of the market.[43] In the demise of the DDS and its restructuring as a conventional Internet service provider,

one can experience how the dissemination of information and communication technologies in the 1990s led to an everyday media routine,
in which the pioneering projects with their mostly artistic and activist
orientation were no longer viable: 'The free Internet services advertised
massively and attracted a customer's pool far removed from the idealis-
tic concerns that used to inform the original Digital City. This resulted
in a substantial quantitative, but more importantly qualitative erosion
of the DDS user base.'[44] Yet, Geert Lovink, despite his disappointment
about the outcome of the project, saw a successful experiment in the
digital city of Amsterdam, since it succeeded in introducing a broad
public to the new media technologies, thus implementing the political
agenda of early net cultures.[45] Hence, the impulse for founding and
maintaining the DDS had come primarily from the activists' conviction
that in the light of an encroaching privatisation of digital and urban
space, a democratic public sphere was needed. And perhaps the high
expectations placed in the digital city as a social-utopian space could
only be disappointed, since the Internet itself became part of a commercial mass culture.

Internationale Stadt

What began in Amsterdam as a participative citizen's net continued
to develop elsewhere in a different form. The DDS was long considered a model for a number of European digital cities, which emerged
in the 1990s. In addition to London, Milan or Kiev, a digital city
also arose in Berlin. The Internationale Stadt (I.S.) was founded
in the mid-1990s in very heterogeneous surroundings: 'A former
sponsor, experiences from the hacker underground, self-organised
but bankrupt media art events, mixed with a healthy portion of
pseudo-science, led to the strange but unique brew of the Internationale Stadt.'[46] In Berlin Mitte, where the local techno as well as
art scene was located, the net art project Handshake rented a space
from the cultural association Botschaft e.V.[47] The spatial proximity
to other initiatives made it possible to share not only ideas, but also
the technical infrastructure. This form of a collective use of physical
resources for the production of artistic and media contents distinguished the Berlin experiment from the Amsterdam one, where the
focus was less on techno-cultural and net-artistic aspects, but more
on the communal–political aspect.

When the Internet provider and sponsor of Handshake dissolved in late 1994,[48] the scene simply took over its equipment and initiated the I.S. on 1 January 1995. From the beginning, I.S. was planned as a collective endeavour to provide the necessary infrastructure for self-managed art and cultural projects. Not least because of this background, an innovative interface design was of central value to the project: in the beginning, the I.S. was thus depicted by a kind of 'bone' (self-description), which consisted of a rectangle of pipes that condensed into balls at the corners. This form was intended to refer to the underground system of Berlin and, consequently, to serve as an orientation and navigation tool. Unlike the more conventional representation of the Amsterdam model with its cafes, post offices and city districts, the interface in Berlin remained highly abstract, even after migrating to the graphical World Wide Web.

In its second, expanded version, the interface was programmed in the form of a shell system, whereby the dynamically changing shells each represented a thematic area. This was intended to depict a global discourse within the I.S., as well as a 'local structure with digital clubs, newspapers, galleries, and many other information resources within the global world of the Internet'.[49] In order to facilitate the exchange between the local and the global, new tools were developed to migrate the classical Internet services (Internet Relay Chats, Newsgroups or BBS) to the World Wide Web. Using a toolbar, the roughly 300 users could navigate through the individual thematic areas (such as media, music, municipal issues, environment and market) and therefore evade the pitfalls of an all- too rigid order: 'Unlike the real city, the centre of the Internationale Stadt is the pattern of activities initiated by its inhabitants.'[50] In this sense, buildings were replaced by content, which resulted from the interaction of the users. Whereas the private area of each user was protected by a password, the inhabitants of I.S. could work on collective pages and decide whether the content should be made available to the public or not. The idea of such a self-determined media practice was also mirrored in the interface, which prompted the users to take part in its development.

The 'social architecture'[51] of the I.S. was intended to make the users independent from the operators, who should provide only the functions needed to build and navigate the city. Hence, the focus of I.S. was not on the simulation of urban space, but rather on the bidirectional communication between the participants. The central aim was to enable social

Figure 5.4   Screenshot of Internationale Stadt Berlin (1995–1997).

networking practices, both on the net and in real space. Public terminals were set up in Berlin's techno clubs, in order to make Internet services, such as chat forums and discussion boards, available to as many people as possible. Taking social-utopian concepts into consideration, I.S. saw itself as an 'ideal city' in electronic space, which had to assert itself against the commercial area: 'The idea of social networking through technology is certainly not new, but has … a perhaps one-time chance to subject communicative action in electronic networks not exclusively to monetary aims.'[52]

In Berlin, the digital city was understood as public sphere. What was essential in this context was that access – such as via the afore-mentioned terminals – was to be free of charge or at least affordable, in order to maintain a clear distinction 'between commercial interests and citizens' right to "basic informational supply."'[53] However, since the *political price* for membership in the I.S. (29 DM per month for Internet access without traffic or time limitations) was not sufficient to finance the infrastructure, commissions for designing commercial web sites (including Deutsche Telekom, Daimler-Benz, Hewlett-Packard) had to be accepted. The I.S. as a self-organising system was not able to sustain itself, not least because financial support from the city of Berlin was not forthcoming. As Joachim Blank, one of the initiators of the I.S., summarised quite soberly: 'The local, localised approach of the I.S. or other digital cities only functioned in a very limited way, because most of the users were not interested.'[54] Even though – or especially because – the concept was transferred to other German cities such as Bremen and Cologne, commercial Internet providers soon superseded the independent Internet providers. The attempt to position projects like I.S. beyond the commercial media sector eventually failed. When the Berlin Senate decided on 28 October 1997 to set up its own electronic information service in the form of a public–private partnership, the last hope for public financial support was gone, and I.S. had to close its gates in the following year.

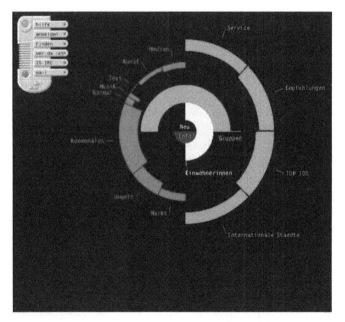

Figure 5.5   General map of Internationale Stadt Berlin (1995–1997).

Wien.at

A shared characteristic of digital cities was the demand for access for all, which was regarded a necessary precondition for the redemocratisation of public and urban spaces. In the beginning of the 1990s, however, the monopoly position of single telecommunication companies, particularly in Europe, hindered the development and expansion of an affordable infrastructure, which was further exacerbated by the fact that 'the introduction of the Internet did not come from a national strategy, but was instead part of a global marketing strategy'.[55] This is one of the reasons why state initiatives to introduce the Internet on a mass basis repeatedly failed – not least in Austria. Since 1990, there had been a dedicated line based on the TCP/IP standard, which connected the University of Vienna with the Internet, but networking efforts developed very slowly. The postal company Post und Telegraphen AG (PTA), which regarded the opening of electronic networks less as an opportunity, but rather as a danger to its business model, was actively impeding the work of independent Internet providers.[56] Outside of the universities' ACOnet, which was reserved for research and educational institutions, a connection to the Internet was possible only through the company Eunet Dienstleistungs-GmbH, founded in 1992 as the first commercial Internet provider in Austria.[57]

Against this background, various interest groups met in early 1995 in the city hall of Vienna to consult on the possibility of non-commercial web hosting, together with open online forums and public Internet terminals in the city.[58] As was the case in Amsterdam and Berlin, there was already an existing net culture scene in Vienna. Especially the Blackbox, a BBS system founded in 1992 by members of the Socialist Youth, was very popular and was by then one of the largest social networks in Europe.[59] The Blackbox was then also the one being commissioned by the city administration to coordinate the digital city project in Vienna, while its commercial spin-off, DatenWerk Kommunikations-GmbH, was to take over operations. On the website 'wien.at' the metaphor of the city was continued underground: five subway lines, which stood for the thematic areas of politics, society, city life, education and culture, were meant to lead users through the data space and provide them with information on the real city. Such a 'virtual doubling of Vienna'[60] implied veritable leaps of metaphors between the city and the net, which often led to an overextension of concepts. Yet, the discrepancy between the shared notional space and the actual interface persisted, leaving the stations of the digital underground largely vacant. As Oliver Marchart commented: 'The whole concept breathed the charm of the Viennese communal bureaucracy, which repeatedly anticipated serving the data works.'[61]

The lack of attractiveness might be explained by the fact that the founding context of the digital city was too much anchored in the city administration. Hence, for the Austrian Social-Democratic Party governing at that time, the cyber discourse presented an opportunity to prove their own progressiveness with respect to the new media technologies. This was done, however, less in the sense of a participatory implementation of net technologies, to which independent Internet providers could have contributed in a significant way, but rather in the paternalist style of Vienna's imperial and royal tradition. After the digital city was launched in December 1995, it was already integrated in the official information system of the Viennese municipal administration (*Wien Online*) by July 1996. Consequently, '[t]he internal flow of communication soon stalled, many jumped off the train, so the work was left up to only a few, and the critical mass was not reached'.[62] So, instead of developing a community of its own, the project was turned into a service platform for tourists and citizens. As was already the case in Amsterdam and Berlin, 'cyber-philosophers and -metaphors were no longer in demand', because in Vienna 'the city administration did not want to close itself to the [users'] wishes for content, services, and

Figure 5.6   Network map of Wien.at (1995–1996).

faster retrieval of information, so it concentrated more on the existing presence of Wien Online'.[63] What *too little* meant in Berlin, which was the lack of support from the city administration, turned into the opposite: in Vienna the data space was regarded as the virtual expansion of the administrative space, with the result that the online community was turned into 'a further symptom of Austrian Josephinism'.[64] Even before the underground of wien.at could go into operation, its symbolic value was already exhausted.

Despite their ultimate failure, the examples of Amsterdam, Berlin and Vienna clearly show how a digital urban space was imagined and produced in the surroundings of the European net cultures, which was radically different from the info cities, implemented only shortly before. The digital city no longer saw itself as a mere representation of digital space, but rather as a place of socio-technical networking. It can therefore be seen as an attempt to practically implement net critique by tying together virtual and physical space. The reasons for this differed in each example, depending on the respective local context: whereas the focus in Amsterdam was on the communal–political aspect, in Berlin it was primarily the desire for an autonomous and collectively used infrastructure for artistic and media content. In Vienna, on the other hand, it was the paternalism typical of the city that suffocated every attempt to develop a self-determined community from the start. What all three cities had in common was that they wanted to develop a self-reliant structure of Internet services independent from commercial interests. In this way, the digital cities often created not only the first Internet access for local initiatives, groups and individuals (especially in the field of art and culture), but also the possibility to collectively produce, store and share information. They provided the first groupware, which was no longer limited to a certain circle (e.g. academic staff), but was potentially available to everyone. This was also the reason why the interface of the digital cities, especially in Berlin, was conceived as an *open process* to allow users to design their very own shared network environment (i.e. the WWW server). And although the call to participate was seldom taken up, the virtual collaboration did enable a whole series of technical innovations, which today are among the standard repertoire of Internet applications.[65]

Despite its innovative character, the digital city was challenged by a remarkable anachronism: like traditional communities, it was distinguished by being tied to a specific place. Even though attempts were undertaken – as can be seen in the example of Amsterdam – to connect the local to the global space, the digital cities ultimately remained bound to their local context. This may be one of the reasons for the clumsy metaphors, which often were more reminiscent of village structures than the complexity of a globally networked space. Somehow inferior to the network metaphor itself, the digital city was not able to mediate between the global and local, but remained in the imagination of local communities. The nostalgic narrative of the loss of community is mirrored in the digital city, whereby the community was to be revived with the help of new information and communication technologies. This constriction led to the already familiar problem of technicist reduction: because of their focus on access for all, these projects took over the ideological shortcut of netism, according to which social participation was seen as a consequence of technological networking. Instead of demanding active and political participation in all areas, the digital cities limited themselves to the technical simulation of local communities.[66]

VIRTUAL COMMUNITIES

Already some time before the World Wide Web turned the Internet into a mass medium, first online communities emerged in association with Bulletin Board Systems (BBS), which are based on a program called Modulator-Demodulator (modem) written by Ward Christensen and Randy Suess in 1977. After logging into the BBS, users can exchange data, call up messages and communicate with each other – either through e-mail and Internet forums or through online chat.[67] Similar to Usenet, the success of BBS was based on its grassroots approach: 'For less than the cost of a shotgun, a BBS turns an ordinary person anywhere in the world into a publisher, an eyewitness reporter, an advocate, an organizer, a student or teacher, and potential participant in a worldwide citizen-to-citizen conversation.'[68] Howard Rheingold, social scientist and net enthusiast from the start, defined these new communities as 'social aggregations that emerge from the net when enough people carry on … public discussions long enough, with sufficient human feeling, to form webs of personal relationships in cyberspace'.[69] What is important in this perspective is the idea of socio-technical connections, which make it possible to communicate over long distances and in real time, as well as to form communities beyond the traditional barriers of class, race, gender, age or sexuality.[70] Hence, with the new technologies, the foundation for entirely new forms of communal life was believed to be found.[71]

At the electronic frontier, the hope of a revitalisation of communitarian spirit arose. As Pierre Lévy wrote, 'The "desire" of the members of virtual communities is linked ... with the ideal of deterritorialised, transversal, and free human relationships.'[72] In this perspective, the virtual communities were a means to dissolve social hierarchies and enable a self-government of emancipated citizens. Here, another set piece of the Internet ideology comes to light: According to the tele-democrats, more network technology led to more knowledge and thus led to more democracy. Hence, the mere introduction of new information and communication technologies was deemed sufficient to induce a 'new Attic age' (Al Gore). In the *electronic agora*, information was mutually exchanged, which was considered to revive and expand the public sphere. As in comparable techno-utopias before, cyber democracy was regarded as being the result of technological progress: 'This is a technologically supported continuation of a long-term shift to communities organized by shared interests rather than by shared neighborhoods or kinship groups.'[73] With the network technologies, the issue of democratic self-government beyond traditional social cohesion finally seemed to be solved.[74]

The virtual community thus appeared on the horizon of a general crisis of governance triggered by the postmodern dissolution of the social. In this sense, the community, understood as a set of voluntary relationships, based on shared interests, was taken into account as a counter concept to the notion of an association compelled by society, or, more precisely, by the state. Community then contained only the we-feeling of a specific group identity, which is 'strengthened through rituals of self-assurance and mutual internal recognition and ultimately constituted through the distinction from "others"'.[75] Out of this, a new governmental practice arose, based on 'the instrumentalization of personal allegiances and active responsibilities'.[76] For the British sociologist Nikolas Rose, this corresponds to a political programme that attempts to dissolve society on behalf of individual freedom: 'These new forms of government through freedom multiply the points at which the citizen has to play his or her part in the games that govern them.'[77] Those who want to be part of a community must identify with it, which is why the participation of the individual becomes obligatory with reference to a communitarian aim. In other words, this is not simply a form of domination exercised with force, but rather a mode of governing that relies on freedom, self-determination and self-responsibility. Individuals form communities on the basis of what they have in common, that is, on the basis of shared interests and consensual rules of behaviour, to which they voluntarily subject themselves.

This kind of 'government through community' superseded the old concept of social solidarity, leaving behind a disparate field of individual responsibilities. Accordingly, the digital cities with their virtual communities followed the liberal definition of democracy: 'Clearly, the discourse or even the mythology of the Digital City project is one largely built up around Habermasian notions of the public sphere.' They may therefore be regarded as an experimental field for a new sociability, whose aim is no longer found in an antagonistic public sphere, but rather in consensual partial publics. Instead of insisting on democratic plurality as a means of radical politics, the 'notion of bridging the gap, and responding to a "crisis" in democracy, ... seems to have failed, or at least has not met up with the grand expectations being thrust forth at the beginning'.[78] The communitarisation and commercialisation of the social, as well as the fragmentation of the urban, marks the most recent wave of a neo-liberal transformation and corresponds to the binary logic of digital computer networks, which functions on the basis of inclusion and exclusion. Inherent to this form of networked governance, however, is always the danger that 'there is little chance of social change *within* a given network or network of networks'.[79] Because of the capacity of networks to simply switch off incompatible nodes, or to integrate dissent into their own mode of functioning, the possibilities of an articulatory practice are lessened, which eventually means the possibilities of democracy itself.[80]

NOTES

1. See Paul Virilio, 'Speed and Information: Cyberspace Alarm!', in *Reading Digital Culture*, ed. David Trend (Malden/Oxford: Blackwell, 2001), 23–27.

2. Friedrich Kittler, 'The City Is a Medium', *New Literary History* 27:4 (1996): 725.

3. Peter Weibel, 'Die virtuelle Stadt im telematischen Raum', in *Mythos Metropole*, ed. Gotthard Fuchs et al. (Frankfurt a.M.: Suhrkamp, 1995), 212.

4. See Kevin Lynch, *The Image of the City* (Cambridge/London: MIT Press, 1960).

5. Christine Boyer, *CyberCities: Visual Perception in the Age of Electronic Communication* (New York: Princeton Architectural Press, 1996), 6.

6. See Boyer, *CyberCities*.

7. See Mike Davis, *City of Quartz. Excavating the Future in Los Angeles* (London/New York: Verso, 1990).

8. See Christa Maar and Florian Rötzer, eds., *Virtual Cities. Die Neuerfindung der Stadt im Zeitalter globaler Vernetzung* (Basel: Birkhäuser, 1997).

9. See Toru Ishida and Katherine Isbister, eds., *Digital Cities: Technologies, Experiences and Future Perspective*, (Berlin/Heidelberg: Springer-Verlag, 2000).

10. See Florian Rötzer, *Telepolis. Urbanität im digitalen Zeitalter* (Mannheim: Bollmann, 1995). 'Telepolis' was also the title of a conference series that took place in October and November in 1995 in Munich and Luxembourg, organised by Armin Medosch, Florian Rötzer and others. Together, Rötzer and Medosch founded the online magazine of the same name in early 1996, which has been published since then by Heise publishing.

11. See Martin Pawley, 'Auf dem Weg zur digitalen Desurbanisierung', in *Virtual Cities. Die Neuerfindung der Stadt im Zeitalter globaler Vernetzung*, ed. Christa Maar et al. (Basel: Birkhäuser, 1997), 17–29.

12. William J. Mitchell, *City of Bits. Space, Place, and the Infobahn* (Cambridge: MIT Press, 1996), 109.

13. See William J. Mitchell, *e-topia* (Cambridge/London: MIT Press, 2000).

14. See Oliver Marchart, *Die Verkabelung Mitteleuropas. Medienguerilla – Netzkritik – Technopolitik* (Vienna: edition selene, 1998), 35–38.

15. See Jay David Bolter, 'Electronic technology and the metaphor of the city', *telepolis*, March 1, 1996, accessed April 4, 2017, https://www.heise.de/tp/features/Electronic-technology-and-the-metaphor-of-the-city-3445801.html.

16. David Gelernter, *Mirror Worlds* (Oxford: Oxford University Press, 1993), 31.

17. See Andreas Dieberger, *Navigation in Textual Virtual Environments using a City Metaphor*, Ph.D. Thesis (Vienna: University of Technology, 1994).

18. See Andreas Dieberger, 'The Information City – A Metaphor for Navigating Hypertexts' (research paper presented at the BCS-HCI'93, Loughborough, 1993).

19. Andreas Dieberger and Andrew U. Franck, 'A City Metaphor for Supporting Navigation in Complex Information Spaces', *Journal of Visual Languages and Computing* 9 (1998): 597–622, here 598.

20. Dieberger, 'A City Metaphor', 598.

21. Ibid., 605.

22. For a differentiation between diegetic and non-diegetic interfaces, see Alexander Galloway, *The Interface Effect* (Hoboken: John Wiley & Sons, 2012), 25–53.

23. Andreas Dieberger was not the first to make use of this approach. In *The Legible City* (1988 and 1991), media artist Jeffrey Shaw asked visitors of the installation to use a stationary bicycle, in order to navigate through the streets of a city projected on a screen. Instead of a built environment, the users passed by letters, words and whole sentences, so that a separate narrative strand resulted each time with a different interpretation of the legible city (see Oliver Grau, 'Immersion and Interaction: From circular frescoes to interactive image spaces', *MedienKunstNetz* (2004), accessed March 3, 2017, http://www.medienkunstnetz.de/themes/overview_of_media_art/immersion/20/.

24. Flavia Sparacino et al., 'City of News', *interactive cinema* (1997), accessed December 29, 2016, http://ic.media.mit.edu/Publications/Conferences/CityOfNewsArs/HTML.

25. Sparacino et al., 'City of News.'

26. Bolter, 'Electronic Technology.'

27. Douglas Schuler, 'Community Networks: Building a New Participatory Medium', *Communications of the ACM* 37:1 (1994):, 39–51, here 39. Probably the most famous Freenet was the Cleveland Freenet designed by Tom Grundner in 1986. Although it was operated in the beginning as a BBS for health issues, the network grew rapidly because of its openness towards other topics. The interface was orientated to the metaphor of the city and had its own post office, a public square, an administration building and a hospital and artist house. The service was closed in 1999.

28. See Armin Medosch, *Freie Netze. Geschichte, Politik und Kultur offener WLAN-Netze* (Hannover: Heise Verlag, 2004).

29. The idea of a socially produced space goes back to Henri Lefebvre. He speaks of a trialectic of the social space, consisting of the spatial practice as what is perceived, the representations of space as what is conceived, and the representation spaces as lived space (see Henri Lefebvre, *The Production of Space*, trans. Donald Nicholson-Smith [Oxford/Cambridge: Blackwell, 1991]).

30. The Hacktic Network emerged in 1992 as a part of the hacker magazine *Hack-Tic*, which was published between 1989 and 1993 by Rop Gonggrijp. After the last issue was published, the Internet provider XS4ALL grew out of the network. It was soon separated from the hacker organisation and turned into an independent enterprise with commercial aims. In December 1998, XS4ALL was sold to Royal KPN N.V. (see Shuschen Tan, 'Digital City, Amsterdam. An Interview with Marleen Stikker', in: *ctheory*, 1995, accessed December 29, 2016: http://www.ctheory.net/articles.aspx?id=65).

31. Geert Lovink, *Dark Fiber. Tracking Critical Internet Culture* (Cambridge: MIT Press, 2002), 43.

32. See Lovink, *Dark Fiber*, 47.

33. See Inke Arns, *Netzkulturen* (Hamburg: eva, 2002), 52–53.

34. Joost Flint, 'Das Amsterdamer-Freenet 'De Digitale Stad' (DDS)', in *Virtual Cities. Die Neuerfindung der Stadt im Zeitalter globaler Vernetzung*, ed. Christa Maar et al. (Basel: Birkhäuser, 1997), 58. Quote translated by author.

35. Geert Lovink, 'The Digital City Amsterdam. Creating a Virtual Public', in *Welcome to the Wired World*, ed. Ars Electronica (1995), accessed April 21, 2017, http://90.146.8.18/en/archives/festival_archive/festival_catalogs/festival_artikel.asp?iProjectID=8627%22.

36. Lovink, 'The Digital City.'

37. See Kirsten Wagner, 'Architektonika in Erewhon. Zur Konjunktur architekturaler und urbaner Metaphern', *Wolkenkuckucksheim. Internationale Zeitschrift für Theorie und Wissenschaft der Architektur* 3:1 (1998), accessed December 29, 2016, http://www.cloud-cuckoo.net/openarchive/wolke/deu/Themen/981/Wagner/wagner_t.html.

38. Tan, 'Digital City.'

39. See Peter Hinssen, 'Life in the digital city', *Wired* 3.06 (1995), accessed December 30, 2016, www.wired.com/wired/archive/3.06/digcity.html.

40. To this end, three subsections were created: firstly, a commercial business section, which offered web-based services for private customers; secondly, a design section, which developed new applications for businesses; and thirdly, a section for social experimentation, which was to carry out the original intention of the DDS as a virtual community (see Geert Lovink, 'Die Digitale Stadt Amsterdam', in *Internet & Politik. Von der Zuschauer- zur Beteiligungsdemokratie?*, ed. Claus Leggewie et al. [Cologne: Bollmann, 1998], 295).

41. Geert Lovink and Patrice Riemens, 'Amsterdam Public Digital Culture 2000', *Telepolis* (2000), accessed December 30, 2016, https://www.heise.de/tp/features/Amsterdam-Public-Digital-Culture-2000-3447524.html.

42. See Lovink and Riemens, 'Amsterdam Public Digital Culture 2000.'

43. See Lovink, *Dark Fiber*, 55–56.

44. Geert Lovink, 'The Rise and Fall of the Digital City Metaphor and Community in 1990s Amsterdam', in *The Cybercities Reader*, ed. Stephen Graham (London/New York: Routledge, 2004), 376.

45. In contrast, Oliver Marchart took a critical stance to this approach: 'Instead of alienating people from technology to even enable a sober, enlightened use in the first place, there is an attempt to bring the technology "closer", to simplify it, which permanently undermines the degree of intelligence of the prospective users' (Oliver Marchart, *Die Verkabelung Mitteleuropas*, 33. Quote translated by author). For Marchart, this 'how-do-I-explain-it-to-my-children pedagogy' also explains the inflationary use of the metaphor of the city on the net: 'Little house icon, circle around the village square. Here is the city hall, there is the shopping centre, there the post office. The user must not get lost and should feel at home' (Ibid.).

46. Joachim Blank, 'Internationale Stadt Berlin. Notizen aus der Provinz', in *Virtual Cities. Die Neuerfindung der Stadt im Zeitalter globaler Vernetzung*, ed. Christa Maar et al. (Basel: Birkhäuser, 1997), 70. Quote translated by author.

47. The project Handshake, which was founded in late 1993 by Barbara Aselmeier, Joachim Blank, Armin Haase and Karl Heinz Jeron, originated in a loose association of media artists called LUX LOGIS, which was the driving force behind the Berlin media art festival Electronic Arts Syndrom (1991 and 1992). As an interactive spatial installation, Handshake focused on developing a participatory media environment on the basis of new network technologies (see Gottfried Kerscher, 'brave new city: Eine Einleitung und ein Interview mit einem der Mitbegründer der Internationalen Stadt Berlin, Joachim Blank', in: *Kritische Berichte* 1 [1998]: 10–16).

48. Contributed Software GbR a.D., co-founded by Thomas Kaulmann (aka Thomax), was among the first private Internet providers in Berlin. Thomax was also responsible for the programming of the *Internationale Stadt* and operated the *Radio Internationale Stadt*.

49. Internationale Stadt e.V. 'Internationale Stadt. Die ideale Stadt im Internet', *digitalcraft* (1995), accessed December 30, 2016, www.digitalcraft.org/dateien/islang2.pdf. This and the following quotes translated by author.

50. Internationale Stadt e.V., 'Internationale Stadt.'

51. Joachim Blank, 'Die Stadtmetapher im Datennetz', *digitalcraft* (1995), accessed December 30, 2016, www.digitalcraft.org/dateien/357_0730163813.pdf.

52. Internationale Stadt e.V., 'Internationale Stadt.'

53. Joachim Blank, 'Die Stadtmetapher im Datennetz.' Quote translated by author.

54. Tilman Baumgärtel, 'Die Zeit der digitalen Städte ist vorbei. Interview mit Joachim Blank von der Internationalen Stadt Berlin', *Telepolis* (1998), accessed December 30, 2016, www.heise.de/tp/r4/artikel/3/3167/1.html. Quote translated by author.

55. Hans W. Zeger, 'Das Internet in Österreich. Media-Hype und die sozialen Anforderungen', in *Informationsgesellschaft. Sozialwissenschaftliche Aspekte*, ed. Frank Hartmann (Vienna: Forum Sozialforschung, 1998), 23. Quote translated by author.

56. To prevent the shared use of dedicated lines by the Vienna Backbone System (VBS), an association of the Internet providers inode, Silver Server and ATNet, the PTA installed blocks in various DP connections. This 'post terror' finally ended when the new telecommunications law went into effect on January 1, 1998, with which the Austrian telecommunication market was adapted to EU guidelines. (see Harald Kapper, 'Standleitungen für Alle! Vienna Backbone Service – Ein Konzept mit Zukunft für den urbanen Raum', *Telepolis* [1998], accessed January 3, 2017, https://web.archive.org/web/20050131071757/http://www.heise.de/tp/r4/artikel/1/1404/1.html).

57. The *Eunet Dienstleistungs-GmbH* (EUnet) was founded on February 13, 1992 by the Unix User Group Austria (UUGA) and soon became Austria's leading Internet provider (see Thomas Schartner, '20 Jahre universitäres Internet, 18 Jahre kommerzielles Internet in Österreich', *ISPA News* 02 [2010], accessed March, 3 2016, https://www.ispa.at/filedl/0/0/1488903499/2576e 17aba2f539bdc50fb810139fc46a2ae081e/fileadmin/content/5_Wissenspool/ ISPA_News/2010/News_2010/2010_02_ispa_news.pdf).

58. Present during the meeting were the mailbox community Blackbox, the Internet provider Ping, the Group of Dedicated Computer Experts and the Public Voice Lab.

59. In late 1997, the Blackbox community counted around 4000 active users. However, the BBS system increasingly lost its significance with the rise of private Internet providers and the increasing internationalisation of the Internet, which is why it was shut down in its original form at the end of 1999 (see Daniel AJ Sokolov, 'Online-Community 'Blackbox' sagt nach 20 Jahren Adieu', *Der Standard*, November 6, 2012, accessed April 25, 2017, http://derstandard. at/1350260413960/Online-Community-Blackbox-sagt-nach-20-Jahren-Adieu).

60. See Oliver Marchart, *Die Verkabelung Mitteleuropas*, 32–34.

61. Ibid., 33–34. Quote translated by author. The culture line of the Digital City Vienna was supposed to be run by the net institutions Public Netbase, Silver Server, and Thing.at – although none of them were asked beforehand. The attempted implementation from above was vehemently opposed, especially since the three cultural servers had already their own infrastructures (see Armin Medosch, 'Public Netbase Wien. Netzbasis für Kulturschaffende', *Telepolis* [1998], accessed January 4, 2017: https://www.heise.de/tp/features/Public-Netbase-Wien-3441239.html).

62. Andreas vom Bruch, 'Der Niedergang der Digitalen Stadt Wien', *Telepolis* (1997), accessed January 4, 2017: www.heise.de/tp/artikel/1/1208/1.html. Quote translated by author.

63. Presse- and Informationsdienst der Stadt Wien, 'Zur Geschichte von wien.at', accessed January 4, 2017, https://www.wien.gv.at/pid/wienat-online/ zehnjahresjubilaeum. Quote translated by author.

64. Oliver Marchart, *Die Verkabelung Mitteleuropas*, 33. Quote translated by author.

65. The I.S. Berlin, for instance, invented the first web chat suitable for mass communication.

66. At the same time, they can be seen as a kind of *re-enactment* of civic media projects, for example the Community Memory Project in Berkeley during the 1970s. In this sense, digital cities were yet another wave in a long line of attempts to build community media.

67. One of the most popular BBS networks was FidoNet, founded in 1984 by Tom Jennings. It was able to offer transregional communication at affordable prices and connected more than 10,000 users within only a few years. In

the 1980s, the first BBS was implemented in Europe: with MausNet, Zerberus-Netz, Quicknetz, T-Netz and RaveNet, there were a number of German BBS which understood themselves as citizens' networks (see Medosch, *Freie Netze*, 206–212).

68. Howard Rheingold, *The Virtual Community. Homesteading on the Electronic Frontier* (New York: Harper Perennial, 1994), 131.

69. Rheingold, *The Virtual Community*, 5. The research on virtual communities in the 1990s was determined by two positions: one was the psychologically orientated analysis of virtual identities, which dealt mostly with the self-image of single individuals within digital environments (see Sherry Turkle, *Life on the Screen: Identity in the Age of the Internet* [New York/London/Toronto/Sydney: Simon & Schuster, 1995]); the other focused on social relationships and changing sociability in online communication (see Barry Wellman, 'The Network Community: An Introduction', in *Networks in the Global Village. Life in Contemporary Communities*, ed. Barry Wellman [Boulder: Westview, 1999], 1–47).

70. See Howard Rheingold, 'A Slice of Life in My Virtual Community',' in *Global Networks: Computers and International Communication*, ed. Linda M. Harasim (Cambridge: MIT Press, 1993), 57–80.

71. One of the most famous BBS was the Whole Earth Lectronic Link (The WELL), founded in 1985 by Stewart Brand and Larry Brilliant. The self-proclaimed 'birthplace of online communities' was located in the Californian Bay Area, where the communitarian spirit of the hippies had already connected with the cybernetic idea of self-steering, self-managing and self-governing virtual communities (see Fred Turner, *From Counterculture to Cyberculture: Stewart Brand, the Whole Earth Network, and the Rise of Digital Utopianism* [Chicago: University of Chicago Press, 2006]). While the WELL began as a Bulletin Board System, it was turned into a commercial Internet Service Provider (ISP) in the beginning of the 1990s. With the introduction of the WWW, the services of the WELL were integrated into a web-based environment and the ISP was sold to the company Salon.com. Following a series of financial problems, the community ultimately collected money to buy the WELL back from the Salon Media Group in September 2012.

72. Pierre Lévy, 'Cyberkultur', in *Kursbuch Internet Anschlüsse an Wirtschaft und Politik, Wissenschaft und Kultur*, ed. Stefan Bollmann et al. (Reinbeck: Rowolth, 1998), 80. Quote translated by author.

73. Barry Wellman et al., 'Computer Networks as Social Networks: Collaborative Work, Telework and Virtual Community', *Annual Review of Sociology* 22 (1996): 224.

74. Of course, the distinction between virtual and real communities is always a problematic one. The very *real* community of the nation-state, for example, also holds a virtual part, specifically in the sense of a nation-state

imaginary (e.g. founding myths, flags and anthems). For this reason, Mark Poster already noted early on: 'Just as virtual communities are understood as having the attributes of "real" communities, so "real" communities can be seen to depend on the imaginary: what makes a community vital to its members is their treatment of the communications as meaningful and important.' (Mark Poster, 'Postmodern Virtualities', in: Cyberspace/Cyberbodies/Cyberpunk. Cultures of Technological Embodiment, eds. Mike Featherstone, Roger Burrows [London/Thousand Oaks/New Delhi: Sage, 1995], 90).

75. Claus Leggewie, 'Demokratie auf der Datenautobahn. Wie weit geht die Zivilisierung des Cyberspace', in *Internet und Politik*, ed. Claus Leggewie et al. (Köln: Bollmann, 1998), 43. Quote translated by author.

76. Nikolas Rose, 'The Death of the Social? Re-Figuring the Territory of Government', *Economy and Society* 25:3 (1996): 332.

77. Nikolas Rose, 'Governing Cities, Governing Citizens', in *Democracy, Citizenship and the Global City*, ed. Engin F. Isin (London/New York: Routledge, 2000), 97.

78. Stefan Wray, 'Paris Salon or Boston Tea Party? Recasting Electronic Democracy, A View from Amsterdam', *The Thing* (1998), accessed January 6, 2017, www.thing.net/~rdom/ecd/teaparty.html.

79. Manuel Castells, 'Materials for an Exploratory Theory of the Network Society', in *Social Theory Re-Wired. New Connections to Classical and Contemporary Perspectives*, ed. Wesley Longhofer et al. (New York/London: Routledge, 2016), 182.

80. In his 'Postscript on the Societies of Control', Deleuze already described this binary logic of (digital) code: 'The numerical language of control is made of codes that mark access to information, or reject it.' (Gilles Deleuze, 'Postscript on the Societies of Control', *OCTOBER* 59 [1992]: 5).

Chapter 6

Network Dispositif

The Internet as a place for yearning corresponded with the neo-liberal paradigm of the 1990s.[1] The network supplied a model, with which the postmodern confusion was supposed to be overcome and a new form of governing to be tried out. In contrast to social-mediating institutions such as the state, political parties and trade unions, the virtual community held the promise of placing individuals directly in relation with one another. It was not least of all this ideological construction of the Internet as a self-sufficient system that first made it attractive to the business world. The community, in this perspective, promotes a new form of governance that seems to fit capitalist demands for flexible organisation and a permanent self-optimisation.[2] This may explain why, in the eyes of many, the Internet ultimately did not bring the often-invoked democratisation, but rather a new governmentalisation of society, which is based on a protocological mode of organisation.[3] Herein lies a fundamental transformation in the exercise of power: it is no longer primarily exerted through force, but rather through the invocation of the freedom of subjects who are now supposed to govern themselves in the name of a common good. The call for more participation thus led to a communitarian exercise of power, which implies that political concerns and organisational difficulties are being outsourced to the community.[4]

The desire for an all-encompassing connectivity gave rise to a new dispositif, which incorporated the network model. The network dispositif is thus composed of 'lines of visibility and enunciation, lines of force, lines of subjectification, lines of splitting, breakage, fracture, all of which criss-cross and mingle together, some lines reproducing or giving rise to others, by means of variations or even changes in the way they are grouped'.[5] What is important in this context is the fact that a dispositif is always marked by a transition and already refers to possible other dispositifs; we are part of a specific dispositif and act within it, therefore always changing its composition. To this extent, a critical analysis of the status quo is needed, in order to question and identify predominant assumptions in relation to the current network model, in particular its reduction to evenly distributed nodes and lines. The idea of a per se democratic network obscures the real topology of the net, which is characterised not only by a horizontal, but also by a vertical, structure. So, in order to investigate the implicit power relations within the network dispositif, it is necessary to describe and understand networks, as they correspond to our networked reality.[6]

This also affects the subjectivity engendered by the network dispositif: the *networked individual* is an expression of a mode of subjectification that has become the predominant form of sociability today.[7] From a genealogical perspective, this means that the mode of subjectification is to be investigated not only in its repressive form, but also in its activating function. Subjects are not simply networked with one another, but are indeed produced by network technologies and their imaginaries. In this sense, one can speak of a strategic field of subjectification that allows independent subjectivities to emerge.[8] The network dispositif therefore is both, the arrangement of discursive, institutional, regulating, theoretical and practical elements that produces the social, economic and cultural hegemony of the networked society, and the basis for alternative imaginaries to reverse its mechanisms.[9] In this sense, technical connectivity is indeed the precondition for a social collectivity, but is not its sole purpose. Digital network technologies are not merely a means of networking, but rather part of the social relationships themselves.

Hence, the idea of technical connectivity came up just as social collectivity started to crumble. In relation to the network dispositif, one has therefore to look at the specific context of the 1990s, when the neo-liberal attack on social institutions coalesced with a new network imaginary.

DISTRIBUTED NETWORKS

One of the most basic definitions of a network is Mark Newman's description in his standard work on networks: 'A network is ... a collection of points joined together in pairs by lines.'[10] The Internet, for instance, consists of a series of computers connected to one another by data lines. And from the perspective of such a simplified network thinking, society itself is composed of a series of individuals connected with one another through various relations. Networks are usually understood as topological formations, and the task of network theory is to describe the structure and properties of these topologies: 'Unless we know something about the structure of these networks, we cannot hope to understand fully how the corresponding systems work.'[11] The idea to analyse social or technical systems as networks goes back to the work of the Austrian psychologist Jacob Levy Moreno. His sociometry describes societies on the basis of their formal and informal structures, which consist of a network of social relationships.[12] Soon, just about anything was imagined as a network, especially since the network in its most abstract form can be applied to almost everything. This model, however, is limited in many respects, especially since it does not cover the dynamic aspects of networks. Unlike a system, which is defined by a boundary between itself and its environment, networks are distinguished by open structures, which are potentially infinite and cannot be closed. Hence, the network does not simply form the entirety of the nodes connected in it, but is instead an ever-changing set of nodes and lines.[13]

Like a network, a dispositif is distinguished by a constant transition 'between what we are (what we already no longer are) and what we are becoming'.[14] Even though the emergence of modern society had always depended on technological networks, as the development of electrical, railway or telephone networks in the nineteenth century shows, the Internet marked a qualitatively new stage: the *network of networks* has become the basis for a networked sociability, which transforms the way we see and imagine ourselves as a collective.[15] In particular the horizontal structure of the Internet represents a form of organisation that is different from a centralised, but also a decentralised, one. The distributed network suggests an even distribution of nodes, with the result that each node has, on average, the same amount of links as all the other nodes within the network.[16] Accordingly, the Internet, respectively the military ARPANET, was initially designed as a distributed communication infrastructure, in order to be able to withstand a nuclear first strike.[17] Unlike centralised command structures, which are vulnerable to targeted attacks, the method of 'packet switching' via distributed nodes was intended to compensate the outage of central nodes by simply rerouting the data packets through other nodes in the network.[18]

With the establishment of the Internet as a mass medium, the network prevailed as the guiding metaphor of the 1990s. This led to the assumption of a de-hierarchising function of the Internet, which was expected to undermine traditional forms of organisation: 'This was one of the first systems to present itself as a multiplicitous, bottom-up, piecemeal, self-organizing network which ... could be seen to be emerging without any centralized control.'[19] In this netism, the heterarchic and autopoetic nature of biological systems was taken as a model for technical networks.[20] Especially Kevin Kelly, executive editor of *Wired* magazine in the 1990s, saw a direct parallel between the Internet and a self-regulating ecosphere. In his widely read book *Out of Control*,[21] Kelly propounded the thesis that the Internet as a human-made system had achieved the complexity level of eco systems: 'As very large webs penetrate the made world, we see the first glimpses of what emerges from that net – machines that become alive, smart and evolve – a neo-biological civilization.'[22] In this way, Kelly, like many of his digiphile colleagues, was of the opinion that biological, social and technical systems conformed to the same non-hierarchical principle of self-organisation. So, instead of emphasising their social construction, technical networks were seen as biological, which means naturally given systems, therefore reducing their political complexity to the cybernetic ideal of a self-regulating organism.[23]

In contrast, Alexander Galloway saw the 'emergence of distributed networks [as] part of a larger shift in social life. The shift includes a movement away from central bureaucracies and vertical hierarchies toward a broad network of autonomous social actors.'[24] In this sense, the development of the Internet was marked not only by a Cold War military invention, nor by the new economy rhetoric, but also by new social movements. The desire for more participation yielded a form of political, social and economic organisation, which was brought into play against the traditional model of capitalist-industrial modernism.[25] Sovereign power based on top-down institutions was supposed to be superseded by a distributed form of power, made possible by the development of computer networks. While centralised or decentralised networks are both vertically structured, a distributed network, like the Internet, allows for a horizontal networking of single nodes. However, and this is Galloway's point, technical protocols are needed to connect and eventually control these nodes. Hence, the flip side of the distributed network, which was supposed to have a democratic effect on society, is the emergence of a new protocological regime of control. Instead of its elimination, sovereign power re-enters the stage through the backdoor of Internet protocols, which are central in digital media infrastructure.[26]

This is the reason why the network does not merely represent an abstract metaphor, but is described by its functionality and power structure. Hence, it is less a question of what a network is, but rather how it works and whom it works for.[27] The network, according to Eugene Thacker, cannot be described by some kind of inner logic or topology, but has to be analysed in its doing. It therefore represents a new mode of governance, which is less based on a centralised system of power, but rather on a flexible control regime. This does not mean, of course, that hierarchical forms of organisation have vanished, but 'power relations are in the process of being transformed in a way that is resonant with the flexibility and constraints of information technology'.[28] Digital networks, defined by their contingency, horizontality and flexibility, have become the material foundation of a social transformation, which distinguishes present forms of sociality from those of the past. Hence, instead of assuming a specific nature of networks, from which politically desired (or undesired) qualities are derived, we may take a closer look into the material basis as well as social tendencies, in order to better understand the socio-technical processes of the network dispositif.

SCALE-FREE NETWORKS

A closer look at the current network dispositif shows that hierarchical and centralising forces have not disappeared from either the technical or the social field. As the physicist Albert-László Barabási shows, we are dealing less with horizontal networking, but rather with major effects of inequality in network topology. In particular, complex networks, such as those in nature or society, but also the Internet itself, contain a small number of well-connected nodes, whereby the majority of the network nodes remains insignificant.[29] This dominance of individual hubs contradicts the egalitarian approach of distributed networks, in which each node is randomly connected and therefore has the same number of links. Barabási, on the other hand, speaks of scale-free networks, because here the individual nodes no longer have an average degree of connection. This is significant to the extent that it addresses the power law as an organisational principle of complex networks: 'In contrast to the democratic distribution of links seen in random networks, power laws describe systems in which a few hubs, such as Yahoo and Google, dominate.'[30]

It may well have been the intention of the founding fathers to build a distributed network, but precisely because of the principle of openness the Internet has led to a type of network different from what was originally planned. In fact, the structure of the Internet exhibits a strong centrality, not least because of a common property of networks: new nodes usually seek out the proximity of already well-connected nodes, so that the latter unfold an even greater force of attraction.[31] This process, called preferential attachment, is one of the distinguishing characteristics of scale-free networks, enabling the 'small-world phenomenon' highly regarded in network research.[32] This means that most nodes join together in their immediate proximity by means of fewer, but much stronger connections, whereas a few nodes connect these clusters with one another.[33] To get from one side to another, we do not traverse the entire network, but instead take shortcuts through central hubs. These hubs assume a strategic position within scale-free networks, because they become increasingly important as the network grows: '[T]his "rich get richer" process will generally favor the early nodes, which are more likely to eventually become hubs.'[34] Such a *Matthew effect* of accumulated advantage has profound impacts on the distribution of power within scale-free networks.[35]

The finding of scale-free distributions following a power law is henceforth challenging the conventional notion of a network that, in many cases, is still seen as a horizontal entity, evoking an emancipatory hope among political activists. For Rodrigo Nunes, recent political upheavals have shown that the organisational form of protest cannot be characterised by horizontality anymore, but rather by what he calls 'distributed leadership'.[5] Ever since the *alterglobalisation movement* in the late 1990s, collective political actions have changed fundamentally in their organisation: even if classical institutional players such as political parties, unions or interest groups still play a crucial role in the ability of a movement to organise itself, they do not *naturally* seize leadership within the movement anymore. This does not correspond to the libertarian dream of a movement without leadership, but, in fact, there are multiple leaders, on different layers, reorganising the movement over time. As Nunes states, new social movements 'are not leader*less*, but … leader*ful*',[36] taking into account that the leadership role can, potentially, be occupied by anyone within the movement. A look at new collectives such as the loosely connected transnational network called Anonymous may help to clarify this idea. In its self-conception, the group identifies itself as an 'Internet gathering' with 'a very loose and decentralized command structure that operates on ideas rather than directives'.[37] Thus, Anonymous and its many offshoots and associations, such as LulzSec, AntiSec, TeamPoison and the Peoples Liberation Front, no longer resemble a classical NGO like, let's say, Greenpeace, with its statutes, official members and formal hierarchies. In contrast, Anonymous' gatherings assemble different, and sometimes even differing individuals, groups and interests, without forming a political entity. This does not, however, mean that the collective itself is power*less*, in the sense that it would not be able to make decisions over its actions. On the contrary, the diversity of actions associated with Anonymous has shown how power*ful* distributed leadership, based on scale-free networks, can be; even if it is not always clear how decisions are being made and who is speaking in the name of whom.

It is not equality, but rather inequality that is one of the essential characteristics of scale-free networks. This means that a few, strongly connected hubs ensure the overall stability and therefore have to be strongly protected. Today's 'citadels of Web 2.0'[38] are run by semi-automated databases, which organise data flows in the form of search engines, social media and online portals. To fill these databases, every-one can and should participate, but only under the conditions defined by the Internet platforms. This participatory ideology addresses the user as potential customer, for whom it is not necessary anymore to understand all that much about the technical, but also social composition of the network. Quite a number of Internet companies offer their services to activate users within the net: tools provided free of charge, unlimited cloud storage capacity and the invitation to create one's own profile page serve the aim to fix the users within the respective network and elicit as much data as possible. At the same time, ever more sophisti-cated procedures are developed to virtually connect users, in order to make them comparable by means of algorithmic calculation. Powerful algorithms decide which information users want to receive, based on data not only about the user, but also about his or her immediate sur-roundings. This kind of 'personalization' involves the danger of an increasing homogenisation of information, which ultimately leads to an isolation of the individual users in their informational world view.[39]

Because of the way scale-free networks work, they allow not only for the commodification of user-generated content, but also for the reintroduction of a power regime that was already believed lost. Today's platform capitalism[40] yields new centres of power within the Internet, where sovereign knowledge about individuals and groups gets aggregated. This knowledge can then be used to intervene in the socio-technical structure of society and manipulate it according to commercial or political goals. These are the preconditions of the network dispositif, which is by no means simply characterised by a horizontal distribution of power, but equally by a vertical concentration of power relations. So, instead of a purely quantitative growth of individual nodes, there is the qualitative capacity to optimise the connection between these nodes, using 'algorithms to determine and at the same time inflect the identity of the user'.[41] In this sense, the emancipatory practice of 'collaborative text filtering' (nettime) has become a bio-political instrument of power consisting of myriads of clicks, likes, commentaries, friend requests and web searches, which together create the strategic field of social networking sites. By constantly being prompted to update their status, subjects of the network are constituted as individual users, which need to be connected via commercial online platforms, rather than addressing them as a collective from the start.[42] To be able to question the underlying ideology of the network dispositif, we must therefore investigate the mode of subjectification associated with it.

NETWORKED INDIVIDUAL

Media technologies enable communication between individuals and groups, without determining or relying on any specific type of social relationship. The sociality established by network technologies is not so much based on a meaningful narrative, such as the family, the nation or the like, but rather on an informational connectivity.[43] In the 'network sociality', Andreas Wittel therefore sees a new form of subjectification, which is central to the network society: 'I think it is worthwhile translating this macro-sociology of a network society into a micro-sociology of the information age. That is to say, not to focus on networks themselves, but on the making of networks.'[44] Unlike the historical model of mass media, the public sphere in network society consists between spatially distributed individuals. This mirrors the increasingly fragmented and networked mode of organisation and production in late capitalism, as expressed in networked individualism.[45] For Castells, the Internet forms the material basis upon which new subjectivities can emerge. The networked individual is thus not merely a consequence of technological development, but rather the Internet reinforces the global trend of people individually connecting, communicating and exchanging on the basis of computer-based networks. This development contrasts traditional ties, whether they are established through communities, such as the neighbourhood, the workplace or associations, or through large hierarchical bureaucracies. The networked individual is consequently not a stable subject centred around a certain spatial social relationship, but rather unstable, multiple and diffuse, which ultimately corresponds to the postmodern situation discussed before.

Since the 1990s, the neo-liberal discourse has transformed the traditional solidarity principle into a connectivity paradigm. This means that individuals are no longer bound together by society, but merely connected with one another via network technologies. Social thus ties into technical transformation, as the previous structure of society is dissolved and digital networks are drawn across the yawning gaps. Fixed in these digital networks, the networked individual becomes a source of permanent data production, which, in turn, builds the foundation of info-capitalism and makes governing under late-capitalist conditions possible. The individual is ultimately responsible for his or her position within the network, which means that inequalities between individuals are traced back to the respective networking achievement. On the basis of the neo-liberal notion of self-steering and self-responsibility, the emancipatory potential of digital network technologies now impels the internal colonisation of psychological, sexual, political, professional and affective spheres: 'These signals of belief and desire are eminently susceptible to interception, storage in databases, and transformations into statistics, which can be used as guidelines for the informed manipulation of our environment, and thus of our behaviour.'[46] By invoking permanent participation and interaction, social network sites enable an economic model that knows how to make profit from the desire for individual self-realisation.

With the constant growth of the information sector, it became possible to extend the model of the 'flexible personality'[47] to other areas of life. As a consequence, the boundaries between work and leisure, necessity and liberty, consumption and production have become permeable: the networked individual is not only flexible, mobile and always reachable, but is also supposed to contribute to the exploitation and further development of his or her communicative, social and cognitive abilities. 'Social networks are as old as humankind. But they have taken on a new life under informationalism because new technologies enhance the flexibility inherent in networks while solving the coordination and steering problems that impeded networks, throughout history, in their competition with hierarchical organizations.'[48] A new mode of governing emerged from the wish for flexibility on the basis of an imperative to participate: as is the case in the virtual communities, access to the respective network is granted only to those who actively partake in them and interact according to the parameters of the network.

By commodifying user-generated content, new online platforms turned the idea of user participation into a profitable business model, thereby helping capitalism out of the predicament of a networked environment that is not based on commodities anymore. The relational character of social media allowed for a new culture of connectivity in the form of an 'advanced strategy of algorithmically connecting users to content, users to users, platforms to users, users to advertisers, and platforms to platforms'.[49] In this sense, the initial dream of egalitarian communication systems was incorporated by a new platform capitalism, to the effect that users became the source of permanent data production, while at the same time being targeted by ubiquitous advertising. Unlike the net cultures of the 1990s, which focused on non-commercial networking practices, today we are dealing with the commodification of these practices. The business model of online platforms is, however, not so much based on the direct exploitation of labour, but 'in the realization of "rents" based on enclosure and appropriation'.[50] The horizontal exchange among users is inserted in a vertical relationship between the users and the owners of the platforms, in order to skim off the value produced by networking activities.

The mode of subjectification associated with the network dispositif is characterised by a capture of the emancipatory potential of network technologies. As is the case with all dispositifs, the 'problem cannot be properly raised as long as those who are concerned with it are unable to intervene in their own processes of subjectification, any more than in their own apparatuses, in order to then bring to light the Ungovernable, which is the beginning and, at the same time, the vanishing point of every politics'.[51] If we want to take the socio-technical processes of today's networks seriously, we must take an antagonistic stance to the connectivity paradigm, which ultimately only allows for a neo-liberal networking imaginary. Hence, a genuine alternative to the networked individual can be found only in a reformulation of the network model itself: instead of the neo-liberal network of self-managing individuals, a network of social relationships has to be imagined. So, opposite to the networked individual, which exists merely as an already defined node within the network that is connected according to capitalist needs, we have to invoke the formation of new collectives on the basis of new media technologies, especially since they have already reorganised the way we work, communicate and live together.

NOTES

1. See Paul Treanor, 'Der Hyperliberalismus des Internet', *Telepolis* (1996), accessed October 31, 2016: www.heise.de/tp/r4/artikel/1/1052/1.html.

2. See Steven G. Jones, 'Understanding Community in the Information Age', in *Cybersociety. Computer-Mediated Communication and Community*, ed. Steven G. Stones (Thousand Oaks/London/New Delhi: Sage, 1995), 25–26.

3. See Alexander R. Galloway, *Protocol: How Control Exists after Decentralization* (Cambridge/London: The MIT Press, 2004).

4. See Clemens Apprich, 'It's the Community, Stupid! Urbane Regierungstechniken der Selbstverwaltung', in *Phantom Kulturstadt. Texte zur Zukunft der Kulturpolitik II*, ed. Konrad Becker et al. (Wien: Löcker, 2009), 244–250.

5. Gilles Deleuze, 'What is a dispositif?', In Michel Foucault, Philosopher, ed. Timothy J. Armstrong. (New York: Routledge, 1992), 162.

6. See Albert-László Barabási, *Linked. How Everything Is Connected to Everything and What It Means for Business, Science, and Everyday Life* (New York: Plume, 2003).

7. See Lee Rainie and Barry Wellman, *Networked. The New Social Operating System* (Cambridge: MIT Press, 2012).

8. According to Giorgio Agamben: 'At the root of each [dispositif] lies an all-too-human desire for happiness' (Giorgio Agamben, *What is an Apparatus and Other Essays* [Stanford: Stanford University Press, 2009], 17). The net euphoria of the 1990s can be understood in this sense, to the extent that it can be read as an expression of a desire for more freedom.

9. See Michel Foucault: 'The Confession of the Flesh', in Power/Knowledge: Selected Interviews and Other Writings, ed. Colin Gordon (New York: Pantheon Books, 1980), 194–228.

10. Mark Newman, *Networks. An Introduction* (Oxford: Oxford University Press, 2010), 1. In network theory, the points are also called 'nodes' and the lines connecting them 'edges'.

11. Newman, *Networks*, 2.

12. See Jacob L. Moreno, *Sociometry, Experimental Method and the Science of Society: An Approach to a New Political Orientation* (Boston: Beacon House, 1951). For a further discussion of Moreno and Social Network Analysis, see Yuk Hui and Harry Halpin, 'Collective Individuation: The Future of the Social Web', in *Unlike Us Reader. Social Media Monopolies and Their Alternatives*, ed. Geert Lovink et al. (Amsterdam: INC, 2013), 103–116.

13. In this sense, the network and the system are mutually incompatible, assuming that a network is neither stable nor fixed, but comes into being only during the process of network building itself. A system can become a network, though, by dissolving its boundaries, because every node within a network can be seen as a transit point with potentially endless connections going through it (see Stefan Weber, *Medien – Systeme – Netze. Elemente einer Theorie der Cyber-Netzwerke* [Bielefeld: transcript, 2001], 48).

14. Gilles Deleuze, 'What is a dispositif?', 164.

15. See Wendy Hui Kyong Chun, 'Networks NOW: Belated too Early', in *Postdigital Aesthetics. Art, Computation and Design*, ed. David M. Berry et al. (London: Palgrave Macmillan, 2015), 290–316.

16. This idea goes back to the model of random networks, which was first developed by Paul Erdős and Alfréd Rényi (see Paul Erdős, Alfréd Rényi, 'On Random Graphs', *Publicationes Mathematicae Debrecen* 6 [1959]: 290–297). In accordance with a distributed network, the points of a random graph are equally distributed, whereby the lines between the nodes are randomly drawn. This results in a *democratic effect* of the network (see Albert-László Barabási, *Linked. How Everything Is Connected to Everything and What It Means for Business, Science, and Everyday Life* [New York: Plume, 2003], 21–23).

17. The basic idea of the ARPANET goes back to the work of US engineer Paul Baran. He worked in the 1960s as a scientist for the RAND Corporation, a think-tank associated with the US military. In this function, he was commissioned in 1962 – at the height of the Cuba Crisis – to develop a communication system that would be able to withstand a nuclear first strike (see Paul Baran, 'On Distributed Communications', *RAND Publications* [1964], accessed November 3, 2016, www.rand.org/pubs/research_memoranda/RM34 20.html).

18. In fact, it was not Paul Baran who first gained the attention of the American Advanced Research Projects Agency (ARPA) for his idea of a distributed computer network, but Donald Davies from the UK, who was working

on exactly the same idea at the National Physical Laboratory in Teddington. Whereas Baran originally spoke of 'message blocks', it was Davies who introduced the concept of 'data packets'. Plans for the ARPAnet, however, were ultimately based on Baran's study, 'On Distributed Communications', published in 1964.

19. Sadie Plant, *Zeros + Ones. Digital Women + The New Technoculture* (New York: Doubleday, 1997), 49.

20. The idea of self-organisation already came up in the cybernetic discourse of the 1960s. Heinz von Foerster described autonomous systems, which are closed in themselves and organise according to their own rules (see Heinz von Foerster, 'On Self-Organizing Systems and Their Environments', in *Understanding Understanding: Essays on Cybernetics and Cognition*, ed. Heinz von Foerster [New York: Springer, 2003], 1–19).

21. See Kevin Kelly, *Out of Control. The New Biology of Machines, Social Systems, and the Economic World* (New York: Basic Books, 1994).

22. Kelly, *Out of Control*, 202.

23. Kelly's hive-minded organism soon became a metaphor for the emerging New Economy and thus corresponded to late-capitalist *technoscience*, which was a wild amalgam of set pieces from biology, cybernetics, physics, mathematics, economy, information theory and system theory.

24. Galloway, *Protocol*, 32–33.

25. See Luc Boltanski, Eve Chiapello, *The New Spirit of Capitalism*, trans. Gregory Elliott (London, New York: Verso, 2005).

26. See Galloway, *Protocol*. Deleuze already said in an interview with Antonio Negri in 1990: 'One can of course see how each kind of society corresponds to a particular kind of machine – with simple mechanical machines corresponding to sovereign societies, thermo-dynamic machines to disciplinary societies, cybernetic machines and computers to control societies' (Gilles Deleuze, *Negotiations, 1972–1990*, trans. Martin Joughin [New York: Columbia University Press, 1995], 175). He added, however: '[T]he machines don't explain anything, you have to analyze the collective apparatuses of which the machines are just one component' (Ibid.).

27. See Eugene Thacker, 'Foreword: Protocol Is as Protocol Does', in *Protocol: How Control Exists after Decentralization*, Alexander Galloway (Cambridge/London: The MIT Press, 2004), xi–xxii.

28. Thacker, 'Foreword', xix.

29. See Barabási, *Linked*, 55–64. Barabási uses the image of the American air traffic network to illustrate a scale-free network: unlike the highway network, which principally corresponds to a distributed network, because the individual nodes (i.e. cities) indicate an average degree of connection, the air traffic network is distinguished by a very small number of larger and well-connected airports as well as a large number of small and less well-connected

airports. To get from one point to another, we do not traverse the entire network, but instead take shortcuts through central hubs (see Barabási, *Linked*, 69–72). Such a power law is missing, however, in Alexander Galloway's explanations, who compares the Internet with the US highway network, thus depicting it as a distributed network (see Galloway, *Protocol*, 38).

30. Albert-László Barabási and Eric Bonabeau, 'Scale-Free Networks', *Scientific American* 288 (2003): 53. It should be noted here that scale-free networks themselves can only be a description of real-real world phenomena, such as the power law. Unfortunately, it seems that the discussion around scale-free networks often tends to new essentialisations, similar to the ones regarding random networks.

31. See Albert-László Barabási and Réka Albert, 'Emergence of Scaling in Random Networks', *Science* 286 (1999): 509–512.

32. See Duncan J. Watts, 'Networks, Dynamics, and the Small-World Phenomenon', *American Journal of Sociology* 105:2 (1999): 493–527.

33. The sociologist Mark Granovetter speaks of the 'strength of weak ties' in this context (see Mark S. Granovetter, 'The Strength of Weak Ties', *American Journal of Sociology* 78:6 [1973]: 1360–1380).

34. Barabási and Bonabeau, 'Scale-Free Networks', 55.

35. Until now a lot of effort has been put into scrutinising the topological properties of scale-free networks, in particular power hubs. However, the existence of power hubs contradicts the emergence of new players, which are gaining a strategic role within the network. Here, Rodrigo Nunes may be of help, when he mentions the possibility of a node which is not a hub to 'act as a vector of collective action' (Rodrigo Nunes, *The Organisation of the Organisationless: Collective Action After Networks* [London: Mute, 2014], 38). This is deemed important, because it means that a node (e.g. a member of a network) can occupy a 'vanguard-function' over a specific period of time, without necessarily becoming a hub or permanent leader in the process.

36. Nunes, *The Organisation of the Organisationless*, 33.

37. 'ANON OPS: A Press Release', last modified December, 2010, https://www.wired.com/images_blogs/threatlevel/2010/12/ANONOPS_The_Press_Release.pdf.

38. See Martin Warnke, 'Databases as Citadels in the Web 2.0', in *Unlike Us Reader: Social Media Monopolies and Their Alternatives*, ed. Geert Lovink et al. (Amsterdam: INC, 2013), 76–88.

39. The Internet activist Eli Pariser speaks of 'filter bubbles', due to which users are less and less confronted with opinions contrary to their own. According to Pariser, this results in the loss of an ability that is crucial to democracy, namely that of bridging gaps between heterogeneous social groups and individuals (see Eli Pariser, *The Filter Bubble: How the New Personalized Web Is Changing What We Read and How We Think* [New York: Penguin Press, 2011]).

40. See Nick Srnicek, *Platform Capitalism* (Cambridge/Malden: Polity Press, 2017).

41. Galloway, *Protocol*, 114.

42. See Wendy Hui Kyong Chun, *Updating to Remain the Same. Habitual New Media* (Cambridge: MIT Press, 2016), 21–23.

43. See Andreas Wittel, 'Towards a Network Sociality', *Theory, Culture & Society* 18:6 (2001): 51–76.

44. Wittel, 'Towards a Network Sociality', 52.

45. See Manuel Castells, 'Communication, Power and Counter-power in the Network Society', *International Journal of Communication* 1 (2007): 238–266.

46. Brian Holmes, 'Signals, Statistics and Social Experiments: The Governance Conflicts of Electronic Media Art', *nettime* (2004), accessed December 12, 2016, http://amsterdam.nettime.org/Lists-Archives/nettime-l-0411/msg00067.html.

47. See Brian Holmes, 'The Flexible Personality. For a New Cultural Critique', *transversal* (2002), accessed December 12, 2016, http://transversal.at/transversal/1106/holmes/en.

48. Manuel Castells, 'Epilogue. Informationalism and the Network Society', in *The Hacker Ethic. A Radical Approach to the Philosophy of Business*, Pekka Himanen (New York: Random House, 2002), 166. Not least of all, the integration of women in the labour market contributed to a further flexibilisation of the work force. Workers preferred by information-processing industries in the second half of the twentieth century were 'educated, married women, who can afford to be less demanding in terms of wages, and who will provide skills in information-processing activities at a lower cost than would be incurred by employing men' (Manuel Castells, *The Informational City. Information Technology, Economic Restructuring and the Urban-Regional Process* [Oxford: Blackwell, 1991], 160).

49. José van Dijck and Thomas Poell, 'Understanding Social Media Logic', *Media and Communication* 1:1 (2013): 9.

50. Steffen Böhm, Chris Land, Armin Beverungen, *The Value of Marx: Free Labour, Rent and ›Primitive‹ Accumulation in Facebook* (Working Paper, University of Essex, 2012), 15.

51. Agamben, *What Is an Apparatus*, 23–24.

Chapter 7

Transindividuality

In the 1990s, the distributed network raised the hope for a largely horizontal communication infrastructure, which was supposed to yield a new democratic media culture. More recently, though, the utopian idea of self-governing individuals and communities has given way to the dystopian vision of a protocological control society.[1] However, neither the idea of absolute freedom nor that of absolute control corresponds with the socio-technical features of complex networks, but rather tend to consider digital media simply as tools, as *means* of communication. Instead of describing technologies as something separate from us, ultimately turning them into projection surfaces for our own fantasies and fears, they should be considered as part of human culture. As Mark Poster already reminded us: 'Discussions of these technologies ... tend often to miss precisely this crucial level of analysis, treating them as enhancements for already formed individuals to deploy to their advantage or disadvantage.'[2] Technologies should therefore not be considered merely as an extension of the human being, as an instrument of networking, but rather as conditions of the possibility of a socio-technical network itself. In this perspective, technologies become the starting point for new forms of collectivity that differ from a mere connectivity of social media.

This raises the question of new modes of subjectification, which have emerged on the basis of the current network dispositif. Since digital information and communication technologies increasingly co-determine the formation of a networked subjectivity, a better understanding of the socio-technical framework is needed, in which this subjectivity is embedded. For this reason, a 'technical culture' will be described in the following paragraphs, on the basis of some considerations of the French philosopher Gilbert Simondon. In contrast to a media-technical a priori (including Kittler and McLuhan) or an anthropocentric approach (including Habermas), with Simondon, new forms of concatenations between humans, non-humans and their technical environment can be described. In such a media-ecological perspective, technical knowledge is needed to understand the genuine, reciprocal relationship between humans and technology, humans and nature, and among humans themselves. The culture of technology has become the culture of society.

For Simondon, 'The technical world offers an indefinite availability of groupings and connections.'[3] This description does not only come very close to our networked reality, but also promises to offer alternatives to the current network model. Rather than being a separate and self-contained realm of its own, 'technical reality lends itself remarkably well to being continued, completed, perfected, extended'.[4] In this sense, the network society is not so much characterised by a total horizontality or a total verticality, but can instead be understood as a continuous process in the interplay between discipline and control, between centrality and distribution. We should therefore not focus so much on the alleged oppression or liberation of an already constituted individual, but look at the emergence of the individual within the network itself. This implies an alternative entanglement between human and non-human collectives and opens the way for a new form of solidarity, based on digital networks.

SOCIO-TECHNICAL COLLECTIVES

Media technologies have so far been mostly regarded as devices for processing, storing and distributing information. Print media, for instance, were ultimately understood only from their use side, that is, as the preferred instrument of a bourgeois public sphere. This brings us to a distinction typical for the debate about media technologies, namely between a world of meaning on the one side and a world of use on the other: while the former depends on a subject that produces meaning, such as the well-informed citizen of a bourgeois public sphere, the latter refers to technical apparatuses in the narrower sense – which can be used for either the emancipation or the manipulation of the subject. This long-standing dichotomy between culture and technology starts to crumble, however, the moment new object cultures begin to emerge with the increasing digitisation and networking of our world. As media philosopher Erich Hörl writes: 'These object cultures, with which we are intimately coupled, are truly techno-logical, in an eminent sense of the term, and they ultimately unhinge the sovereignty and authority of the transcendental subject.'[5] So, instead of maintaining an old culture of meaning on the basis of the bourgeois subject, today's object cultures are capable of producing their own technological condition 'with a new nonintentional, distributed, technological subjectivity that is informed by machinic processes and speeds'.[6]

A media-ecological orientation of this kind goes back to the work of French philosopher Gilbert Simondon. In the late 1950s, Simondon already raised the question of the extent to which the 'crisis of human culture' could be understood as a crisis of humans' way of dealing with technology: 'We would like to show that culture ignores a human reality within technical reality and that, in order to fully play its role, culture must incorporate technical beings in the form of knowledge and in the form of a sense of values.'[7] In his work *On the Mode of Existence of Technical Objects* (original title: *Du mode d'existence des objets techniques*), Simondon describes the emergence of technical objects, which takes place on three levels: on the level of the element, the individual and the ensemble. Whereas elements usually represent a simple technical object, for example a hammer, technical individuals are complex machines that emerged in the course of the Industrial Revolution.[8] The thermodynamic machine, however, was only the most basic technical individual for Simondon. For it was only with the rise of information theory before and during World War Two (based on works by Claude E. Shannon and Norbert Wiener) that technical processes successively opened up, which made it possible for technical individuals to join together at a next higher level of organisation to form technical ensembles. Simondon sees in this informational turn the most progressive form of technologisation up to the present.[9] It is the *open* technical object that first allows a reciprocal exchange of information and thus the formation of complex technical ensembles.[10]

At the level of ensembles, it now becomes possible to introduce the technical being into human culture. For Simondon, overcoming this difference implies a radical break with the European understanding of technology: it is no longer to be conceived merely as an object of use, but rather to be comprehended in its very own logic. In order to experience technical ensembles, the human must be transposed into concrete technological situations: 'In the same way one used to consider journeys as a means for acquiring culture, because they constituted a mode of placing man into a situation, one should also consider the technical experiences of being placed into a situation with respect to an ensemble, with effective responsibility, as having cultural value.'[11] To be conscious of our technical situatedness, as it becomes necessary today because of the ubiquity of digital media, is also a way to undermine a falsely understood humanism, specifically in the form of a reflex-like defence of human culture against technology. Humanism in this sense represents technology as the always already *other*, that is not as part of the human environment, but as a threat to it.[12]

However, as Simondon continues in *On the Mode of Existence of Technical Objects*, this kind of threat is not evoked by technology itself, but is instead the consequence of a widespread misunderstanding in the relation of the human and the machine: '[M]an has for so long played the role of the technical individual that the machine, once it has become a technical individual, still appears like a man occupying the place of another man, when it is, on the contrary, man who in fact provisionally replaced the machine before truly technical individuals could emerge.'[13] Hence, the reason for human alienation in an increasingly technified world is found in a misjudgement of technology itself: humans have so far delegated their humanness to the machine, which has thus become a replica of the human.[14] This has resulted in an utilisation of the machine, which means that the technical object has thus far remained subordinated to human work: 'The work paradigm is what pushes us to the consideration of the technical object as a utilitarian one; the technical object does not carry its utilitarian aspect within itself as an essential definition.'[15] The technical object is recognised only by means of human work, in other words as an instrument, which gains its meaning through the work paradigm, but not for itself.[16]

According to Simondon, the human being relates to the world in two ways: through a community based on work, which mediates between human and technology; or through a direct relationship between the human individual and the technical object, understood as the concretisation of human creativity. In keeping with the distinction between a closed and an open technical object, Simondon refers here to the difference between the community as a socially closed system and society as an open exchange between individuals: 'The immediate relation between individuals defines a social existence in the proper sense of the word, whereas the communitarian relation prevents individuals to directly communicate with each other, but instead constitutes a totality through which they communicate indirectly and without a precise awareness of their individuality.'[17] This does not necessarily imply the idea of immediate communication, as it predominated, for example, in some parts of radical net cultures,[18] but rather the observation that the technical object is always already open and participable, therefore allowing individuals to liberate themselves from the constraints of the community. In this perspective, a social association of psychic, technical and collective individuals can happen only in transition to a society based on technology: 'An inter-human relation that is the model *transindividuality* is thus created through the intermediary of the technical object.'[19] A transindividual collectivisation, as it occurs in society, requires the technical object, because it 'carries with it something of the being that has produced it'.[20] This specifically does not mean the purported humanness in the machine (in other words, the aforementioned humanisation of technology), but rather addresses the 'weight of nature that is preserved with the individual being'.[21] Nature in the technological sense refers to what is potentially common, thus to the pre-individual, which serves as the basis of socio-technical collectives.[22]

Because of the association between human and non-human individuals within the transindividual, the anthropological tendency of Western thinking is circumvented, as is the cybernetic reduction of society to the automated machine.[23] For Simondon, the automaton represents the lowest level of technological development, specifically because it reduces the complexity of social processes to the mere problem of regulation. His focus, in contrast, is on new kinds of ensembles of physical, psychic and collective individuals, as they are produced by technical culture: 'The technical world is a world of the collective, which is adequately thought neither on the basis of the brute social [fact], nor on the basis of the psyche.'[24] The collective consists of individuals that have – each for itself and similarly to the technical object – gone through a process of individuation on the basis of pre-individual reality. This process is never finished, though, because the pre-individual, which all individuals share, cannot be fully realised in one individual. 'According to Simondon, within the collective we endeavor to refine our singularity, to bring it to its climax. Only within the collective, certainly not within the isolated subject can perception, language, and productive forces take on the shape of an individuated experience.'[25] As the Italian philosopher Paolo Virno further explains, a transformation takes place here of the individuated 'I' to the social 'I', that is, from the individual to the transindividual.[26]

The collective individual surpasses the psychic individual because of the common experience that makes up the pre-individual, such as language, modes of perception or the historically conditioned mode of production. In this sense, it is a 'network of individuals'[27] who have gone through the process of individuation on the basis of their pre-individual reality. At the same time, the psychic individual is neither a stable state nor an identity, but is considered to be the never-completed end point of this development and not – as is the case in liberalism – its starting point. Consequently, the psychic individuation is always already inscribed in a process of collective or social individuation. It is therefore not a matter of integrating (or even assimilating) the singular individual into an already existing collective, but rather the interaction *between* the individuals is what first engenders this collective. For this interaction to take place, technology is needed: whereas work simply links already individuated individuals with one another, thus creating inter-individual communities, technology refers to the pre-individual, that is, collective experience, which forms the basis of a transindividual society. In order to form collectives, we need technology, not in the sense of a prosthesis-like extension of human work, but rather as the foundation of a collective world-building.[28]

If it is true that technology, understood as a pre-individual reality, is necessary for the participation in the process of collective individuation, then the opposite is also true; there is no collective individuation without psychic individuals being individuated and – even more important – without the active decision of these individuals to join the process of transindividuation. In this process, the pre-individual serves as an unstable or meta-stable state, as pure potency, which must be realised in the act of individuation. Today, it is the technical experience of an increasingly networked world, which is essential for the individuation process. Following Simondon, it could be said that the technical ensembles of digital networks engender a new transindividuality, which, in contrast to the inter-individuality of the modern labour society, is characterised by connections between human and non-human individuals. Hence, the expansion of human culture by non-human technology contains a 'political and social value: it can give man the means for thinking his existence and situation according to the reality that surrounds him'.[29] We are living in a technological sense culture, which fundamentally transforms our modes of cognition and being.[30]

Today this concern is more topical than ever, given the fact that our environment is more and more permeated by digital technologies. In particular in cities, where 'a sensor-based ubiquitous computing across urban infrastructure' has been implemented, a new regime of environmental governance is emerging.[31] Like the Internet, urban infrastructure is run by commercial interests, which tend to atomise individuals in order to reconstitute them as codifiable and exploitable nodes within the network. Today's predominant network model thus does not serve a collective transindividuation in the Simondonian sense, but instead promotes the individual self, which is compelled by networking sites to constantly update its status according to predetermined datasets. What happens to this data, how it is analysed and combined, is beyond our grasp, therefore reinforcing the feeling of a loss of social cohesion. At the same time, however, digital technologies offer the possibility of developing alternative modes of individuation within the network, which means creating new forms of subjectivity that may show a way out of the walled gardens of platform capitalism.[32]

INDIVIDUAL AS NETWORK

The mode of subjectification that has become hegemonic in network society is based on the liberal premise of atomised individuals. Not only does the individual precede the collective, but it is itself bifurcated into a myriad of data points. Since the content produced by users does not have any intrinsic value per se, commercial Internet platforms are dependent on the 'relational character' of network technologies, that is the fact that value in online communication is not created by digital artefacts (e.g. documents, pictures, entries, audio and video files), but rather by the relations between these artefacts (e.g. sharing, commenting and comparing).[33] Hence, 'capitalist productivity derives from [the] expropriation and exploitation of communicative processes'.[34] For Jodi Dean, this means that capitalism has subsumed communication, especially since network technologies make it possible to directly extract value from social relations. This is a crucial point, because it implies a shift from value production based on labour to a value production based on communication.[35] The valorisation of intellect and language, of information and communication, of creativity and politics, has superseded the old dualities between work and leisure, production and consumption, with the effect that the subject becomes an endlessly exploitable source of data production.[36] What becomes apparent here is the social character of network technologies, which, until now, has been captured only by commercial Internet platforms. As a networked individual, the subject is interwoven in digital networks of social relations, thus already pointing to a new transindividual, who holds the potential to go beyond the community based on work relations. It is not the isolated, private and atomised individual, as we know it from platform capitalism, that is of importance here, but rather a social individual integrated in various kinds of networks. Such an individual is open to its environment, whether it is of human, technical or social nature. Prototypical for this could be an open model, such as that expressed in wikis: within these networks the identity of an individual is usually not fixed, so it is not necessary to know who the other is in order to cooperate on a collaborative project. Instead of being fixed within the network, as is the case with commercial platforms, the individual individualises by traversing through several of these open networks. This is what distinguishes the individual as network from the networked individual: individuality is not something given, assembled and connected according to the needs of preset data structures, but instead it emerges in the process of networking itself. This is why a knowledge of the technical but also of the social potential of networks is needed, a knowledge that does not allow itself to be sealed off by commercial interests. Particularly in postfordism, the new information and communication technologies have led to a socio-economic assemblage, which builds the basis for a new subjectivity. A subjectivity formulated like this unites two contradictory movements: on the one hand, a tendency to convergence, made possible by the emergence of technological standards and protocols; on the other hand, a social diversity, engendered by the openness of the network. The juxtaposition of vertical and horizontal developments is typical for our 'post-media age',[37] in particular since digital media have permeated almost all areas of life. For Félix Guattari, the potential of new media technologies consists in social, technological and psychological ensembles, which engender new forms of a collective mode of expression. Yet, post-media is not to be seen simply as a succession from majoritarian to minoritarian media, but rather – in keeping with Lyotard's concept of postmodern revision[38] – as a mutual intertwining of reterritorialisation and deterritorialisation, an interlocking of mass media and new forms of expression.[39] Digital technology therefore 'perpetuates the modern desire for control and mastery through networks, databases, algorithms and simulations'.[40] Thirty years after Les Immatériaux, it is obvious that digital media are no longer just a code for socio-technical transformation, but have instead become the foundation of this transformation. Instead of taking them merely as media apparatuses for one purpose or another, the material basis has to be investigated, which is built directly into the technological protocols.

According to Alexander Galloway, a computer protocol contains certain rules, which steer and control possible behaviour within a heterogeneous network. In their function, they correspond to a diplomatic protocol, which also defines the framework for possible actions between two (or more) parties: 'Like their diplomatic predecessors, computer protocols establish the essential points necessary to enact an agreed-upon standard of action.'[41] They specify how a network operates, by setting the rules for the transmission of data from one computer to another, from one application to another, but also from one protocol to another.[42] The Internet, therefore, has little to do with the common perception of an uncontrolled space of data distribution, but is governed by highly formalised rules. Protocols are, in other words, technical objects, which, following Simondon, enable the creation of technical ensembles. In this sense, protocols are the basis for both, new regimes of control and new modes of communication. Galloway therefore sees no way to simply bypass protocological control: 'It is *through* protocol that we must guide our efforts, not against it.'[43] This also applies to biological life, which itself is protocological in the sense that it is increasingly depicted as informational flow (e.g. the genetic code), leading to the development of biotechnologies as a protocol-based network.[44]

Network technologies play a crucial role in the cultural logic of late capitalism, because they enable new forms of transindividuation. The material basis for this is the Internet, which in its function as a top-level ensemble connects a series of sub-ensembles – in other words, computer networks that are compatible with TCP/IP. This results in new assemblages between human and non-human elements, an ongoing, never-finished process of protocols generating other protocols, and networks conjoining with other networks. In this socio-technical milieu, 'It is necessary for every man employed with a technical task to ... have an understanding of it in some way, and to look after its elements as well as its integration into the functional ensemble.'[45] The human subject operates as a kind of curator within the technical process, which implies that progress is not only technical progress, as it is expressed in technological determinism, but rather must always be a human-technological progress.[46] Conversely, the technical object must be recognised by humans as such, in order to be able to engender a truly technical culture. This is where the potential of transindividuality is found: 'The merit of a dialogue between the individual and the technical object is to conserve the human effort and to create a transindividual domain, in which, distinct to the community, the notion of liberty takes on meaning, and which transforms the notion of individual destiny, without annihilating it.'[47] Such a dialogue enables the individual to be in different social spheres at the same time. The individual is thus traversed by different networks, remaining open to diverse associations as the precondition for a genuine – because collective – subjectivity.

DIGITAL SOLIDARITY

Related to the question of how new collectives can emerge in our post-media era is the question of how they can counter the capitalist tendency to destroy collective experiences and get beyond the liberal idea of individual identities? Félix Guattari situates his answer in the modular transition from consensual mass media to dissensual post-media, as a new social ecology emerges in this transformation: 'An essential programmatic point for social ecology will be to encourage capitalist societies to make the transition from the mass-media era to a post-media age, in which the media will be reappropriated by a multitude of subject-groups capable of directing its resingularization.'[48] In this sense, the reappropriation of digital media technologies by new kinds of subject groups entails a continual process of differentiation on the basis of a common solidarity.[49] The transversal nature of socio-technical networking indicates a mode of subjectification, which has the potential to confront a one-dimensional, data-driven mass-media subjectivity with a 'pluralism of forces, able to positively feedback on their comparative strengths'. As Srnicek and Williams further explain, a new organisational ecology 'requires mobilisation under a common vision of an alternative world, rather than loose and pragmatic alliances'.[50] So, instead of simply criticising the strategic field of platform capitalism, thereby repeating the same ontological presuppositions of today's network dispositif, a pluralism of forces must be organised, in order to unleash 'new collective assemblages of enunciation'.[51]

Networked digital media give way not only to new forms of capitalist exploitation, but also to new modes of existence. In fact, algorithmic governance, itself dependent on a multitude of technological protocols, has become prevalent in our daily lives, ranging from finance, to logistics, to medicine, to urban planning, to creative expression. By breaking with the imaginative power of 'capitalist realism',[52] Tiziana Terranova sees a way to put algorithms to different social ends and to constitute 'a new political rationality around the concept of the "common."'[53] For her, a post-capitalist mode of production, consumption and distribution based on networked digital media has to go beyond the dichotomies of the state versus the market, the public versus the private, in order to deploy the concept of the common as a new imaginary of digital cultures. Algorithms play a crucial role here, because they provide a 'genealogical line' in the ongoing automation of capitalism. Hence, the automaton of the thermo-mechanical model of the industrial age, that is, in Simondon's view, the lowest level of the technical object, has been superseded by electro-computational networks, which form the material basis of capitalism today. As open technical objects, these networks allow for a post-capitalist common, exemplified in Terranova's account on virtual money, social networks and bio-hypermedia, all of which hold the promise to free time and energy from our work-based mode of existence.[54]

A commons-based peer production can thus serve as a starting point to think about self-managed resources and infrastructures that are neither commercially driven nor state owned. The term, which was initially coined by Yochai Benkler,[55] describes a collaborative way of producing, where single persons freely cooperate to create common goods. This indicates a new social mode of production, which is based on the principles of openness, sharing and the common realisation of projects. For Benkler, a prominent example is the Free Software movement, which 'suggests that the networked environment makes possible a new modality of organizing production: radically decentralized, collaborative, and non-proprietary; based on sharing resources and outputs among widely distributed, loosely connected individuals who cooperate with each other without relying on either market signals or managerial commands'.[56] What becomes apparent in this description is the influence of the aforementioned netism, in particular its unbroken belief in the distributed network. However, the self-imposed rules of Free Software, its protocols so to say, prevent the privatisation of resources, because the outputs built through a collaborative process are available to all participants.[57] The emerging commons are not necessarily anti-capitalist, but indicate a radical change in the mode of production. Hence, the collaborative approach, based on the principles developed by Free and Open Source Software (FOSS) movement, can be applied to a variety of other fields, which apply a social rather than a commercial culture of production, distribution and consumption.[58]

For media sociologist Felix Stalder, such a socio-economic transformation is contingent on digital network technologies, since they provide the material infrastructure needed for new forms of cooperative and coordinated action: 'Over the last few years, the infrastructure as a whole has become so differentiated that it enables co-operation in socially nuanced ways, ranging from close-knit trust circles to more or less complete anonymity.' New infrastructures of cooperation, together with a whole new ecology of digital tools, enable collective forms of organisation. 'Depending on the type of co-operation intended, mainstream tools might be fully sufficient, but there are also more specialised tools, available on central servers, or those which can be installed in a decentralised way under full user control.'[59] This mixed ecological field of commercial as well as non-commercial applications is crucial, because it fosters a socio-technological learning process through collaborative platforms and practices, which, following Simondon once more, lies at the heart of collective individuation. Moreover, it shows that cooperative processes have been part of Internet cultures from the beginning on, as the example of digital cities demonstrates. In fact, network technologies were developed with the goal to facilitate the free sharing of information among peers.[60]

What should be noted here is that the experience with participatory media as well as technical infrastructure reveals that 'a sustainable, open and collaborative practice is difficult to achieve and that new specialized approaches must be developed in order to sustain the fine balance between openness and a healthy signal/noise ratio'.[61] To this end, the active co-creation of protocols is needed. As was mentioned before, they establish social and technical obligations, which must be upheld by the human and non-human individuals, so that they can exchange information with one another. Hence, a network can spread out only as far as its protocols reach. If the protocols are open, as is the case in the Open and Free Software movement, principally endless concatenations of technical ensembles can be formed. Conversely, closed or hierarchical protocols, such as those found with commercial online platforms, can easily establish relationships of dependency and pave the way for a privatisation of knowledge and information. This holds an immediate political question: How can collective action, built on socio-technical protocols, contribute to strengthen a social solidarity? As Stalder writes: 'Such solidarity, embedded in new narratives and creating new shared horizons for action, can provide the basis for novel cultural, economic and political forms.'[62] The history of net cultures is thus marked not only by the development of technical standards, but also by the general framework of socio-economic development. With the financial crisis in 2008, the old model of organisation seems to have lost ground, whereas new forms of solidarity have emerged.[63]

It is not the community based on work but a society rooted in the principle of solidarity that is able to produce commons as 'long-term social and material processes'.[64] Rather than focusing solely on commons as material goods, we should consider the creation of commons as an immanent political process: 'If we understand *the commons* to refer both to the material context and the consequence of practices of peer-production, *the common* is the political potential immanent in such practices.'[65] Hence, the common as social substance builds the basis for a cooperative mode of existence, which enables individuals to recognise each other and to individuate themselves through the collective. Beyond the distinction between a mechanical and an organic solidarity, digital media hold the promise of a social solidarity, which is neither based on kinship ties nor on work-based relations.[66] To this effect, a universal principle is needed, which does not exhaust itself in a particular goal, as was the case in virtual communities, but allows for a collective individuation based on collaboration and information sharing. In this sense, the notorious reference to the Free Software movement as a success story involves the danger of reducing the overall social process to this one example. Instead, the socio-technical culture must be considered as a whole if we want to avoid the communitarian snares of 1990s.

NOTES

1. See Alexander R. Galloway, *Protocol: How Control Exists after Decentralization* (Cambridge/London: The MIT Press, 2004). On the protocological side, Galloway's description of a control society is based on an analysis of the Transmission Control Protocol (TCP), where control is already included in the name. Of course, TCP is one of the most important protocols within the IP family, but Galloway's argument would probably be different if he would also include the promiscuous User Datagram Protocol (UDP). Contrary to the connection-orientated TCP, with UDP, there is no guarantee that a data packet will actually arrive. This corresponds more to the wasteful power of the sovereign than to the control society relying on distributed networks.

2. Mark Poster, 'Postmodern Virtualities', in *Cyberspace/Cyberbodies/Cyberpunk. Cultures of Technological Embodiment*, ed. Mike Featherstone et al. (London/Thousand Oaks/New Delhi: Sage, 1995), 80.

3. Gilbert Simondon, *On the Mode of Existence of Technical Objects*, trans. Cécile Malaspina et al. (Minneapolis: Univocal, 2017), 251.

4. Gilbert Simondon, 'Technical Mentality', trans. Arne De Boever, *Parrhesia* 7 (2009), 24.

5. Erich Hörl, 'The Technological Condition', trans. Anthony Enns, *Parrhesia* 22 (2015), 3.

6. Hörl, 'The Technological Condition', 4.

7. Simondon, *On the Mode of Existence of Technical Objects*, 15.

8. In this context, it is important to emphasise that the individuation of a technical object is only possible in an *associated milieu*: 'No individual would be able to exist without a milieu that is its complement, arising simultaneously from the operation of individuation: for this reason, the individual should be seen as but a partial result of the operation bringing it forth' (Muriel Combes, *Gilbert Simondon and the Philosophy of the Transindividual*, trans. Thomas LaMarre [Cambridge/London: MIT Press, 2013], 4) This means that the individuation of technical objects can be seen as an external resonance in the sense of a mutual causality between the technical individual and its associated milieu.

9. See Simondon, 'Technical Mentality', 18.

10. Here, the open technical object is contrasted with a self-contained cybernetic machine, because it requires a certain scope of indeterminacy to be receptive to external information (expansion of the mode of functioning). The emphasis on the openness of technical objects is thus a direct critique of (second order) cybernetics: as highly as Simondon praises cybernetic theory (Norbert Wiener) for its inductive understanding of the machine, to the same extent he criticises its fixation on a certain type of technical object: the automaton (see Jean-Hugues Barthélémy, 'Simondon – Ein Denken der Technik im Dialog mit der Kybernetik', in *Die technologische Bedingung. Beiträge zur Beschreibung der technischen Welt*, ed. Erich Hörl [Berlin: Suhrkamp, 2011], 93–109).

11. Simondon, *On the Mode of Existence of Technical Objects*, 235.

12. This felt threat manifests itself in the cultural representation in two ways: either in the form of a complete obliteration of human culture by machines, for example in films like *Terminator* or *Matrix* or through the instrumentalisation of the machine as an instrument of domination, such as in Fritz Lang's film *Metropolis*.

13. Simondon, *On the Mode of Existence of Technical Objects*, 81.

14. That is a projection surface for human fantasies, as is manifested in the figure of the robot, the cyborg, but ultimately also in the idea of the Internet as an urban environment.

15. Simondon, *On the Mode of Existence of Technical Objects*, 251.

16. For Simondon work, is a historical sequence of technicity and not – as previously assumed – technicity a historical sequence of work. This is significant, because technology, not work, thus becomes the centre point of human reality: 'To this day, the reality of the technical object has been relegated to the background behind the reality of human work. The technical object has been apprehended through human work, thought and judged as instrument, adjuvant, or product of work. However, one ought to be capable, in favor of man himself, to carry out a reversal that would enable what is human in the technical object to appear directly, without passing through the relation of work' (Simondon, *On the Mode of Existence of Technical Objects*, 247). Akin to Baudrillard's critique of use value as the 'mirror stage of Marxism' (Jean Baudrillard, *Le miroir de la production ou l'illusion critique du matérialisme historique* [Paris: Galilée, 1985]), one can see a radical abandonment of the Marxist concept of labour and utility here. For Simondon, it is labour, respectively work, that is the source of human alienation, rather than alienation being due to work relations induced by capitalism. The capitalist separation of the workers from the means of production exacerbates the process of alienation, but is not its cause (see Simondon, *On the Mode of Existence of Technical Objects*, 253).

17. Gilbert Simondon, *L'individuation à la lumiére des notions de form et d'information* (Grenoble: Éditions Jérôme Millon, 2005), 514. Quote translated by author.

18. See Hakim Bey, 'Immediatism', in *Immediatism. Essays by Hakim Bey*, Hakim Bey (Edinburgh/San Francisco: AK Press 1994), 7–12.

19. Simondon, *On the Mode of Existence of Technical Objects*, 253.

20. Ibid.

21. Ibid.

22. Every subject is charged with a pre-individual reality, which goes beyond the human and non-human individual (see Paolo Virno, *Grammar of the Multitude*, trans. Isabella Bertoletti et al. [Los Angeles: semiotext(e), 2004], 76–80).

23. See Barthélémy, 'Simondon', 94–95.

24. Simondon, *On the Mode of Existence of Technical Objects*, 258.

25. Paolo Virno, *Grammar of the Multitude*, 79.

26. Paolo Virno equates the pre-individual (i.e. language, affects, perception, certain productive forces) with Marx' 'General Intellect' and the entirety of 'social individuals' with the multitude. With this he undertakes an attempt to adapt Marxist theory to Simondon's philosophy: 'It may seem paradoxical, but I believe that Marx's theory could (or rather should) be understood today, as a realistic and complex theory of the individual, as a rigorous individualism: thus, as a theory of individuation' (Virno, *Grammar of the Multitude*, 80). Accordingly, for Virno, it is not a matter of a mere integration (or assimilation) of the individual into the collective (as is the case in the community), but rather of constant negotiation between the individual and the multitude. Ultimately this is possible only through forms of non-representative democracy (see Virno, *Grammar of the Multitude*, 13).

27. Virno, *Grammar of the Multitude*, 76.

28. Sybille Krämer speaks of a productive meaning of media technologies, which is not so much found in human work, but rather in world production (see Sybille Krämer, 'Das Medium als Spur und als Apparat', in *Medien, Computer, Realität. Wirklichkeitsvorstellungen und Neue Medien*, ed. Sybille Krämer [Frankfurt a.M.: Suhrkamp, 1998], 73–94).

29. Simondon, *On the Mode of Existence of Technical Objects*, 20.

30. See Hörl, 'The Technological Condition'.

31. See Gabrys, Jennifer. 'Programming Environments: Environmentality and Citizen Sensing in the Smart City'. *Environment and Planning D: Society and Space* 32:1 (2014): 30–48.

32. See Nick Srnicek, *Platform Capitalism* (Cambridge/Malden: Polity Press, 2017).

33. See Søren Mørk Petersen, 'Loser Generated Content: From Participation to Exploitation', *First Monday* 12:3 (2008), accessed January 8, 2017, http://firstmonday.org/article/view/2141/1948.

34. Jodi Dean, 'Communicative Capitalism and Class Struggle', *spheres – Journal for Digital Cultures* 1 (2014), accessed April 30, 2017, http://spheres-journal.org/communicative-capitalism-and-class-struggle.

35. See Virno, *Grammar of the Multitude*, 56–59.

36. See danah boyd and Kate Crawford, 'Critical Questions for Big Data', *Information, Communication & Society* 15:5 (2012): 662–679.

37. See Félix Guattari, 'Towards a Post-Media Era', in *Provocative Alloys: A Post-Media Anthology*, ed. Clemens Apprich et al. (London: Mute, 2013) 26–27.

38. See Jean-François Lyotard, 'Note on the Meaning of 'Post'', in *The Postmodern Explained*, ed. Julian Pefanis et al. (Minneapolis: University of Minnesota Pres, 1992), 75–80.

39. See Gary Genosko, Gary (2013): 'The Promise of Post-Media', in *Provocative Alloys: A Post-Media Anthology*, ed. Clemens Apprich et al. (London: Mute, 2013), 15–25.

40. Yuk Hui and Andreas Broeckmann, 'Introduction', in *30 Years after Les Immatériaux: Art, Science, and Theory*, ed. Yuk Hui et al. (Lüneburg: meson press, 2015), 16.

41. Galloway, *Protocol*, 7.

42. As Alexander Galloway explains, individual protocols are always nested within other protocols: 'Take, for example, a typical transaction of the World Wide Web. A web page containing text and graphics (themselves protocological artefacts) is marked up in the HTML protocol. The protocol known as Hypertext Transfer Protocol (HTTP) encapsulates this HTML object and allows it to be served by an Internet host. However, both client and host must abide by the TCP protocol to ensure that the HTTP object arrives in one piece. Finally, TCP is itself nested within the Internet Protocol, a protocol that is in charge of actually moving data packets from one machine to another. Ultimately, the entire bundle (the primary data object encapsulated within each successive protocol) is transported according to the rules of the only "privileged" protocol, that of the physical media itself' (Galloway, *Protocol*, 10–11).

43. Alexander R. Galloway, 'Protocol, or, How Control Exists after Decentralization', *Rethinking Marxism* 13:3/4 (2001): 88.

44. See Alexander R. Galloway and Eugene Thacker: *The Exploit. A Theory of Networks* (Minneapolis: University of Minnesota Press, 2007), 47–53.

45. Simondon, *On the Mode of Existence of Technical Objects*, 80.

46. See Gilbert Simondon, 'The Limits of Human Progress: A Critical Study', *Cultural Politics* 6:2 (2010): 229–236.

47. Simondon, *L'individuation à la lumiére des notions de form et d'information*, 515. Quote translated by author.

48. Félix Guattari, *The Three Ecologies*, trans. Ian Pindar et al. (London/ New Brunswick: The Athlone Press, 2000), 61.

49. See Guattari, *The Three Ecologies*, 69.

50. Nick Srineck and Alex Williams, *Inventing the Future. Postcapitalism and a World Without Work* (London: Verso, 2015), 163.

51. Félix Guattari, 'Remaking Social Practices', in *The Guattari Reader*, ed. Gary Genosko, (Oxford/Cambridge: Blackwell, 1996), 263. For Guattari, the autonomous radio stations of the 1970s and 1980s represented such 'new collective assemblages of enunciation'. Radio Alice, for example, a radio station, which was operated from 1976 to 1977 by a collective in Bologna, pursued a twofold strategy: on the one hand the programme was to be made by as many groups and individuals as possible; on the other hand, however, they were not supposed to speak on behalf of anyone else. Guattari saw in this experiment a subversive resingularisation and deconstruction of mass-media logic (see Genosko, 'The Promise of Post-Media', 20–22).

52. See Mark Fisher, *Capitalist Realism. Is there no alternative?* (Winchester: Zero Books, 2009).

53. Tiziana Terranova, 'Red Stack Attack! Algorithms, Capital and the Automation of the Common', *EuroNomade* (2014), accessed April 30, 2017, http://www.euronomade.info/?p=2268.

54. See Terranova, 'Red Stack Attack!'

55. See Yochai Benkler, *The Wealth of Networks: How Social Production Transforms Markets and Freedom* (New Haven: Yale University Press, 2006).

56. Benkler, *The Wealth of Networks*, 60.

57. Copyleft is an inverted copyright licensing scheme and practice, in which an author offers people the right to freely distribute copies and modified versions of his or her work with the stipulation that the same rights have to be preserved in all the following derivative works (see 'What is Copyleft?', Free Software Foundation, accessed April 30, 2017, https://www.gnu.org/licenses/copyleft.en.html).

58. This non-commercial orientation does not imply a post-capitalist vision per se. In fact, the ideas on how to go about FOSS differ widely, ranging from communist positions, such as Terranova's, to more market-conform ones, such as Benkler's model of a liberal commons-based peer production.

59. Felix Stalder, *Digital Solidarity* (London: Mute, 2013), 25.

60. See Eric Raymond, 'A Brief History of Hackerdom', (2002), accessed April 25, 2017, http://www.catb.org/esr/writings/homesteading/hacker-history.

61. Felix Stalder and Jesse Hirsh, 'Open Source Intelligence', *First Monday* 7:6 (2002), accessed April 25, 2017, http://www.firstmonday.org/ojs/index.php/fm/article/view/961/882. According to Stalder and Hirsh, such approaches include collaborative filtering (mailing lists), collaborative editing (wikis) and collaborative moderation (open-source platforms).

62. Stalder, *Digital Solidarity*, 30.

63. Michel Bauwens, for instance, speaks of a new 'P2P economy' (see Michel Bauwens, 'Thesis on Digital Labor in an Emerging P2P Economy', in *Digital Labor. The Internet as Playground and Factory* [New York/London: Routledge, 2013], 207–210).

64. Stalder, *Digital Solidarity*, 31.

65. Ned Rossiter and Soenke Zehle, 'Acts of Translation: Organizing Networks as Algorithmic Technologies of the Common', in *Digital Labor: The Internet as Playground and Factory*, ed. Trebor Scholz (London/New York: Routledge, 2013), 226. In their most recent book *Declaration*, Michael Hardt and Antonio Negri therefore also speak of the 'double combat' (Michael Hardt, Antonio Negri, *Declaration* [Allen: Argo-Navis, 2012], 80). This combat implies not only the defence of certain resources (i.e. *commons*) against their privatisation, but also the struggle for a new political sphere, which has to be constituted outside the realm of the market and the state (i.e. *the common*).

66. Émile Durkheim already distinguished between mechanical and organic solidarity (see Émile Durkheim, *The Division of Labor in Society*, trans. William D. Halls [New York: Free Press, 1997]). While mechanical solidarity refers to the social integration of a society, whose members are characterised by homogeneity (that is similar values, beliefs, work, educational and religious training in traditional and small-scale societies), organic solidarity implies a social integration, which is based on interdependent but heterogeneous individuals (because of the specialisation of work and differentiation of people in modern and industrial societies).

Chapter 8

Critical Infrastructures

While the implementation of network technologies in the 1990s was accompanied by a veritable net euphoria, recent years have brought a general disillusion vis-à-vis the Internet. In particular, the revelations of Edward Snowden mark a break with the long-lasting belief in the emancipatory power of network-based media. This does not necessarily have to be a bad thing, given the fact that socio-technical developments have repeatedly run into the danger of mistaking dreams for reality, thus obscuring the social, legal, political, cultural and economic antagonisms embedded in these developments. To see through the 'phantasmagorias'[1] propagated by marketing departments of IT companies, we have to focus on the material structure of digital cultures, especially since these have always been the site of negotiation, communication and conflict. For a critical theory of the Internet, it is therefore important to counter the ideological 'fantasy of a society without antagonism',[2] as it has been central to the emergence of the Internet as a mass medium. This is all the more important since cultural theory seems to move away from a critical understanding of and engagement with politico-economic questions of digital cultures. As Wendy Chun writes: 'Rather than engaging in decisive political action, we defer and extend action: we are arguably forever searching, but never finding.'[3] As a consequence, we can witness a longing for a new ontological grounding of media philosophy, characterised by discussions around the anthropocene, the posthuman and the singularity, thereby repeating the quietistic attitude of early cyberculture.

137

A critical network theory differs from an ontological media theory in the sense that it does not query the ahistorical *essence* of network technologies, but rather analyses these technologies in terms of their genesis. Instead of a speculative discussion about nodes, links and the web, its focus is on the concrete socio-technical situation that must be considered in its media-genealogical formation. Digital networks are not merely metaphors, but are indeed material technologies that allow for certain social, political and cultural practices, and prevent others. Conversely, this approach does not imply a techno-determinist view: rather than describing technology as something external, it is seen as part of human culture and society. In keeping with Simondon's position, we can actually say that there is no society without technology and no technology without society. To this extent, technology is always already embedded in social, political and economic processes, a fact that was already understood by critical net culture in the 1990s and has since then become evident. In particular, current debates about the Internet of Things, Smart Cities and Ubiquitous Computing thus necessitate a critique of the political economy of the net, which eventually means an analysis of the power relations embedded in network technologies and its infrastructure.

In recent years, one can discern an increasing interest in the material foundation of our networked society.[4] Network infrastructures, understood as collective assemblages of human, social and technological individuals, are typically concealed behind server rooms, industrial buildings and underground facilities, thus recalling what Lewis Mumford once called the 'invisible city'.[5] While infrastructures often come along with – or are even conditioned by – processes of concentration, centralisation and accumulation,[6] they are, at the same time, complicated, vulnerable and amenable to modification through the activities of tactical intervention, as well as strategic debates about the commons and shared resources.[7] In this sense, infrastructures are critical, because they are always already in crisis, and therefore open to *détournements* and misappropriation. At the same time, they are critical, because they yield critical knowledge, which is able to challenge and transform the currently predominant network model, represented by corporate Internet platforms such as Amazon, Facebook and Google. Hence, a post-media strategy, as it will be proposed in the following with reference to Félix Guattari,[8] pleads for the development of counter-imaginaries, in order to destabilise today's social media domination and develop alternative infrastructures for our digital cultures.

POLITICAL ECONOMY OF THE NET

The media change we have been witnessing over the past thirty years does not simply involve a change from analogue to digital media. Rather, since the early days of the twentieth century, electronic media have always found themselves in a constant interchange between old and new media formats. The introduction of television, for instance, was accompanied by critical debates about the one-way media structure of radio or the press. As was addressed by Nam June Paik's 'Participation TV' (1963–1966), the passivity of media consumption was supposed to be transformed into an active media participation.[9] Yet, after television had itself developed into the epitome of one-way communication infrastructure, hope for a participative turn was tied to digital media. The difference between analogue and digital media is thus due less to the fact that the latter have supplemented the first, but rather that the mass-mediated public sphere has been profoundly reconfigured with the arrival of the Internet.[10] Similar to the logic of mass media,[11] the power of Internet media consists in being able to transfer their mode of functioning to other areas of society. Through the standardisation of economic, social and technological norms, it is possible for them to naturalise their specific logic. However, '[f]ar from being neutral platforms for everyone, social media have changed the conditions and rules of social interaction'.[12] Online platforms with their well protected databases constitute the new centres of power, which produce the knowledge necessary for a new sociability, but only under the conditions of the rules defined by the networking sites.[13]

The emergence of Internet platforms occurs in accordance with the same discourse that already accompanied the formation of the net cultures in the 1990s: 'Key terms used to describe social media's functionality, such as the "social", "collaboration", and "friends", resonate with the communalist jargon of early utopian visions of the Web as a space that inherently enhances social activity.'[14] Unlike the attempts of digital cities to build communities with the help of collaborative software, commercial online platforms foster an atomisation of subjects, in order to connect them according to their preset categories (e.g. friend, follower and subscriber). The user, in this model, is an already fixed point, an identifiable, thus exploitable node within the network. Consequently, the socio-metrical portrayal of reality as nodes and links reinforces the neo-liberal thinking that society is simply a conjunction of individuals seen as social atoms; from now on only mediated by network technologies.[15] This indicates, not least of all, a societal shift, in which formerly state-regulated tasks, such as education, health, housing and transport are gradually commodified and managed by capitalist platforms. In this 'postwelfare model of capitalism',[16] individuals are no longer governed by means of social institutions such as parties, unions and state organisations, but rather through data-driven intermediaries, which form the basis of a new economic model, often referred to as the sharing economy.[17]

Although such a sharing, or rather renting, economy is often praised and marketed as a way to introduce community values into the production, distribution and consumption process, it has very little to do with the actual idea of sharing common resources. Instead, it can be seen as an attempt to monetise the access to the last idle resources within society and to subsume shared goods to a market-based logic. However, in the light of the most recent developments of capitalism, that is the push for flexibilisation and precarisation of working conditions, 'the sharing is just part of a much larger socioeconomic ecosystem, one that is dominated by the use of computing and satellite technology to coordinate workforces and create global transnational supply chains and that enables just-in-time manufacturing through the production of low-wage labor and the exploitation of outsourced workers'.[18] In this sense, the *digital revolution* is not only closely entangled with neo-liberal transformation, but appears to be its driving force, which makes the market the structuring principle in Western societies. Though the state is still expected to create the legal and infrastructural framework, in order to secure private business interests, it should no longer interfere in issues relevant to society as a whole, let alone organise 'forms of collective agency, action, or means of generating the kind of solidarity that might be able to challenge this state of affairs'.[19] In an increasingly globalised and networked world, the state does no longer precede the market, but rather it is the globally networked market that first engenders the state as a political society.[20]

Since the 1990s, digital information and communication technologies have been held accountable for transforming society according to the needs of global capital. However, the Internet cannot be seen as a natural means of transnational capitalism, not least because it itself is part of the society, which is being transformed. 'The Internet is a prime example of how technologies do not automatically bring about social change on their own, but how they are "redesigned" by hegemonic discursive practices – a capitalism dominated by "neoliberalism" from 1973 onward, but especially so since 1989/90.'[21] For Jens Schröter, the discourse of a 'frictionless capitalism' was central to this transformation: After the Berlin Wall came down the idea of a market-driven revolution, apt to solve all problems of capitalism, was in full swing in Europe and the United States, as the programmatic documents of the 1990s – from Al Gore's 'National Information Infrastructure', to the European 'Bangemann Report', to the neo-conservative 'Magna Carta of the Knowledge Age' – show.[22] It was thus the political discourse of that time that encouraged the privatisation and deregulation of electronic space, by imagining a medium independent from social, political and economic conflict. This was fortified by an almost totalitarian vision, which ran through this discourse: 'Barriers are broken, global expansion (of markets) is predicted, and limitless, universal competition and concurrent unlimited access to the internet is not only demanded, but more or less commanded.'[23]

This is why we need a critique of the political economy of the net, because the network, like the commodity form or the sign before, has become an ineluctable reality. One cannot not want to be networked today. By creating the dream of a medium that was already democratic by itself, the desire for participation has turned into a paradigm of connectivity, in other words a normative imperative of networking without an alternative. However, as was discussed previously, the network itself is subject to different interpretations. In fact, the notion of an all-inclusive distributed network, which was seen as a means of either total freedom or total control, has made way for the idea of scale-free networks, which makes it possible to leave the two-dimensional space of distributed networks behind and open up a new perspective: that of power. Complex networks, structured by a power law, allow us to depict a three-dimensional space of networked reality.[24] Rather than hiding existing inequalities behind the flattening and therefore mystifying figure of the distributed network, scale-free networks permit to identify power hubs within the network and make them contestable. This is important if we want to understand the move to the Internet as a platform, which ultimately breaks with the idea of a unified electronic space with equally distributed nodes. The danger here is the segregation of network society in single communities organised and confined by social networking sites. These communities necessarily remain virtual, because they are no longer capable of constituting themselves as political assemblies. This kind of 'inconsequential cultural self-administration of a however-defined collective'[25] corresponds to the neo-liberal mode of governing, as it is hiding behind digital culture's unbroken myth of a communitarian self-organisation.

The self-sufficient community, which becomes manifest in almost all of today's Internet platforms (just think of Amazon's or Apple's attempt to become a self-contained system), corresponds to the automaton, which is usually found at the lowest level of technological development. Both strive for an inner stabilisation by warding off external influences and potential changes in their structure: 'A community behaves like an automaton; it develops a code of values destined to hinder structural change.'[26] As Simondon reminds us, the community is not able of putting itself into question, thereby impeding any form of innovation. Thus, a possible reason for the failure of the digital cities in the 1990s can be seen in their wish to set up a rather strict 'symbolic order'[27] in data space. In other words, they attempted to counter the 'confusion of harddisks, BBS systems, small servers, partially computerised institutions, and dispersed groups'[28] by means of virtual communities, an attempt, which resulted in a constriction of their actual innovative power, namely being places of open networking practices. From the communities with an initially mostly emancipatory orientation, ultimately only their commercial branches survived. Whereas early citizens' networks were characterised by a striving to 'realise social aims, such as creating a social consciousness, encouraging participation in local decision-making, or developing economic possibilities for disadvantaged communities',[29] the New Economy saw in the *electronic agora* simply a new marketplace. As a consequence, the communal collectives, which were locally anchored and organised around common themes, have transformed into an abstract connective.[30]

However, such a critique applies not only to commercial media platforms (e.g. Facebook, Google and eBay), but also to a digital ecosystem based on crowd-sourced value production (e.g. Amazon's Mechanical Turk, Crowdflower and Netflix), as well as rapidly growing Smart Cities with their privatised infrastructures (e.g. New Songdo City, Masdar City and PlanIT Valley). In particular, the latter can be seen as the new technotopia, not least because they offer a test bed for new forms of urban life.[31] Like Facebook and Google, smart cities represent enclosed spaces, whose purpose it is to collect and assess as much data as possible from the *users* of the city. Here, the 'phrase *smart city* can feasibly be applied to a large number of diverse international projects that range from the updating of telecommunication infrastructures to the construction of entirely new, planned cities'.[32] What all these projects have in common is that the envisioned city is built upon a physical computing infrastructure, composed of ubiquitous sensing technologies, advanced data management and novel visualisation methods. As is the case in New Songdo City, for instance, citizens themselves become sensors, in order to produce the data necessary for the permanent self-optimisation of the urban environment. Smart cities, therefore, work like centralised Internet platforms: being a fixed node within the information network, the citizen is the source of data production and the subject of data-driven governance; whereas the control over and management of this data remains in the hands of privately owned IT-businesses.[33]

The utopian potential of these digitally enhanced urban environments consists in their promise to provide a means to live, work and participate in a more peaceful, productive and efficient way. In accordance with the urban vision of the 1990s, the smart city aims to banish the problems of the modern world by building an experimental playground for neo-liberal governance. While in the early days of the Internet the city came into the net, in order to structure the newly formed data space, today the net comes into the city, in order to provide the necessary data to govern it. Both the digital city of the 1990s and the smart city of today are considered to be ideal spaces of information, designed to integrate computational systems with architectural knowledge. In this sense, the networked platform of the city becomes a new model of governance, which makes use of new urban environments. This form of 'environmentality' is based on massive data extraction and algorithmic calculation, thus producing new power arrangements between human and non-human agencies.[34] The shift towards a more abstract and automated form of socio-technical governance must not only be seen in terms of a control society. In fact, it holds the potential to generate a different mode of organising the digital that goes beyond a communitarian understanding of technology: 'The technological infrastructure of the twenty-first century is producing the resources by which a very different political and economic system could be achieved.'[35] This might be the starting point for a technotopian vision, which is based on collective solidarity, rather than individual networking.[36]

POST-MEDIA STRATEGY

The crucial question with regard to digital cultures today is whether technical media have truly been responsible for alienating the human subject from its *natural* environment or whether this perceived estrangement is not in fact an effect of the very discourse around media. In particular, Californian Ideology is bound to the communitarian notion of a self-reproducing automaton. According to this logic, technology serves some kind of intrinsic will, which, in consequence, has to be deciphered and put to use. The problem with this is that technology is not being recognised in its own logic, but rather seen as a means for something else – typically the liberation of the individual from the constraints of society. So, instead of acknowledging the socio-technical potential within it, technology is submitted to a communitarian thinking, which is predominantly defined by capitalist economy. Conversely, post-capitalist values, as they are expressed in recent debates about the commons and shared resources, are themselves all too often locked in 'the ideology of the new cognitive working class'.[37] Here, digital technology, providing the basis for a peer-to-peer production, is presented as an ideal condition for cognitive work, which only has to be freed from the limits of intellectual property and waged labour.[38] But here is the thing: there is no frictionless society, not even if it is mediated by digital media technology. The image of a hyperproductive info-capitalism, freed from the fetters of the industrial world, is deeply deceptive, because it conceals the underlying complexity of the problem. In Marx' words: 'The real barrier of capitalist production is capital itself.'[39] This implies that with the capitalisation of media technologies new dynamics were set in motion, which eventually resulted in a crisis of the existing mode of production. The Internet is thus not only an instrument for the smooth functioning of capitalism, but also a site of possible critique.[40]

In this respect, net critique of the 1990s, which arose as a 'pragmatic form of negative thinking',[41] can provide us with a reference point as to how such a critique may or may not look like today. Net critique's position was less defined by an ideological concept or prospective idea, but rather by its ongoing practices: 'Our Net Criticism has nothing to do with a monolithic or dialectic dogma, like "neo-Luddism" or "digital Marxism". It is more a behaviour than a project, more a parasite than a strategic position, more based on a diffuse corpus of works than an academic knowledge, it is heavily interfered by contradictions and techno-pleasure, and it keeps vivid in this way.'[42] The happy negatives therefore created tactical media as hit-and-run actions to undermine the mainstream discourse, dominated by public broadcasters and large media corporations. Following Michel de Certeau's distinction between strategies and tactics,[43] tactical media's claim was not to occupy a stable ideological space, but rather to attack the strategic field of mass media by tactical means. However, these short-term interventions necessitated the invention of new forms and formats of media, as can be seen from numerous experiments of artistic and activist groups, hacker collectives, as well as tactical media initiatives that mushroomed in the 1990s. The alleged powerless had at their command a rather good infrastructure of cultural centres, art festivals and communication channels, which helped them to get their message through. In this sense, critical net cultures themselves did not strictly distinguish between tactical interventions and strategic positioning, not least because they incorporated the legacy of former alternative media projects with their political agenda of setting up autonomous communication infrastructures.[44] Tactical media indeed tried to occupy an ideological space by building communities around specific values. As much as they were defined by hit-and-run interventions, they also applied a general strategy, a fact very obvious in the attempts to create sustainable networks for media production.[45]

Anticipating a global alternative media infrastructure, of which Indymedia then became only one, albeit a very important part, net critique in the 1990s had already discussed the outline of a new ecological field of artistic and activist media. In this field, new forms of cooperation and exchange, of production and distribution had emerged, able to subvert the dominant 'mass-media subjectivity'.[46] Inspired by Manuel de Landa's historical account of the machinic,[47] a systematic description of media ecology in association with tactical media was attempted: 'The media ecology is a machine composed of several distinct levels: the levels of media and related tools and instruments; the level of tactics, in which individuals and media are integrated into formations; the level of strategy, in which the campaigns conducted by those formations acquire a unified political goal; and finally, the level of logistics, of procurement and supply networks, in which media practice is connected to the infrastructural and industrial resources that fuel it.'[48] The media-ecological machine thus includes both the level of tactics and the level of strategy. Contrasting the focus on ephemeral practices, tactical media also refer to a political dimension found in the media-ecological disposition of our time.

Digital media technologies have spread tremendously in recent years, so that media practices, in their multiple usage of digital technologies, have penetrated into nearly every area of daily life. Yet, a paradox seems to arrive from this: while technologies, in the form of end-user tools, have become more affordable and thus accessible than ever before, the infrastructure behind these tools gets increasingly concentrated in the hands of a few, private corporations. Hence, the promise of an all-encompassing media ecology is contrasted by a political economy of exclusion, which forms the basis of today's platform capitalism. Here, a new imaginary of media is needed if we want to co-shape the technological condition we live in. Rather than just leaving it up to commercial interests, we need social networks worthy of this name; that means infrastructural policies that impel the formation of new collectivities beyond state anxieties and the corporate sector. With reference to Félix Guattari, we could speak of the social potential of the 'enunciative dimensions of communication'.[49] In contrast to the reductionist concepts of information theory, Guattari is not so much interested in the mere sending and receiving of information, but rather in the interactions between transmitter and recipient. Unlike Baudrillard, for whom the use of electronic media inevitably leads to a schism between encoder and decoder, that is a systemic form of non-communication, Guattari did not reject the new information and communication technologies, but rather called for a new heterogeneous composition of the human–machine relationship. For him, a 'computerized subjectivity'[50] did not imply a further step in the dissolution of the social, but rather entailed the possibility of repositioning of humans in relation to their socio-technical environments.

New forms of expression beyond the dichotomy of transmitter and receiver, encoder and decoder, client and server are needed to escape the quietism of the postmodern, which has 'accustomed us to a vision of the world drained of the significance of human interventions, embodied as they are in concrete politics and micropolitics'.[51] Guattari understood these micropolitics as a transversal process, which can itself be experienced as a process of greater freedom.[52] Contrary to the limiting subjectification of mass media, which is ultimately always orientated to the majoritarian subjectivity, new media technologies enable a sociotechnical ensemble, which, like a network, is not defined by a starting or an end point, but rather by the entirety of lines traversing it. The network liberates itself from the individual node, so to speak, and in its transversal movement it now conjoins all the other points that are in a permanent process of becoming. From this perspective, there is no antagonism between the individual and the collective, as is claimed in liberalism with its one-sided emphasis on the individual, rather they are always mutually conditional. This is the compelling insight resulting from Simondon's philosophy. However, this perspective itself must be radicalised, especially since Simondon still presumed that 'one cannot change the network, one doesn't construct a network of one's own'.[53] For him, the network ultimately remained a static system; one can join it, adapt to it, participate in it, but one cannot create it or even become a network oneself. But what if that has become possible with digital network technologies? What if the network is no longer merely understood as an already constituted system, but rather as a socio-technical association, in the sense that it is engendered by individuals using network technologies to associate themselves?

Unlike the belief in a distributed, thus per se democratic network, a genuine transindividualism contains a political act, an active decision to join a collective subjectivity. A post-media strategy, therefore, has to disengage from the mass media logic of today's social networking sites, whose *identity politics* hinder the formation of any collectivity. As long as the individual continues to be the premise of the collective, the actual possibilities of social networking remain unrecognised. A genuine alternative to conventional social media platforms, by contrast, consists of 'organised networks' as new media assemblages, which 'emerge from within the technics of digital communication media'.[54] By recognising the existing power structures of network technologies, these collective organisations provide a pragmatic approach to new institutional and socio-political forms of organisation: 'Institutions function to organise social relations. It follows then, that the social-technical dynamics peculiar to a range of digital media technologies (mailing lists, collaborative blogs, wikis, content management systems) institute new modes of networked sociality.'[55] Whereas tactical media merely aimed for short-term interventions, thereby affirming the disruptive business models of platform capitalism, organised networks acquire an institutional formation, in order to reappropriate media, social and political terrain.[56] The strategic dimension of a post-media approach is evident in this, in particular as Guattari's focus was not only on refusing the current media status, but also on remaking social practices, thereby searching 'for new social interactivities, for an institutional creativity and an enrichment of values'.[57] Not the one large-scale counterproposal, but rather the multiple counterprojects, nesting in the hegemonic network like spiderwebs, provide a post-media response to state surveillance and market-driven control.[58]

COUNTERIMAGINARIES

Post-mediality holds the promise of producing your own media as the material basis of collective organisation. What is important for this work is the fact that this potential was already present in critical net cultures of the 1990s, specifically in the form of collaborative platforms, such as Public Netbase in Vienna, Deckspace in London, E-Lab in Riga, Ljudmilla in Ljubljana and c-base in Berlin. During the *short summer* of digital counterculture, at a time, when the critical potential of the Internet was fiercely debated, there was 'a relief from capital's tyranny of specialization that forces us to perform as if we are a fixed set of relationships and characteristics, and to repress or strictly manage all other forms of desire and expression'.[59] Collective infrastructures opened up the possibility of overcoming existing modes and norms of production and enabled the experimentation with new subjectivities through transversal forms of networking. For social change to happen, new imaginaries are needed, which no longer considers social groups as stable entities, but as a 'collective arrangement of enunciation'.[60] Such counterimaginaries are important, if we want to take up the fight for an alternative disposition of digital cultures and its infrastructures.[61] In order to appropriate them for other ends than data mining and advertising, we need collective strategies. As Guattari already knew: 'Obviously, we cannot expect a miracle from these technologies: it will all depend, ultimately, on the capacity of groups of people to take hold of them, and apply them to appropriate ends.'[62]

But how can we collectively develop infrastructures when confronted with algorithmic power and data economies? How can we sustain these infrastructures vis-à-vis an overly powerful platform capitalism, which, to cap it all, is dressed up as a sharing economy? Of course, there can be no clear-cut answer, since critique of the status quo has to be articulated at all possible level, by all media necessary. Opening the 'black box' of digital cultures requires new coalitions of voices, not only from a media-technological standpoint, but also from that of culture, economics and politics. Instead of looking only at large-scale infrastructural studies, we should also consider the multiplicity of micropolitics hidden behind the infrastructural black box of the *network of networks*.[63] This means that media technologies cannot be understood without the norms, values and desires that accompany them, since these ultimately find expressions in the way networks are conceived and developed as they emerge in the form of digital infrastructures.[64] In this sense, infrastructures are historical materialities that intersect, overlap, reinforce, transform and compete against one another, as is exemplified by the struggle over specific yet often unforeseen standardisation processes. These *structures in the making* are therefore deeply entangled in the politics of technology, which, in turn, are grounded in questions of ownership and property regimes.[65] Challenging these regimes has become central to current forms of political activism, not least because in recent years open-source and free software principles have been extended to new fields of society, in order to unleash alternative test cases, prototypes and blueprints for our techno-cultural future.[66]

This shift from tactical media to the commons can be seen in some of today's most prolific art and media projects, which counter the privatisation and commercialisation of the media infrastructure by producing shared resources to collaboratively build, learn and edit. In particular, Do-It-Yourself projects in Latin America register alternative modes of knowledge production in order to rethink dominant assumptions about how politics, economics and culture are reassembled by digital networks, while also opening new approaches to the invention of infrastructures.[67] A critical perspective emanating from infrastructural experiments in Non-Western net cultures has generated novel expressions of what it means to collectively design and produce digital infrastructures. In Brazil, for instance, the emphasis on the civic and participatory potential of electronic media in the early 2000s created new practices in art and media on the basis of collaboration, media access and hands on technology.[68] One example of infrastructural meddling is the network MetaReciclagem. Since 2002 the reuse of recycled computers has provided the infrastructure for artistic interventions and collective reappropriation of technology to facilitate new social possibilities in mainly rural parts of Brazil. MetaReciclagem is neither a formal NGO nor a specific group of people, but a name everyone can adopt. Rather than being a fixed point within the network, the individual, in this perspective, becomes an operational device open to any number of misappropriations and recalibrations of relation that in a strict computational sense would be defined as a protocological failure. Thus, even though MetaReciclagem itself has ceased to exist, the institutional as well symbolic infrastructure of the network is still being recycled and re-emerges in different places. It is to these examples that we might turn in order to reassess and reimagine the potentialities of infrastructures for activism and art production aimed at inducing social change.[69]

Instead of exploring current subjectivity by means of algorithmic and protocological control, a rearticulation of net critique may also look at projects which effectively challenge property regimes at the very root of information and knowledge production. An example is the self-organised education platform the Public School, which was initiated in 2007 and meanwhile exists in many cities. This is a school which has no curriculum and no degrees, but instead takes the *public* serious by reclaiming knowledge resources, that are endangered by the increasing privatisation of the educational systems. The expansion of these techno-regimes of enclosure also applies to publicly funded knowledge in general. Here, commercial publishers do not only fail to support the transformation of knowledge based on commons-based peer production, but actively hinder any further development and innovation. As a consequence, so-called *shadow libraries* such as Library Genesis, Aaaaarg, Monoskop, Ubuweb and Memory of the World have the mission to return knowledge resources to a commons not circumscribed by the gated enclaves of university libraries, commercial publisher or platform monopolies.[70] By inventing knowledge resources as social infrastructures liberated from the political economy of intellectual property regimes, these libraries constitute new institutional forms that engender the emergence of a new political subjectivity. Such a desire is clearly invoked by Marcell Mars, Manar Zarroug and Tomislav Medak in their manifesto on the public library: 'Today nobody lacks the imagination necessary to see public libraries as part of a global infrastructure of universal access to knowledge for literally every member of society.'[71] What is important here is less the claim of an access for all, which repeats the dictum of the 1990s, than the observation that infrastructures are not limited to the materiality of media alone, but are integrated with the power of the imaginary.

Of course, we cannot easily construct our own global infrastructure, thus competing with monopolies such as Amazon, Apple, Google, Facebook and Microsoft, but we can take control of how we organise our metadata.[72] This is the lesson of the Public Library and the wider movement around disrupting ownership regimes and platform capitalism in the interests of open systems that make possible the collective experience with technical infrastructures: 'When everyone is librarian, library is everywhere.'[73] The socio-technical reappropriation of knowledge resources requires a common endeavour, in other words the *common* described before, in order to create the foundation of a new solidarity built on digital networks. As Armin Medosch writes: 'The potential of empowerment through and with digital technologies is not a foregone conclusion – there is not automated utopia sitting there like a ghost in the machine – but can be considered a project: a projection of what can be attained if people fight for it, combining political will, collective action, and creativity.'[74] The ability of people to produce, edit and share information engenders a social mode of production, which is neither enclosed in the walled gardens of commercial platforms nor reduced to a communitarian understanding of practice. Instead, social networks must seek out niches within the dominant economic system, in which they can experiment with collective forms of production, exchange and property. What will be crucial here is the ability to address society as a whole and to ultimately lobby the state to create appropriate conditions to foster these collective practices of knowledge transfer – as it did for wage labour, the financial system and free trade before. At the intersection of the technical imaginable and the socially feasible, new knowledge fields could thus emerge, capable of countering the control regime of current info-capitalism. A critical network theory must therefore follow the examples that create and maintain autonomous and open infrastructures, such as the recycling network MetaReciclagem, the learning platform the Public School and the social institution the Public Library. These technotopian projects can provide us with an example as to how we can develop a new imaginary of digital cultures and its infrastructures. This is also where the legacy of the early net cultures might be found: thinking about the preconditions of media alone is not enough; instead, we need to co-shape these conditions, in order to be able to intervene in our socio-technical future.

NOTES

1. See Walter Benjamin, *The Arcades Project*, trans. Howard Eiland and Kevin McLaughlin (Cambridge/London: Harvard University Press, 1999), 14–15.

2. Jodi Dean, *Blog Theory. Feedback and Capture in the Circuits of Drive* (Cambridge/Malden: Polity Press, 2010), 8.

3. Wendy Hui Kyong Chun, 'Networks NOW: Belated too Early', in *Postdigital Aesthetics. Art, Computation and Design*, ed. David M. Berry et al. (London: Palgrave Macmillan, 2015), 290.

4. Representatively, see Keller Easterling, *Extrastatecraft. The Power of Infrastructure Space* (London: Verso, 2014); Finn Brunton and Gabriella Coleman, 'Closer to the Metal', in *Media Technologies. Essays on Communication, Materiality, and Society*, ed. Tarleton Gillespie et al. (Cambridge/London: MIT Press, 2014), 77–97; Tung-Hui Hu, *A Prehistory of the Cloud* (Cambridge/London: MIT Press, 2015); Nicole Starosielski, *The Undersea Network* (Durham/London: Duke University Press, 2015).

5. An alternative approach to study network infrastructures offers Nicole Starosielski: 'Instead of seeing fiber-optic cables as part of an invisible city, I suggest that we view them as a material system whose visibility must be continually constructed in order to maintain a smooth and effective sphere of global communication' (Nicole Starosielski, "Warning: Do Not Dig': Negotiating the Visibility of Critical Infrastructures', *Journal of Visual Culture* 11:1 [2012]: 41).

6. See, for instance, Thomas P. Hughes, *Networks of Power: Electrification in Western Society, 1880–1930* (Baltimore/London: The Johns Hopkins University Press, 1993).

7. See Brett M. Frischmann, *Infrastructure. The Social Value of Shared Resources* (New York: Oxford University Press, 2012).

8. See Félix Guattari, 'Towards a Post-Media Era', in *Provocative Alloys: A Post-Media Anthology*, ed. Clemens Apprich et al. (London: Mute, 2013), 26–27.

9. See Dieter Daniels, 'Television—Art or Anti-art? Conflict and cooperation between the avant-garde and the mass media in the 1960s and 1970s', *MedienKunstNetz* (2004), accessed December 12, 2016, http://www.medienkunstnetz.de/themes/overview_of_media_art/massmedia.

10. Today, we are dealing with a fragmentation of the public sphere, as the formerly homogeneous public sphere produced by mass media (print, radio and TV) has dissolved into heterogeneous partial public spheres with the arrival of digital media – both online and offline. This does not mean, however, that we are dealing simply with a distributed public sphere, which would reintroduce the old myth of the democratic network. Instead, we could speak of scale-free public spheres, since these do not evince an average degree of networked opinions (in the sense of Habermas' ideal model of a bourgeois public sphere), but are rather dominated by a few, central opinion-makers (well-connected blogs, for instance, but also traditional media publishers).

11. See David L. Altheide and Robert P. Snow, *Media Logic* (Thousand Oaks: Sage, 1979).

12. José van Dijck and Thomas Poell, 'Understanding Social Media Logic', *Media and Communication* 1:1 (2013): 2.

13. See Martin Warnke, 'Databases as Citadels in the Web 2.0', in *Unlike Us Reader. Social Media Monopolies and their Alternatives*, ed. Geert Lovink et al. (Amsterdam: Institute of Network Cultures, 2013), 76–88.

14. Dijck and Poell,Understanding', 13.

15. See Yuk Hui and Harry Halpin, 'Collective Individuation: The Future of the Social Web', in *Unlike Us Reader. Social Media Monopolies and Their Alternatives*, ed. Geert Lovink et al. (Amsterdam: INC, 2013), 106.

16. Gary Hall, *The Uberfication of the University* (Minneapolis: University of Minnesota Press, 2016), 13.

17. See Juliet Schor, 'Debating the Sharing Economy', *Great Transition Initiative* (October 2014), accessed, May 5, 2017, http://greattransition.org/publication/debating-the-sharing-economy. The sharing economy does not oppose inequality or injustice in society, but actually tends to increase them. In this sense, it leads to a new intensification of social homophily (see Hall, *Uberfication*, 16).

18. Hall, *Uberfication*, 11.

19. Ibid., 13.

20. See Philip Mirowski, 'Postface: Defining Neoliberalism', in *The Road from Mont Pelerin. The Making of the Neoliberal Thought Collective*, ed. Philip Mirowski et al. (Cambridge: Harvard University Press, 2009), 417–455.

21. Jens Schröter, 'The Internet and "Frictionless Capitalism"', *Triple C* 10:2 (2012): 302.

22. For a discussion of these documents, see chapter 4.

23. Schröter, 'Internet', 306.

24. Again, this can only mean an approximation to reality, not an essentialisation of it, as it all too often happens in the discussion around networks in general and scale-free networks in particular.

25. Diedrich Diederichsen, 'Wie aus Bewegungen Kulturen und aus Kulturen Communities werden', in *Mythos Metropole*, ed. Gotthard Fuchs et al. (Frankfurt a.M.: Suhrkamp, 1995), 134. Quote translated by author.

26. Gilbert Simondon, *L'individuation à la lumiére des notions de form et d'information* (Grenoble: Éditions Jérôme Millon, 2005), 519. Quote translated by author.

27. Geert Lovink, Pit Schultz, *Jugendjahre der Netzkritik. Essays zu Web 1.0 (1995–1997)* (Amsterdam: INC, 2010), 31. Quote translated by author.

28. Ibid.

29. Douglas Schuler, 'Community Networks: Building a New Participatory Medium', *Communications of the ACM* 37:1 (1994), 1994, 41.

30. See José van Dijck, *The Culture of Connectivity. A Critical History of Social Media* (New York: Oxford University Press, 2013).

31. See Orit Halpern et al., 'Test-Bed Urbanism', *Public Culture* 25:2 (2013): 273–306.

32. Ibid., 276.

33. See Adam Greenfield, *Against the Smart City* (New York: Do projects, 2013), 83–90.

34. See Jennifer Gabrys. 'Programming Environments: Environmentality and Citizen Sensing in the Smart City', *Environment and Planning D: Society and Space* 32:1 (2014): 30–48.

35. Srnicek, Nick and Alex Williams, *Inventing the Future. Postcapitalism and a World Without Work* (London: Verso, 2015), 12.

36. To this extent, it might be appropriate to speak of the net, rather than the net*work*, since the latter is still based on the schema of work and usability, in other words technology as tool.

37. Michel Bauwens, 'Thesis on Digital Labor in an Emerging P2P Economy', in *Digital Labor: The Internet as Playground and Factory*, ed. Trebor Scholz (London/New York: Routledge, 2013), 207.

38. For a critical discussion of the double-exploitation of living labour, understood as wage and free labour, see Tiziana Terranova, 'Free Labor', in *Digital Labor: The Internet as Playground and Factory*, ed. Trebor Scholz (London/New York: Routledge, 2013), 33–57.

39. Karl Marx, 'Capital. A Critique of Political Economy – Volume III: The Process of Capitalist Production as a Whole', in *Marx and Engels Collected Works*, Vol. 37, ed. Friedrich Engels (New York: International Publisher, 1998), 248.

40. See Armin Medosch, 'Shockwaves in the New World Order of Information and Communication', in *Blackwell Companion to Digital Art*, ed. Christiane Paul (Hoboken: Wiley-Blackwell, 2016), 355–383.

41. Geert Lovink, 'From Speculative Media Theory to Net Criticism', Lecture at ICC, Tokyo, 19.12.96: http://www.nettime.org/Lists-Archives/nettime-l-9701/msg00032.html (accessed September 6, 2016).

42. Geert Lovink and Pit Schultz, quoted from: Geert Lovink, *Dark Fiber* (Cambridge: MIT Press, 2002), 82.

43. See Michel de Certeau, *The Practice of Everyday Life* (Berkeley/Los Angeles: University of California Press, 1984). For Certeau, the distinction was primarily focused on the subversive power of reading as a deviant consumption of signs. His understanding of tactics might in fact have been quite different to what tactical media had in mind (see Joanne Richardson, 'The Language of Tactical Media', *subsol* (2002), accessed May 5, 2017, http://subsol.c3.hu/subsol_2/contributors2/richardsontext2.html).

44. See Felix Stalder, '30 Years of Tactical Media', in *Public Netbase: Non Stop Future. New Practices in Art and Media*, ed. Branka Ćurčić et al. (Frankfurt a.M.: Revolver, 2008), 191–193.

45. For example, the Virtual Platforms in Austria and the Netherlands, as well as the European Cultural Backbone. See also chapter 3.

46. Félix Guattari, *The Three Ecologies*, trans. Ian Pindar, Paul Sutton (London/New Brunswick: The Athlone Press, 2000), 33.

47. See Manuel de Landa, *War in the Age of Intelligent Machines* (New York: Zone Books, 1991).

48. Andreas Broeckmann, 'Introduction: Tactical Media', *Next 5 Minutes* (1995), accessed December 15, 2016, http://www.tacticalmediafiles.net/n5m2/media/texts/abroeck.html.

49. Félix Guattari, 'Remaking Social Practices', in *The Guattari Reader*, ed. Gary Genosko, (Oxford/Cambridge: Blackwell, 1996), 266.

50. Félix Guattari, 'Regimes, Pathways, Subjects', in *The Guattari Reader*, ed. Gary Genosko, (Oxford/Cambridge: Blackwell, 1996), 99.

51. Félix Guattari, *The Three Ecologies*, 41. Power in this sense is not to be understood simply as control or domination. 'On the contrary', as Michel Foucault remarked in a lecture in 1978, 'it always has to be considered in relation to a field of interactions, contemplated in a relationship which cannot be dissociated from forms of knowledge. One always has to think about it in such a way as to see how it is associated with a domain of possibility and consequently, of reversibility, of possible reversal' (Michel Foucault, 'What is Critique?' in *The Politics of Truth*, ed. Paul Rabinow [Los Angeles: semiotext(e), 2007], 66).

52. See Gary Genosko, 'The Life and Work of Félix Guattari: From Transversality to Ecosophy', in *The Three Ecologies,* Félix Guattari (London/New Brunswick: The Athlone Press, 2000), 140–141.

53. Simondon, *On the Mode of Existence of Technical Objects*, 229.

54. Geert Lovink and Ned Rossiter, 'The Politics of Organized Networks: The Art of Collective Coordination and the Seriality of Demands',' in *New Media, Old Media: A History and Theory Reader*, 2nd edition, ed. Wendy Hui Kyong Chun et al. (New York/London: Routledge, 2016), 346. See also, Ned Rossiter, *Organized Networks: Media Theory, Collective Labour, New Institutions* (Rotterdam: Nai Publishers, 2007).

55. Ned Rossiter, 'Organised Networks: Transdisciplinarity and New Institutional Forms', *transform* (2006), accessed January 15, 2017, http://transform.eipcp.net/correspondence/1144943951.

56. This is how the concept of organised networks differs from that of 'networked disruption' (See Tatiana Bazzichelli, *Networked Disruption: Rethinking Oppositions in Art, Hacktivism and the Business of Social Networking* [Aarhus: Aarhus Universitet Multimedieuddannelsen, 2013]).

57. Guattari, 'Remaking Social Practices', 272.

58. See Eric Kluitenberg, *Legacies of Tactical Media. Network Notebooks 05* (Amsterdam: Institute of Network Cultures, 2011).

59. Critical Art Ensemble, *Digital Resistance. Explorations in Tactical Media* (New York: Autonomedia, 2001), 6.

60. Critical Art Ensemble, *Digital Resistance. Explorations in Tactical Media*, 6.

61. On the concept of counterimaginaries see also Ned Rossiter, *Software, Infrastructure, Labor: A Media Theory of Logistical Nightmares* (New York/ Oxon: Routledge, 2016), 184–196.

62. Guattari, 'Remaking Social Practices', 263.

63. This includes human as well as non-human decision-making processes (see Florian Sprenger, *Politics of Micro-Decisions*, trans. Valentine A. Pakis [Lüneburg: meson press, 2015]).

64. See Christopher M. Kelty, 'Against Networks', *Spheres – Journal for Digital Cultures* 1 (2014), accessed March 30, 2017, http://spheres-journal.org/against-networks.

65. See Rossiter, *Software*, 143.

66. See Medosch, 'Shockwaves', 372. To coordinate these test models and to bring about social change, it does not necessarily require a vanguard party, as Jodi Dean claims (see Jodi Dean, *Crowds and Party* [London/New York: Verso Books, 2016]), but may also be achieved through the 'vanguard function' of scale-free networks (see Rodrigo Nunes, *The Organisation of the Organisationless: Collective Action After Networks* [London: Mute, 2014]). Nick Srnicek and Alex Williams speak of an ecological organisation in this context: 'We therefore do not seek to promote any single organisational form as the ideal means of embodying transformational vectors. Every successful movement has been the result, not of a single organisational type, but of a broad ecology of organisations. These have operated, in a more or less coordinated way, to carry out the division of labour necessary for political change' (Nick Srnicek and Alex Williams. *Inventing the Future. Postcapitalism and a World Without Work* [London: Verso, 2015], 163).

67. See Clemens Apprich and Paulo Lara, 'Tactical Disenchantments: On the 'Tactical' in Media from a Non-Western Perspective', in *Tactical Media Anthology*, ed. Eric Kluitenberg et al. (Cambridge: MIT Press, in print).

68. See Karla Brunet, 'Internet, Activism and Tactical Media. Practices of Resistance and Enthusiasm in Brazil', *ZEMOS98* (2005), accessed May 10, 2017, http://www.zemos98.org/IMG/article_PDF_article_673.pdf.

69. See Clemens Apprich and Ned Rossiter, 'Sovereign Media, Critical Infrastructures, and Political Subjectivity', in *Across & Beyond: A transmediale Reader on Post-digital Practices*, ed. Ryan Bishop et al. (Berlin: Sternberg Press, 2017), 270–283.

70. See Lawrence Liang, 'Shadow Libraries', *e-flux Journal* 37 (2012), accessed May 10, 2017, http://www.e-flux.com/journal/37/61228/shadow-libraries.

71. Marcell Mars et al., 'Public library (Essay)', in *Public Library*, ed. Tomislav Medak et al. (Zagreb: Gallery Nova, 2015), 78.

72. See McKenzie Wark, 'Metadata Punk', in *Public Library*, ed. Tomislav Medak et al. (Zagreb: Gallery Nova, 2015), 111–119.

73. Mars, 'Public library', 85.

74. Medosch, 'Shockwaves', 376.

Bibliography

Adilkno, *Cracking the Movement*. Brooklyn: Autonomedia, 1994.

Adorno, Theodor W., and Max Horkheimer. 'The Culture Industry: Enlightenment as Mass Deception'. In Theodor W. Adorno and Max Horkheimer, *Dialectic of Enlightenment*, edited by Gunzelin Schmid Noerr, 94–136. Stanford: Stanford University Press, 2002.

Agamben, Giorgio. *What Is an Apparatus and Other Essays*. Stanford: Stanford University Press, 2009.

Altheide, David L., and Robert P. Snow. *Media Logic*. Thousand Oaks: Sage, 1979.

Althusser, Louis. *For Marx*. London/New York: Verso, 2005.

Anonymous. 'ANON OPS: A Press Release'. Last modified December, 2010. https://www.wired.com/images_blogs/threatlevel/2010/12/ANON-OPS_The_Press_Release.pdf.

Apprich, Clemens. 'It's the Community, Stupid! Urbane Regierungstechniken der Selbstverwaltung'. In *Phantom Kulturstadt. Texte zur Zukunft der Kulturpolitik II*, edited by Konrad Becker and Martin Wassermair, 224–250. Wien: Löcker, 2009.

Apprich, Clemens, and Felix Stalder, eds. *Vergessene Zukunft. Radikale Netzkulturen in Europa*. Bielefeld: transcript, 2012.

Apprich, Clemens, and Ned Rossiter. 'Sovereign Media, Critical Infrastructures, and Political Subjectivity'. In *Across & Beyond: A Transmediale Reader on Post-digital Practices*, edited by Ryan Bishop, Kristoffer Gansing, Jussi Parikka, and Elvia Wilk, 270–283. Berlin: Sternberg Press, 2017.

Apprich, Clemens, and Götz Bachmann. 'Media Genealogy: Back to the Present of Digital Cultures'. In *Digitization: Theories and Concepts for Empirical Cultural Research*, edited by G. Koch. London: Routledge, 2017 (in print).

Apprich, Clemens, and Paulo Lara. 'Tactical Disenchantments: On the 'Tactical' in Media from a Non-Western Perspective'. In *Tactical Media*

Anthology, edited by Eric Kluitenberg and David Garcia. Cambridge: MIT Press, 2017 (in print).

Arns, Inke. *Netzkulturen*. Hamburg: eva, 2002.

Arns, Inke, and Andreas Broeckmann. 'Minor Media Normality'. *ZKP4* (1997). Accessed April 1, 2017. http://www.mikro.in-berlin.de/wiki/tiki-index.php?page=Minor+Media+Normality#card_1490110306675_5129.

Bangemann, Martin et al. 'Bangeman Report: Europe and the Global Information Society'. *CORDIS* (1994). Accessed March 25, 2017. http://cordis.europa.eu/news/rcn/2730_en.html.

Barabási, Albert-László. *Linked. How Everything Is Connected to Everything and What It Means for Business, Science, and Everyday Life*. New York: Plume, 2003.

Barabási, Albert-László, and Réka Albert. 'Emergence of Scaling in Random Networks'. *Science* 286 (1999): 509–512.

Barabási, Albert-László, and Eric Bonabeau. 'Scale-Free Networks'. *Scientific American* 288 (2003): 50–59.

Baran, Paul. 'On Distributed Communications'. *RAND Publications* (1964). Accessed November 3, 2016. www.rand.org/pubs/research_memoranda/RM34 20.html.

Barbrook, Richard, and Andy Cameron. 'The Californian Ideology'. In *Proud to be Flesh: A Mute Magazine Anthology of Cultural Politics after the Net*, edited by Josephine Berry Slater and Pauline van Mourik Broekman, 27–34. London: Mute Publishing in Association with Autonomedia, 2009.

Barlow, John Perry. 'Crime and Puzzlement' (1990). Accessed December 21, 2016. https://w2.eff.org/Misc/Publications/John_Perry_Barlow/crime_and_puzzlement.1.txt.

Barlow, John Perry. 'A Declaration of the Independence of Cyberspace' (1996). *Electronic Frontier Foundation*. Accessed March 25, 2017. https://www.eff.org/cyberspace-independence.

Barlow, John Perry. 'Re: <nettime> The Piran Nettime Manifesto'. Posted May 27, 1997 on the nettime mailing list. Accessed March 25, 2017. http://www.nettime.org/Lists-Archives/nettime-l-9705/msg00157.html.

Barthélémy, Jean-Hugues. 'Simondon – Ein Denken der Technik im Dialog mit der Kybernetik'. In *Die technologische Bedingung. Beiträge zur Beschreibung der technischen Welt*, edited by Erich Hörl, 93–109. Berlin: Suhrkamp, 2011.

Baudrillard, Jean. *Le Système des Objets*. Paris: Gallimard, 1968.

Baudrillard, Jean. *The Mirror of Production*. Translated by Mark Poster. St. Louis: Telos Press, 1975.

Baudrillard, Jean. *For a Critique of the Political Economy of the Sign*. Translated by Charles Levin. St. Louis: Telos Press, 1981.

Baudrillard, Jean. 'The Beaubourg-Effect: Implosion and Deterrence', translated by Rosalind Krauss and Annette Michelson. *October* 20 (1982): 3–13.

Baudrillard, Jean. *In the Shadow of the Silent Majorities ... or The End of the Social*. Translated by Paul Foss et al. New York: Semiotext(e), 1983.

Baudrillard, Jean. *Simulations*. New York: Semiotext(e), 1983.

Baudrillard, Jean. *Le miroir de la production ou l'illusion critique du matérialisme historique*. Paris: Galilée, 1985.

Baudrillard, Jean. *Symbolic Exchange and Death*. Translated by Iain Hamilton Grant. Los Angeles/London/New Delhi: Sage, 1993.

Baudrillard, Jean. *Simulacra and Simulation*. Translated by Sheila Faria Glaser. Ann Arbor: The University of Michigan Press, 1994.

Baudrillard, Jean. *The Gulf War Did Not Take Place*. Translated by Paul Patton. Indianapolis: Indiana University Press, 1995.

Baudrillard, Jean. 'Review of Marshall McLuhan's *Understanding Media*'. In *The Uncollected Baudrillard*, edited by Gary Genosko, 39–44. London/Thousand Oaks/New Delhi: Sage Publications, 2001.

Baudrillard, Jean. 'Requiem for the Media'. In *The New Media* Reader, edited by Noah Wardrip-Fruin and Nick Montfort, 277–288. Cambridge/London: MIT Press, 2003.

Baumgärtel, Tilman. '"Beauty and the East"—Nettime-Treffen in Ljubljana. Von Onkel Soros' aufmüpfigen Kindern' (1997). Accessed September 14, 2016. www.heise.de/tp/artikel/3/3086/1.html.

Baumgärtel, Tilman. 'Die Zeit der digitalen Städte ist vorbei. Interview mit Joachim Blank von der Internationalen Stadt Berlin'. *Telepolis* (1998). Accessed December 30, 2016. www.heise.de/tp/r4/artikel/3/3167/1.html.

Bauwens, Michel. 'Thesis on Digital Labor in an Emerging P2P Economy'. In *Digital Labor. The Internet as Playground and Factory*, edited by Trebor Scholz, 207–210. New York/London: Routledge, 2013.

Bazzichelli, Tatiana. *Networked Disruption: Rethinking Oppositions in Art, Hacktivism and the Business of Social Networking*. Aarhus: Aarhus Universitet Multimedieuddannelsen, 2013.

Benjamin, Walter. *The Arcades Project*. Translated by Howard Eiland and Kevin McLaughlin. Cambridge/London: Harvard University Press, 1999.

Benkler, Yochai. *The Wealth of Networks: How Social Production Transforms Markets and Freedom*. New Haven: Yale University Press, 2006.

Bey, Hakim. *T.A.Z. The Temporary Autonomous Zone, Ontological Anarchy, Poetic Terrorism*. Brooklyn: Autonomedia, 1991.

Bey, Hakim. 'Immediatism'. In *Immediatism. Essays by Hakim Bey*, edited by Hakim Bey, 7–12. Edinburgh/San Francisco: AK Press, 1994.

Blank, Joachim. 'Die Stadtmetapher im Datennetz'. *digitalcraft* (1995). Accessed December 30, 2016. www.digitalcraft.org/dateien/357_0730163813.pdf.

Blank, Joachim. 'Internationale Stadt Berlin'. Notizen aus der Provinz'. In *Virtual Cities. Die Neuerfindung der Stadt im Zeitalter globaler Vernetzung*, edited by Christa Maar, Florian Rötzer, 70–74. Basel: Birkhäuser, 1997.

Böhm, Steffen, Chris Land, and Armin Beverungen. *The Value of Marx: Free Labour, Rent and ›Primitive‹ Accumulation in Facebook*. Working Paper, University of Essex, 2012.

Böhme, Hartmut. 'Das Neue Jerusalem. Von der Vernetzung zur Virtualisierung der Städte'. In *Flimmernde Zeiten. Vom Tempo der Medien*, edited by Manuel Schneider and Karlheinz A. Geißler, 309–23. Stuttgart/ Leipzig: Hirzel, 1999.

Bollmann, Stefan. 'Einführung in den Cyberspace'. In *Kursbuch Neue Medien. Trends in Wirtschaft und Politik, Wissenschaft und Kultur*, edited by Stefan Bollmann, 243–249. Cologne: Bollmann, 1995.

Boltanski, Luc, and Ève Chiapello. *The New Spirit of Capitalism*, translated by Gregory Elliott. London, New York: Verso, 2005.

Bolter, Jay David. 'Electronic technology and the metaphor of the city'. *Telepolis* (March 1, 1996). Accessed April 4, 2017. https://www. heise.de/tp/features/Electronic-technology-and-the-metaphor-of-the-city-3445801.html.

Bourdieu, Pierre. *The Logic of Practice*. Stanford: Stanford University Press, 1990.

boyd, danah, and Kate Crawford. 'Critical Questions for Big Data'. *Information, Communication & Society* 15:5 (2012): 662–679.

Boyer, Christine. *CyberCitise: Visual Perception in the Age of Electronic Communication*. New York: Princeton Architectural Press, 1996.

Brecht, Bertolt. 'The Radio as an Apparatus of Communication'. In *Brecht on Theatre: The Developments of an Aesthetics*, edited by John Willett, 51–52. New York: Hill and Wang, 1964.

Broeckmann, Andreas. 'Reflections on Building the European Cultural Backbone'. In *Public Netbase: Non Stop Future*, edited by Branka Ćurčić and Zoran Pantelić, 254–255. Berlin: Revolver Publishing, 2008.

Broeckmann, Andreas. 'Introduction: Tactical Media'. *Next 5 Minutes* (1995). Accessed December 15, 2016. http://www.tacticalmediafiles.net/ n5m2/media/texts/abroeck.html.

Bruch, Andreas vom. 'Der Niedergang der Digitalen Stadt Wien'. *Telepolis* (1997). Accessed January 4, 2017. www.heise.de/tp/artikel/1/1208/1. html.

Brunet, Karla. 'Internet, activism and tactical media. Practices of resistance and enthusiasm in Brazil'. *ZEMOS98* (2005). Accessed May 10, 2017. http://www.zemos98.org/IMG/article_PDF_article_673.pdf.

Brunton, Finn, and Gabriella Coleman. 'Closer to the Metal'. In *Media Technologies. Essays on Communication, Materiality, and Society*, edited by Tarleton Gillespie, Pablo J. Boczkowski, and Kirsten A. Foot, 77–97. Cambridge/London: MIT Press, 2014.

Buchmann, Sabeth. 'Nur soviel: Das Medium ist nicht die Botschaft. Kritik der Medientheorie'. In *Im Zentrum der Peripherie. Kunstvermittlung und Vermittlungskunst in den 90er Jahren*, edited by Marius Babias, 79–102. Dresden/Basel: Verlag der Kunst, 1995.

Byfield, Ted. 'nettime – Fortsetzung folgt … '. In *Vergessene Zukunft. Radikale Netzkulturen in Europa*, edited by Clemens Apprich and Felix Stalder, 39–45. Bielefeld: transcript, 2012.

Callon, Michel. 'Techno-economic networks and irreversibility'. *The Sociological Review* 38 (1990): 132–161.

Castells, Manuel. *The Informational City. Information Technology, Economic Restructuring and the Urban-Regional Process*. Oxford: Blackwell Publishing, 1991.

Castells, Manuel. 'European Cities, The Informational Society, and The Global Economy'. *Journal of Economic and Social Geography* 84:4 (1993): 255.

Castells, Manuel. 'The Rise of the Network Society'. Vol. I. of *The Information Age: Economy, Society and Culture*, edited by Manuel Castells. Oxford/Malden: Blackwell, 1996.

Castells, Manuel. 'The Power of Identity'. Vol. II. of *The Information Age: Economy, Society and Culture,* edited by Manuel Castells. Oxford/Malden: Blackwell, 1997.

Castells, Manuel. 'End of Millennium'. Vol. III of *The Information Age: Economy, Society and Culture*, edited by Manuel Castells. Oxford/Malden: Blackwell, 1998.

Castells, Manuel. 'Epilogue: Informationalism and the Network Society'. In *The Hacker Ethic and the Spirit of the Information Age*, edited by Pekka Himanen, 155–178. New York: Random House, 2001.

Castells, Manuel. *The Internet Galaxy. Reflections on the Internet, Business, and Society*. Oxford: Oxford University Press, 2002.

Castells, Manuel. 'Informationalism, networks, and the network society: a theoretical blueprint'. In *The Network Society. A Cross-Cultural Perspective*, edited by Manuel Castells et al., 36–45. Northampton: Edward Elgar Publishing, 2004.

Castells, Manuel. 'Space of Flows, Space of Places: Notes Towards a General Theory'. In *The Cybercities Reader*, edited by Stephen Graham, 82–93. London: Routledge, 2004.

Castells, Manuel. 'Cities, the Informational Society and the Global Economy'. In *The Global Cities Reader*, edited by Neil Brenner et al., 135–136. London/New York: Routledge, 2006.

Castells, Manuel. 'Communication, Power and Counter-power in the Network Society'. *International Journal of Communication* 1 (2007): 238–266.

164   *Bibliography*

Castells, Manuel. 'Materials for an Exploratory Theory of the Network Society'. In *Social Theory Re-Wired. New Connections to Classical and Contemporary Perspectives*, edited by Wesley Longhofer and Daniel Winchester, 168–183. New York/London: Routledge, 2016.

Certeau, Michel de. *The Practice of Everyday Life*. Berkeley/Los Angeles: University of California Press, 1984.

Chun, Wendy Hui Kyong. 'Networks NOW: Belated too Early'. In *Postdigital Aesthetics. Art, Computation and Design*, edited by David M. Berry, Michael Dieter, 290–316. London: Palgrave Macmillan, 2015.

Chun, Wendy Hui Kyong. *Updating to Remain the Same. Habitual New Media*. Cambridge: MIT Press, 2016.

Cleaver, Harry. 'Sozialismus'. In *Wie im Westen so auf Erden. Ein polemisches Handbuch zur Entwicklungspolitik*, edited by Wolfgang Sachs, 345–372. Reinbeck: Rowohlt, 1993. English translation available online, accessed August 8, 2016. http://la.utexas.edu/users/hcleaver/socialismessay.html.

Combes, Muriel. *Gilbert Simondon and the Philosophy of the Transindividual*. Translated by Thomas LaMarre. Cambridge/London: MIT Press, 2013.

Critical Art Ensemble. *Electronic Civil Disobedience and Other Unpopular Ideas*. New York: Autonomedia & Critical Art Ensemble, 1996.

Critical Art Ensemble. *Digital Resistance. Explorations in Tactical Media*. New York: Autonomedia, 2001.

Daniels, Dieter. 'Television—Art or Anti-art? Conflict and cooperation between the avant-garde and the mass media in the 1960s and 1970s'. *MedienKunstNetz* (2004). Accessed December 12, 2016. http://www.medienkunstnetz.de/themes/overview_of_media_art/massmedia.

Davis, Mike. *City of Quartz. Excavating the Future in Los Angeles*. London/New York: Verso, 1990.

Dean, Jodi. *Blog Theory. Feedback and Capture in the Circuits of Drive*. Cambridge/Malden: Polity Press, 2010.

Dean, Jodi. 'Communicative Capitalism and Class Struggle'. *spheres – Journal for Digital Cultures* 1 (2014). Accessed April 30, 2017. http://spheres-journal.org/communicative-capitalism-and-class-struggle.

Dean, Jodi. *Crowds and Party*. London/New York: Verso Books, 2016.

Debord, Guy. *The Society of the Spectacle*. Translated by Donald Nicholson-Smith. New York: Zone Books, 1994.

Deleuze, Gilles. 'Postscript on the Societies of Control'. *OCTOBER* 59 (1992): 3–7.

Deleuze, Gilles. 'What Is a Dispositif?' In Michel Foucault, Philosopher, *edited by Timothy J. Armstrong, 159–168*. New York, NY: Routledge, 1992.

Deleuze, Gilles. *Negotiations, 1972–1990*. Translated by Martin Joughin. New York: Columbia University Press, 1995.

Dieberger, Andreas. 'The Information City—A Metaphor for Navigating Hypertexts'. Research paper presented at the BCS-HCI'93, Loughborough, 1993.

Dieberger, Andreas. *Navigation in Textual Virtual Environments using a City Metaphor*. PhD diss., Vienna: University of Technology, 1994.

Dieberger, Andreas, and Andrew U. Franck. 'A city metaphor for supporting navigation in complex information spaces'. *Journal of Visual Languages and Computing* 9 (1998): 597–622.

Diederichsen, Diedrich. 'Wie aus Bewegungen Kulturen und aus Kulturen Communities werden'. In *Mythos Metropole*, edited by Gotthard Fuchs, Bernhard Moltmann, and Walter Prigge, 126–139. Frankfurt a.M.: Suhrkamp, 1995.

Diefenbach, Katja. 'Im Interview mit Clemens Apprich'. In *Vergessene Zukunft. Radikale Netzkulturen in Europa*, edited by Clemens Apprich and Felix Stalder, 177–182. Bielefeld: transcript, 2012.

Dijck, José van. *The Culture of Connectivity. A Critical History of Social Media*. New York: Oxford University Press, 2013.

Dijck, José van, and Thomas Poell. 'Understanding Social Media Logic'. *Media and Communication* 1:1 (2013): 2–14.

Durkheim, Émile. *The Division of Labor in Society*. Translated by William D. Halls. New York: Free Press, 1997.

Dyer-Witheford, Nick. *Cyber-Marx. Cycles and Circuits of Struggle in High-Technology Capitalism*. Urbana/Chicago: University of Illinois Press, 1999.

Dyson, Esther, George Gilder, George Keyworth, and Alvin Toffler. 'Cyberspace and the American Dream: A Magna Carta for the Knowledge Age'. *The Progress and Freedom Foundation* (1994). Accessed December 21, 2016. www.pff.org/issues-pubs/futureinsights/fi1.2magnacarta.html.

Easterling, Keller. *Extrastatecraft. The Power of Infrastructure Space*. London: Verso, 2014.

Eckardt, Frank. *Soziologie der Stadt*. Bielefeld: transcript, 2004.

Enzenberger, Hans Magnus. 'Constituents of a Theory of the Media'. In *The New Media Reader*, edited by Noah Wardrip-Fruin and Nick Montfort, 261–275. Cambridge/London: MIT Press, 2003.

Erdős, Paul, and Alfréd Rényi. 'On Random Graphs'. *Publicationes Mathematicae Debrecen* 6 (1959): 290–297.

Fisher, Mark. *Capitalist Realism. Is There No Alternative?* Winchester: Zero Books, 2009.

Flint, Joost. 'Das Amsterdamer-Freenet "De Digitale Stad" (DDS)'. In *Virtual Cities. Die Neuerfindung der Stadt im Zeitalter globaler Vernetzung*, edited by Christa Maar and Florian Rötzer, 57–69. Basel: Birkhäuser, 1997.

Foerster, Heinz von. 'On Self-Organizing Systems and Their Environments'. In *Understanding Understanding: Essays on Cybernetics and Cognition*, edited by Heinz von Foerster, 1–19. New York: Springer, 2003.

Foucault, Michel. 'War in the Filigree of Peace: Course Summary', translated by Ian Mcleod. *Oxford Literary Review* 4:2 (1976): 15–19.

Foucault, Michel. *Power/Knowledge. Selected Interview and Other Writings 1972–1977*. New York: Pantheon Books, 1980.

Foucault, Michel. 'The Confession of the Flesh'. In Power/Knowledge: Selected Interviews and Other Writings, edited by Colin Gordon, 194–228. New York: Pantheon Books, 1980.

Foucault, Michel. 'Nietzsche, Genealogy, History'. In *The Foucault Reader*, edited by Paul Rabinow, 76–100. New York: Pantheon Books, 1984.

Foucault, Michel. *The Use of Pleasure. The History of Sexuality,* vol. 2. Translated by Robert Hurley. New York: Vintage, 1985.

Foucault, Michel. 'Of Other Spaces'. *Diacritics* 16:1 (Spring 1986): 22–27.

Foucault, Michel. 'What Is Critique?' In *The Politics of Truth*, edited by Paul Rabinow, 41–81. Los Angeles: semiotext(e), 2007.

Frischmann, Brett M. *Infrastructure. The Social Value of Shared Resources.* New York: Oxford University Press, 2012.

Fuchs, Gotthard, Bernhard Moltmann, and Walter Prigge, eds. *Mythos Metropole*. Frankfurt a.M.: Suhrkamp, 1995.

Fuller, Matthew. 'The Forbidden Pleasures of Media Determinism'. In *Media After Kittler*, edited by Eleni Ikoniadou and Scott Wilson, 95–110. London: Rowman & Littlefield, 2015.

Gabrys, Jennifer. 'Programming Environments: Environmentality and Citizen Sensing in the Smart City'. *Environment and Planning D: Society and Space* 32:1 (2014): 30–48.

Galloway, Alexander R. 'Protocol, or, How Control Exists after Decentralization'. *Rethinking Marxism* 13:3/4 (2001): 81–88.

Galloway, Alexander R. *Protocol: How Control Exists after Decentralization.* Cambridge/London: MIT Press, 2004.

Galloway, Alexander R. *The Interface Effect*. Hoboken: John Wiley & Sons, 2012.

Galloway, Alexander R., and Eugene Thacker. *The Exploit. A Theory of Networks*. Minneapolis: University of Minnesota Press, 2007.

Garcia, David, and Geert Lovink. 'The ABC of Tactical Media'. Posted May 16, 1997 on the nettime mailing list. Accessed September 6, 2016. www.nettime.org/Lists-Archives/nettime-l-9705/msg00096.html.

Gelernter, David. *Mirror Worlds*. Oxford: Oxford University Press, 1993.

Genosko, Gary. 'The Life and Work of Félix Guattari: From Transversality to Ecosophy'. In *The Three Ecologies,* Félix Guattari, 106–159. London/New Brunswick: The Athlone Press, 2000.

Genosko, Gary. 'The Promise of Post-Media'. In *Provocative Alloys: A Post-Media Anthology*, edited by Clemens Apprich, Josephine Berry Slater, Anthony Iles, and Oliver Lerone Schultz, 15–25. London: Mute, 2013.

Gibson, William. *Neuromancer*. New York: Ace Books, 1984.

Gore, Albert Arnold. 'Remarks on the National Information Infrastructure at the National Press Club'. *ibiblio* (1993). Accessed December 21, 2016. http://www.ibiblio.org/nii/goremarks.

Granovetter, Mark S. 'The Strength of Weak Ties'. *American Journal of Sociology* 78:6 (1973): 1360–1380.

Grau, Oliver. 'Immersion and Interaction: From circular frescoes to interactive image spaces'. *MedienKunstNetz* (2004). Accessed March 3, 2017. http://www.medienkunstnetz.de/themes/overview_of_media_art/immersion/20/.

Greenfield, Adam. *Against the Smart City*. New York: Do projects, 2013.

Guattari, Félix. 'Remaking Social Practices'. In *The Guattari Reader*, edited by Gary Genosko, 262–272. Oxford/Cambridge: Blackwell, 1996.

Guattari, Félix. 'Regimes, Pathways, Subjects'. In *The Guattari Reader*, edited by Gary Genosko, 95–108. Oxford/Cambridge: Blackwell, 1996.

Guattari, Félix. *The Three Ecologies*. Translated by Ian Pindar and Paul Sutton. London/New Brunswick: The Athlone Press, 2000.

Guattari, Félix. 'Towards a Post-Media Era'. In *Provocative Alloys: A Post-Media Anthology*, edited by Clemens Apprich, Josephine Berry Slater, Anthony Iles, and Oliver Lerone Schultz, 26–27. London: Mute, 2013.

Hagen, Wolfgang. 'Discharged Crowds. On the Crisis of a Concept'. In *Social Media – New Masses*, edited by Inge Baxmann, Timon Beyes, and Claus Pias, 123–134. Zürich/Berlin: diaphanes, 2016.

Hall, Gary. *The Uberfication of the University*. Minneapolis: University of Minnesota Press, 2016.

Hall, Stuart. 'Encoding, Decoding'. In *The Cultural Studies Reader*, edited by Simon During, 507–517. London/New York: Routledge, 1999.

Hall, Stuart. 'The Rediscovery of 'Ideology': Return of the Repressed in Media Studies'. In *Cultural Theory and Popular Culture – A Reader*, edited by John Storey, 124–155. Essex: Pearson, 2006.

Halpern, Orit, Jesse LeCavalier, Nerea Calvillo, and Wolfgang Pietsch. 'Test-Bed Urbanism'. *Public Culture* 25:2 (2013): 273–306.

Haraway, Donna. 'Situated Knowledge: The Science Question in Feminism and the Privilege of Partial Perspective'. *Feminist Studies* 14:3 (1988): 575–599.

Hardt, Michael, and Antonio Negri. *Declaration*. Allen: Argo-Navis, 2012.

Hauben, Michael, and Ronda Hauben. *Netizens. On the History and Impact of Usenet and the Internet*. Los Alamitos: IEEE Computer Society Press, 1997.

Heidenreich, Stefan. 'The Situation After Media'. In *Media After Kittler*, edited by Eleni Ikoniadou and Scott Wilson, 135–154. London: Rowman & Littlefield, 2015.

Heinich, Nathalie. 'Les Immatériaux Revisited: Innovation in Innovations'. *Tate's Online Research Journal* 12 (2009). Accessed March 15, 2017. www.tate.org.uk/research/publications/tate-papers/les-immateriaux-revisited-innovation-innovations.

Himanen, Pekka. *The Hacker Ethic. A Radical Approach to the Philosophy of Business*. New York: Random House, 2002.

Hinssen, Peter. 'Life in the Digital City'. *Wired* 3:6 (1995). Accessed December 30, 2016. www.wired.com/wired/archive/3.06/digcity. html.

Holmes, Brian. 'The Flexible Personality. For a New Cultural Critique'. *transversal* (2002). Accessed December 12, 2016. http://transversal.at/transversal/1106/holmes/en.

Holmes, Brian. 'Signals, statistics and social experiments: The governance conflicts of electronic media art'. *nettime* (2004). Accessed December 12, 2016. http://amsterdam.nettime.org/Lists-Archives/nettime-l-0411/msg000 67.html.

Holmes, Brian. 'Swarmachine. Activist Media Tomorrow'. *Third Text* 22:5 (2008): 525–534.

Hörl, Erich. 'The Technological Condition', translated by Anthony Enns. *Parrhesia* 22 (2015): 1–15.

Horn, Eva. 'Editor's Introduction: "There Are No Media."' *Grey Room* 29 (2008): 6–13.

Hu, Tung-Hui. *A Prehistory of the Cloud*. Cambridge/London: MIT Press, 2015.

Hu, Tung-Hui. 'Truckstops of the Information Superhighway: Ant Farm, SRI, and the Cloud'. *Media-N: Journal of the New Media Caucus* 10:1 (2014). Accessed April 1, 2017. http://median.new-mediacaucus.org/art-infrastructures-hardware/truckstops-on-the-information-superhighway-ant-farm-sri-and-the-cloud.

Hudek, Antony. 'From Over- to Sub-Exposure: The Anamnesis of Les Immatériaux'. In *Tate's Online Research Journal* 12 (2009). Accessed March 15, 2017. http://www.tate.org.uk/research/publications/tate-papers/12/from-over-to-sub-exposure-the-anamnesis-of-les-immateriaux.

Hughes, Thomas P. *Networks of Power: Electrification in Western Society, 1880–1930*. Baltimore/London: The Johns Hopkins University Press, 1993.

Huhtamo, Erkki, and Jussi Parikka, eds. *Media Archaeology. Approaches, Applications and Implications*. Berkley/Los Angeles/London: University of California Press, 2011.

Hui, Yuk, and Andreas Broeckmann. 'Introduction'. In *30 Years after Les Immatériaux: Art, Science, and Theory*, edited by Yuk Hui and Andreas Broeckmann, 9–24. Lüneburg: meson press, 2015.

Hui, Yuk, and Harry Halpin. 'Collective Individuation: The Future of the Social Web'. In *Unlike Us Reader. Social Media Monopolies and Their Alternatives*, edited by Geert Lovink and Miriam Rasch, 103–116. Amsterdam: INC, 2013.

Huyssen, Andreas. 'In the Shadow of McLuhan: Jean Baudrillard's Theory of Simulation'. *Assemblage* 10 (1989): 6–17.

Iglhaut, Stefan, Armin Medosch, and Florian Rötzer, eds. *Stadt am Netz. Ansichten von Telepolis*. Mannheim: Bollmann, 1996.

Internationale Stadt e.V. 'Internationale Stadt. Die ideale Stadt im Internet'. *digitalcraft* (1995). Accessed December 30, 2016. www.digitalcraft.org/dateien/islang2.pdf.

Ishida, Toru, and Katherine Isbister, eds. *Digital Cities: Technologies, Experiences and Future Perspective*. Berlin/Heidelberg: Springer-Verlag, 2000.

Jameson, Fredric. *Postmodernism, or, The Cultural Logic of Late Capitalism*. Durham: Duke University Press, 1991.

Jones, Steven G. 'Understanding Community in the Information Age'. In *Cybersociety. Computer-Mediated Communication and Community*, edited by Steven G. Stones, 10–34. Thousand Oaks/London/New Delhi: Sage, 1995.

Kapper, Harald. 'Standleitungen für Alle! Vienna Backbone Service—Ein Konzept mit Zukunft für den urbanen Raum'. *Telepolis* (1998). Accessed January 3, 2017. https://web.archive.org/web/20050131071757/http://www.heise.de/tp/r4/artikel/1/1404/1.html.

Kelly, Kevin. *Out of Control. The New Biology of Machines, Social Systems, and the Economic World*. New York: Basic Books, 1994.

Kelty, Christopher M. 'Against Networks'. *spheres. Journal for Digital Cultures* 1 (2014). Accessed December 21, 2016. http://spheres-journal.org/against-networks.

Kerscher, Gottfried. 'brave new city: Eine Einleitung und ein Interview mit einem der Mitbegründer der Internationalen Stadt Berlin, Joachim Blank'. In *Kritische Berichte* 1 (1998): 10–16.

Kittler, Friedrich. 'Fiktion und Simulation'. In *Philosophien der neuen Technologien*, edited by Ars Electronica, 57–80. Berlin: Merve, 1989.

Kittler, Friedrich. *Discourse Networks 1800/1900*. Translated by Michael Metteer. Stanford: Stanford University Press, 1990.

Kittler, Friedrich. 'Das Internet ist eine Emanation: Ein Gespräch mit Friedrich Kittler'. In *Stadt am Netz. Ansichten von Telepolis*, edited by Stefan Iglhaut, Armin Medosch, and Florian Rötzer, 196–203. Mannheim: Bolmann, 1996.

Kittler, Friedrich. 'The City Is a Medium'. *New Literary History* 27:4 (1996): 717–729.

Kluitenberg, Eric. *Legacies of Tactical Media. Network Notebooks 05.* Amsterdam: Institute of Network Cultures, 2011.

Kluitenberg, Eric. 'On the Archaeology of Imaginary Media'. In *Media Archaeology. Approaches, Applications and Implications*, edited by Erkki Huhtamo and Jussi Parikka, 48–69. Berkley/Los Angeles/London: University of California Press, 2011.

Krämer, Sybille. 'Das Medium als Spur und als Apparat'. In *Medien, Computer, Realität. Wirklichkeitsvorstellungen und Neue Medien*, edited by Sybille Krämer, 73–94. Frankfurt a.M.: Suhrkamp, 1998.

Kroker, Arthur. 'Baudrillard's Marx'. In *The Postmodern Scene. Excremental Culture and Hyper-Aesthetics*, edited by Arthur Kroker and David Cook, 170–188. Hampshire/London: MacMillan, 1988.

Kroker, Arthur, and Michael A. Weinstein. 'Data Trash: The Theory of the Virtual Class'. *ctheory* (1994). Accessed March 25, 2017. http://ctheory. net/book2.asp?bookid=3.

Landa, Manuel de. *War in the Age of Intelligent Machines*. New York: Zone Books, 1991.

Lefebvre, Henri. *The Production of Space*. Translated by Donald Nicholson-Smith. London: Blackwell, 1991.

Leggewie, Claus. 'Demokratie auf der Datenautobahn. Wie weit geht die Zivilisierung des Cyberspace'. In *Internet und Politik*, edited by Claus Leggewie and Christa Maar, 15–51. Köln: Bollmann, 1998.

Leiner, Barry M., Vinton G. Cerf, and David D. Clark et al. 'A Brief History of the Internet'. *The Internet Society* (1997). Accessed December 21, 2016. www.internetsociety.org/internet/what-internet/history-internet/brief-history-internet.

Lévy, Pierre. 'Cyberkultur'. In *Kursbuch Internet. Anschlüsse an Wirtschaft und Politik, Wissenschaft und Kultur*, edited by Stefan Bollmann and Christiane Heibach, 60–87. Reinbeck: Rowolth, 1998.

Lévy, Pierre. *Cyberculture*. Translated by Robert Bononno. Minneapolis/London: University of Minnesota Press, 2001.

Liang, Lawrence. 'Shadow Libraries'. *e-flux Journal* 37 (2012). Accessed May 10, 2017. http://www.e-flux.com/journal/37/61228/shadow-libraries.

Lischka, Gerhard Johann, and Peter Weibel, eds. 'Im Netz der Systeme'. *Kunstforum* 103 (1989).

Lorey, Isabell. 'VirtuosInnen der Freiheit. Zur Implosion von politischer Virtuosität und produktiver Arbeit'. *grundrisse. Zeitschrift für linke Theorie & Debatte* 23 (2007): 4–10. English translation available online, accessed August 8, 2016. http://eipcp.net/transversal/0207/lorey/en.

Lovink, Geert. 'Die Digitale Stadt Amsterdam'. In *Internet & Politik. Von der Zuschauer- zur Beteiligungsdemokratie?*, edited by Claus Leggewie and Christa Maar, 293–299. Cologne: Bollmann, 1998.

Lovink, Geert. 'The Theory of Mixing'. In *Radiotext(e)*, edited by Neil Straus, 114–122. New York: Autonomedia/Semiotext(e), 1993.

Lovink, Geert. 'The Digital City Amsterdam. Creating a Virtual Public'. In *Welcome to the Wired World,* edited by Ars Electronica (1995). Accessed April 21, 2017. http://90.146.8.18/en/archives/festival_archive/festival_catalogs/festival_artikel.asp?iProjectID=8627%22.

Lovink, Geert. 'From Speculative Media Theory to Net Criticism'. Paper presented at ICC, Tokyo, December 19, 1996. Available at *nettime,* accessed August 26, 2016. http://www.nettime.org/Lists-Archives/nettime-l-9701/msg00032.html.

Lovink, Geert. *Dark Fiber. Tracking Critical Internet Culture* Cambridge: MIT Press, 2002.

Lovink, Geert. 'The Rise and Fall of the Digital City Metaphor and Community in 1990s Amsterdam'. In *The Cybercities Reader*, edited by Stephen Graham, 371–377. London/New York: Routledge, 2004.

Lovink, Geert. *Zero Comments: Blogging and Critical Internet Culture.* New York/London: Routledge, 2008.

Lovink, Geert. *Dynamics of Critical Internet Culture.* Amsterdam: INC, 2009.

Lovink, Geert, and Patrice Riemens. 'Amsterdam Public Digital Culture 2000'. *Telepolis* (2000). Accessed December 30, 2016. https://www.heise.de/tp/features/Amsterdam-Public-Digital-Culture-2000-3447524.html.

Lovink, Geert, Pit Schultz. *Jugendjahre der Netzkritik. Essays zu Web 1.0 (1995–1997).* Amsterdam: INC, 2010.

Lovink, Geert, and Pit Schultz. 'Aufruf zur Netzkritik. Ein Zwischenbericht'. In *Netzkritik*, edited by nettime, 5–14. Berlin: ID-Archiv, 1997.

Lovink, Geert, and Ned Rossiter. 'The Politics of Organized Networks: The Art of Collective Coordination and the Seriality of Demands.' in *New Media, Old Media: A History and Theory Reader*, 2nd edition, edited by Wendy Hui Kyong Chun and Anna Watkins Fisher, 335–345. New York/London: Routledge, 2016.

Lynch, Kevin. *The Image of the City.* Cambridge/London: MIT Press, 1960.

Lyotard, Jean-François. 'Lyotard, Answering the Question: What Is Postmodernism?', translated by Regis Durand. In *The Postmodern Condition: A Report on Knowledge*, edited by Jean-François Lyotard, 71–78. Minneapolis: University of Minnesota Press, 1984.

Lyotard, Jean-François. *The Postmodern Condition: A Report on Knowledge.* Translated by Geoff Bennington and Brian Massumi. Minneapolis: University of Minnesota Press, 1984.

Lyotard, Jean-François et al. *Immaterialität und Postmoderne*. Berlin: Merve, 1985.

Lyotard, Jean-François. 'Note on the Meaning of "Post-."' In *The Postmodern Explained*, edited by Julian Pefanis and Morgan Thomas, 75–80. Minneapolis: University of Minnesota Press, 1992.

Lyotard, Jean-François. 'Zone'. In Moralités postmodernes, Collection Débats, edited by Jean-François Lyotard, 25–36. Paris: Galilée, 1993.

Lyotard, Jean-François. 'The Zone'. In *Postmodern Fables*, translated by George Van Den Abbeele and edited by Jean-François Lyotard, 17–32. Minneapolis/London: University of Minnesota Press, 1997.

Maar, Christa, and Florian Rötzer, eds. *Virtual Cities. Die Neuerfindung der Stadt im Zeitalter globaler Vernetzung*. Basel: Birkhäuser, 1997.

Marchart, Oliver. 'Was ist neu an den Neuen Medien? Technopolitik zwischen Lenin und Yogi-Bär'. In *Netzkritik*, edited by nettime, 89–100. Berlin: ID-Archiv, 1997.

Marchart, Oliver. *Die Verkabelung Mitteleuropas. Medienguerilla—Netzkritik—Technopolitik*. Vienna: edition selene, 1998.

Marchart, Oliver. 'Marx und Medien – Eine Einführung'. In *Media Marx*, edited by Jens Schröter, Gregor Schwering, and Urs Stäheli, 45–58. Bielefeld: transcript, 2006.

Marcell Mars, Manar Zarroug, and Tomislav Medak. 'Public library (Essay), in *Public Library*, edited by Tomislav Medak and Marcell Mars, 75–85. Zagreb: Gallery Nova, 2015.

Marx, Karl. 'Capital. A Critique of Political Economy – Volume III: The Process of Capitalist Production as a Whole'. In *Marx and Engels Collected Works*, Vol. 37, edited by Friedrich Engels. New York: International Publisher, 1998.

Marx, Karl. 'Ökonomische Manuskripte 1857/1858'. In *Werke*, vol. 42, edited by Karl Marx and Friedrich Engels. Berlin: Dietz, 1983.

Marx, Karl, and Friedrich Engels. 'Die Deutsche Ideologie'. In *Werke*, vol. 3, edited by Karl Marx and Friedrich Engels. Berlin: Dietz, 1990.

McCarty, Diana. 'Nettime: the legend and the myth' (1997). Accessed March 25, 2017. http://www.nettime.org/nettime/DOCS/1/info3.html.

McLaren, Duncan, and Julian Agyeman. *Shaing Cities: A Case for Truly Smart and Sustainable Cities*. Cambridge: MIT Press, 2017.

McLuhan, Marshall. *Understanding Media. The Extensions of Man*. Cambridge: MIT Press, 1994.

MedienKunstNetz. 'nettime'. Accessed March 25, 2017. http://www.medienkunstnetz.de/works/nettime.

Medosch, Armin. 'Shockwaves in the New World Order of Information and Communication'. In *Blackwell Companion to Digital Art*, edited by Christiane Paul, 355–383. Hoboken: Wiley-Blackwell, 2016.

Medosch, Armin. 'Public Netbase Wien. Netzbasis für Kulturschaffende'. *Telepolis* (1998). Accessed January 4, 2017. https://www.heise.de/tp/features/Public-Netbase-Wien-3441239.html.

Medosch, Armin. *Freie Netze. Geschichte, Politik und Kultur offener WLAN-Netze.* Hannover: Heise Verlag, 2004.

Mirowski, Philip. 'Postface: Defining Neoliberalism'. In *The Road from Mont Pelerin. The Making of the Neoliberal Thought Collective*, edited by Philip Mirowski and Dieter Plehwe, 417–455. Cambridge: Harvard University Press, 2009.

Mitchell, William J. *City of Bits. Space, Place, and the Infobahn.* Cambridge: MIT Press, 1996.

Mitchell, William J. *e-topia.* Cambridge/London: MIT Press, 2000.

Moreno, Jacob L. *Sociometry, Experimental Method and the Science of Society: An Approach to a New Political Orientation.*Boston: Beacon House, 1951.

Mouffe, Chantal. *Agonistics: Thinking the World Politically.* London/New York: Verso, 2013.

Mumford, Lewis. *Technics and Civilization.* Chicago/London: University of Chicago Press, 1962.

Negt, Oskar, and Alexander Kluge. *Public Sphere and Experience. Towards an Analysis of the Bourgeois and Proletarian Public Sphere.* Translated by P. Labanyi et al. Minneapolis/London: University of Minnesota Press, 1993.

Newman, Mark. *Networks. An Introduction.* Oxford: Oxford University Press, 2010.

Nunes, Rodrigo. *The Organisation of the Organisationless: Collective Action After Networks.* London: Mute, 2014.

Old Boys Network. '100 Anti-Theses'. Accessed September 14, 2016. http://www.obn.org/reading_room/manifestos/html/anti.html.

Parikka, Jussi. *What Is Media Archaelogy?* Cambridge/Malden: Polity Press, 2012.

Pariser, Eli. *The Filter Bubble: How the New Personalized Web Is Changing What We Read and How We Think.* New York: Penguin Press, 2011.

Pawley, Martin. 'Auf dem Weg zur digitalen Desurbanisierung'. In *Virtual Cities. Die Neuerfindung der Stadt im Zeitalter globaler Vernetzung*, edited by Christa Maar and Florian Rötzer, 17–29. Basel: Birkhäuser, 1997.

Pawley, Martin. *Terminal Architecture.* London: Reaktion Books, 1998.

Peljhan, Marko. 'Im Interview mit Clemens Apprich'. In *Vergessene Zukunft. Radikale Netzkulturen in Europa*, edited by Clemens Apprich and Felix Stalder, 81–84. Bielefeld: transcript, 2012.

Petersen, Søren Mørk. 'Loser Generated Content: From Participation to Exploitation'. *First Monday* 12:3 (2008). Accessed January 8, 2017. http://firstmonday.org/article/view/2141/1948.

Pias, Claus. 'Der Auftrag. Kybernetik und Revolution in Chile'. In *Politiken der Medien*, edited by Daniel Gethmann and Markus Stauff, 131–153. Zürich/Berlin: diaphanes, 2004.

Pias, Claus. 'Was waren Medien-Wissenschaften? Stichworte zu einer Standortbestimmung'. In *Was waren Medien?*, edited by Claus Pias, 7–30. Zürich/Berlin: diaphanes, 2010.

Plant, Sadie. *Zeros + Ones: Digital Women + The New Technoculture*. New York: Doubleday, 1997.

Poster, Mark. 'Postmodern Virtualities'. In *Cyberspace/Cyberbodies/Cyberpunk. Cultures of Technological Embodiment*, edited by Mike Featherstone and Roger Burrows, 79–95. London/Thousand Oaks/New Delhi: Sage, 1995.

Presse- and Informationsdienst der Stadt Wien. 'Zur Geschichte von wien. at'. Accessed January 4, 2017. https://www.wien.gv.at/pid/wienat-online/zehnjahresjubilaeum.

Rainie, Lee, and Barry Wellman. *Networked. The New Social Operating System*. Cambridge: MIT Press, 2012.

Rajchman, John. 'Les Immatériaux or How to Construct the History of Exhibitions'. *Tate's Online Research Journal* 12 (2009). Accessed March 15, 2017. http://www.tate.org.uk/download/file/fid/7271.

Raley, Rita. *Tactical Media*. Minneapolis: University of Minnesota Press, 2009.

Rancière, Jacques. *Althusser's Lesson*. London/New York: Continuum, 2011.

Raunig, Gerald. *Factories of Knowledge, Industries of Creativity*. Translated by Aileen Derieg. Los Angeles: semiotext(e), 2013.

Reed, S. Alexander. *Assimilate. A Critical History of Industrial Music*. Oxford/New York: Oxford University Press, 2013.

Raymond, Eric. 'A Brief History of Hackerdom' (2002). Accessed April 25, 2017. http://www.catb.org/esr/writings/homesteading/hacker-history.

Rheingold, Howard. 'A Slice of Life in My Virtual Community'. In *Global Networks: Computers and International Communication*, edited by Linda M. Harasim, 57–80. Cambridge: MIT Press, 1993.

Rheingold, Howard. *The Virtual Community. Homesteading on the Electronic Frontier*. New York: Harper Perennial, 1994.

Richardson, Joanne. 'The Language of Tactical Media'. *Subsol* (2002). Accessed May 5, 2017. http://subsol.c3.hu/subsol_2/contributors2/richardsontext2.html.

Ringler, Marie. 'Im Interview mit Clemens Apprich'. In *Vergessene Zukunft. Radikale Netzkulturen in Europa*, edited by Clemens Apprich and Felix Stalder, 271–275. Bielefeld: transcript, 2012.

Roesler, Alexander. 'Bequeme Einmischung. Internet und Öffentlichkeit'. In *Mythos Internet*, edited by Stefan Münker and Alexander Roesler, 171–192. Frankfurt a.M.: Suhrkamp, 1997.

Rose, Nikolas. 'The Death of the Social? Re-Figuring the Territory of Government'. *Economy and Society* 25:3 (1996): 327–365.

Rose, Nikolas. 'Governing Cities, Governing Citizens'. In *Democracy, Citizenship and the Global City*, edited by Engin F. Isin, 95–109. London/ New York: Routledge, 2000.

Rossiter, Ned. 'Organised Networks: Transdisciplinarity and New Institutional Forms'. In *transform* (2006). Accessed January 8, 2017. http:// transform. eipcp.net/correspondence/1144943951.

Rossiter, Ned. *Organized Networks: Media Theory, Collective Labour, New Institutions*. Rotterdam: Nai Publishers, 2007.

Rossiter, Ned. *Software, Infrastructure, Labor: A Media Theory of Logistical Nightmares*. New York/Oxon: Routledge, 2016.

Rossiter, Ned, and Soenke Zehle. 'Acts of Translation: Organizing Networks as Algorithmic Technologies of the Common'. In *Digital Labor: The Internet as Playground and Factory*, edited by Trebor Scholz, 225–239. London/New York: Routledge, 2013.

Rötzer, Florian. *Telepolis. Urbanität im digitalen Zeitalter*. Mannheim: Bollmann, 1995.

Rötzer, Florian. 'Auszug aus der Stadt'. In *Virtual Cities. Die Neuerfindung der Stadt im Zeitalter globaler Vernetzung*, edited by Christa Maar and Florian Rötzer, 11–16. Basel: Birkhäuser, 1997.

Sassen, Saskia. *The Global City: New York, London, Tokyo*. Princeton: Princeton University Press, 1991.

Sassen, Saskia. 'The Global City: Strategic Site/New Frontier'. In *Democracy, Citizenship and the Global City*, edited by Engin F. Isin, 48–61. London: Routledge, 2000.

Schartner, Thomas. '20 Jahre universitäres Internet, 18 Jahre kommerzielles Internet in Österreich'. *ISPA News* 02 (2010). Accessed March 3, 2016. https://www.ispa.at/filedl/0/0/1488903499/2576e17aba2f539bdc50fb81 0139fc46a2ae081e/fileadmin/content/5_Wissenspool/ISPA_News/2010/ News_2010/2010_02_ispa_news.pdf.

Schröter, Jens. 'The Internet and "Frictionless Capitalism."' *Triple C* 10:2 (2012): 302–312.

Schröter, Jens. 'Performing the economy, digital media and crisis. A critique of Michel Callon'. In *Performing the Digital*, edited by Marina Leeker, Imanuel Schipper, and Timon Beyes, 247–275. Bielefeld: transcript, 2017.

Schuler, Douglas. 'Community Networks: Building a New Participatory Medium'. *Communications of the ACM* 37:1 (1994): 38–51

Schultz, Pit. 'From the Archives: Introduction to nettime'. Posted May 7, 2001 on the nettime mailing list. Accessed April 1, 2017. https://nettime. org/Lists-Archives/nettime-l-0105/msg00036.html.

Schultz, Pit. 'The Origins of the Nettime Mailing List. Pit Schultz Interviewed by Pauline van Mourik Broekman'. In *Proud to be Flesh. A Mute Magazine Anthology of Cultural Politics after the Net*, edited by Josephine Berry Slate, Pauline van Mourik Broekman, and Michael Corris, 46–51. London: Mute Publishing, 2009.

Schultz, Pit. 'Im Interview mit Clemens Apprich'. In *Vergessene Zukunft. Radikale Netzkulturen in Europa*, edited by Clemens Apprich and Felix Stalder, 75–79. Bielefeld: transcript, 2012.

Shor, Juliet. 'Debating the Sharing Economy'. *Great Transition Initiative* (October 2014). Accessed, May 5, 2017. http://greattransition.org/publication/debating-the-sharing-economy.

Simmel, Georg. 'The Metropolis and Mental Life' (1903). In *The Blackwell City Reader*, edited by Gary Bridge and Sophie Watson, 11–19. Oxford and Malden, MA: Wiley-Blackwell, 2002.

Simondon, Gilbert. *L'individuation à la lumiére des notions de form et d'information*. Grenoble: Éditions Jérôme Millon, 2005.

Simondon, Gilbert. 'Technical Mentality', translated by Arne De Boever. *Parrhesia* 7 (2009): 7–27.

Simondon, Gilbert. 'The Limits of Human Progress: A Critical Study'. *Cultural Politics* 6:2 (2010): 229–236.

Simondon, Gilbert. *On the Mode of Existence of Technical Objects*. Translated by Cécile Malaspina and John Rogove. Minneapolis: Univocal, 2017.

Smite, Rasa. *Creative Networks, in the Rearview Mirror of Eastern European History*. Amsterdam: INC, 2012.

Soja, Edward D. 'Postmoderne Urbanisierung'. In *Mythos Metropole*, edited by Gotthard Fuchs, Bernhard Moltmann, Walter Prigge, 143–164. Frankfurt a.M.: Suhrkamp, 1995.

Sokolov, Daniel AJ. 'Online-Community 'Blackbox' sagt nach 20 Jahren Adieu'. *Der Standard* (November 6, 2012). Accessed April 25, 2017. http://derstandard.at/1350260413960/Online-Community-Blackbox-sagt-nach-20-Jahren-Adieu.

Sprenger, Florian. *Politics of Micro-Decisions*. Translated by Valentine A. Pakis. Lüneburg: meson press, 2015.

Srineck, Nick, and Alex Williams. *Inventing the Future. Postcapitalism and a World Without Work*. London: Verso, 2015.

Srnicek, Nick. *Platform Capitalism*. Cambridge/Malden: Polity Press, 2017.

Stalder, Felix. '30 Years of Tactical Media'. In *Public Netbase: Non Stop Future. New Practices in Art and Media*, edited by Branka Ćurčić and Zoran Pantelić, 191–193. Frankfurt a.M.: Revolver, 2008.

Stalder, Felix. 'Selbermachen statt teilnehmen'. In *Vergessene Zukunft. Radikale Netzkulturen in Europa*, edited by Clemens Apprich and Felix Stalder, 219–225. Bielefeld: transcript, 2012.

Stalder, Felix. *Digital Solidarity*. London: Mute, 2013.

Stalder, Felix, and Jesse Hirsh. 'Open Source Intelligence'. *First Monday* 7:6 (2002). Accessed April 25, 2017. http://www.firstmonday.org/ojs/index.php/fm/article/view/961/882.

Stalder, Felix, and Manuel Castells. *The Theory of the Network Society*. Cambridge/Malden: Polity, 2006.

Starosielski, Nicole. *The Undersea Network*. Durham/London: Duke University Press, 2015.

Starosielski, Nicole. "Warning: Do Not Dig': Negotiating the Visibility of Critical Infrastructures'. *Journal of Visual Culture* 11:1 (2012): 38–57.

Stiegler, Bernard. 'The Most Precious Good in the Era of Social Technologies'. In *Unlike Us Reader. Social Media Monopolies and their Aeternatives*, edited by Geert Lovink and Miriam Rasch, 16–30. Amsterdam: Institute of Network Cultures, 2013.

Tan, Shuschen. 'Digital City, Amsterdam. An Interview with Marleen Stikker'. *ctheory* (1995). Accessed December 29, 2016. http://www.ctheory.net/articles.aspx?id=65.

Terranova, Tiziana. 'Red Stack Attack! Algorithms, Capital and the Automation of the Common'. *EuroNomade* (2014). Accessed April 30, 2017. http://www.euronomade.info/?p=2268.

Thacker, Eugene. 'Foreword: Protocol Is as Protocol Does'. In *Protocol: How Control Exists after Decentralization*, edited by Alexander Galloway, xi–xxii. Cambridge/London: MIT Press, 2004.

Toffler, Alvin. *The Third Wave*. New York: Bantam, 1984.

Townsend, Anthony M. *Smart Cities: Big Data, Civic Hackers, and the Quest for New Utopia*. New York: W. W. Norton & Company, 2014.

Treanor, Paul. 'Der Hyperliberalismus des Internet'. *Telepolis* (1996). Accessed October 31, 2016. www.heise.de/tp/r4/artikel/1/1052/1.html.

Turkle, Sherry. *Life on the Screen: Identity in the Age of the Internet*. New York/London/Toronto/Sydney: Simon & Schuster, 1995.

Turner, Fred. *From Counterculture to Cyberculture: Stewart Brand, the Whole Earth Network, and the Rise of Digital Utopianism*. Chicago: University of Chicago Press, 2006.

Vattimo, Gianni. *The End of Modernity*. Translated by Jon R. Snyder. Baltimore: John Hopkins University Press, 1991.

Vienna Ad-hoc Committee. 'The Piran Manifesto' (1997). Accessed March 25, 2017. http://www.nettime.org/Lists-Archives/nettime-l-9705/msg00147.html.

Virilio, Paul. 'Speed and Information: Cyberspace Alarm!' In *Reading Digital Culture*, edited by David Trend, 23–27. Malden/Oxford: Blackwell, 2001.

Virno, Paolo. *Grammar of the Multitude*. Translated by Isabella Bertoletti, James Cascaito, and Andrea Casson. Los Angeles: semiotext(e), 2004.

VNS Matrix. 'Cyberfeminist manifesto for the 21st century'. Accessed September 14, 2016. http://www.obn.org/reading_room/manifestos/html/ cyberfeminist.html.

Wagner, Kirsten. 'Architektonika in Erewhon. Zur Konjunktur architekturaler und urbaner Metaphern'. *Wolkenkuckucksheim. Internationale Zeitschrift für Theorie und Wissenschaft der Architektur* 3:1 (1998). Accessed December 29, 2016. http://www.cloud-cuckoo.net/openarchive/wolke/deu/Themen/981/Wagner/wagner_t.html.

Wardrup-Fruin, Noah. 'Introduction to "Constituents of a Theory of the Media."' *The New Media Reader*, edited by Noah Wardrip-Fruin and Nick Montfort, 259–260. Cambridge/London: MIT Press, 2003.

Warnke, Martin. 'Databases as Citadels in the Web 2.0'. In *Unlike Us Reader. Social Media Monopolies and Their Alternatives*, edited by Geert Lovink and Miriam Rasch, 76–88. Amsterdam: INC, 2013.

Wark, McKenzie. 'Metadata Punk'. In *Public Library*, edited by Tomislav Medak and Marcell Mars, 111–119. Zagreb: Gallery Nova, 2015.

Watts, Duncan J. 'Networks, Dynamics, and the Small-World Phenomenon'. *American Journal of Sociology* 105:2 (1999): 493–527.

Weber, Stefan. *Medien – Systeme – Netze. Elemente einer Theorie der Cyber-Netzwerke*. Bielefeld: transcript, 2001.

Weibel, Peter. 'Territorium und Technik'. In *Philosophien der neuen Technologien*, edited by Ars Electronica. Berlin: Merve, 1989.

Weibel, Peter. 'Die virtuelle Stadt im telematischen Raum'. In *Mythos Metropole*, edited by Gotthard Fuchs, Bernhard Moltmann, and Walter Prigge. Frankfurt a.M.: Suhrkamp, 1995.

Wellman, Barry, Janet Salaff, Dimitrina Dimitrova, Laura Garton, Milena Gulia, and Caroline Haythornthwaite. 'Computer Networks as Social Networks: Collaborative Work, Telework and Virtual Community'. *Annual Review of Sociology* 22 (1996): 213–238.

'What is Copyleft?' *Free Software Foundation*. Accessed April 30, 2017 https://www.gnu.org/licenses/copyleft.en.html.

Wilding, Faith, and Critical Art Ensemble. 'Notes on the Political Condition of Cyberfeminism'. *Art Journal* 57:2 (1997): 47–59.

Wilding, Faith, and subRosa, 'Where is Feminism in Cyberfeminism' (2006). Accessed April 1, 2017. www.neme.org/392/cyberfeminism.

Winthrop-Young, Geoffrey. 'Von gelobten und verfluchten Medienländern. Kanadischer Gesprächsvorschlag zu einem deutschen Theoriephänomen', translated by author. *Zeitschrift für Kulturwissenschaften* 2 (2008): 113–127.

Wittel, Andreas. 'Towards a Network Sociality'. *Theory, Culture & Society* 18:6 (2001): 51–76.

Wray, Stefan. 'Paris Salon or Boston Tea Party? Recasting Electronic Democracy, A View from Amsterdam'. *The Thing* (1998). Accessed January 6, 2017. www.thing.net/~rdom/ecd/teaparty.html.

Zeger, Hans W. 'Das Internet in Österreich. Media-Hype und die sozialen Anforderungen'. In *Informationsgesellschaft. Sozialwissenschaftliche Aspekte*, edited by Frank Hartmann, 23–30. Vienna: Forum Sozialforschung, 1998.

Zittrain, Jonathan. *The Future of the Internet—And How to Stop It*. New Haven/London: Yale University Press, 2008.

Index

181